IMAGINARY

MAPS

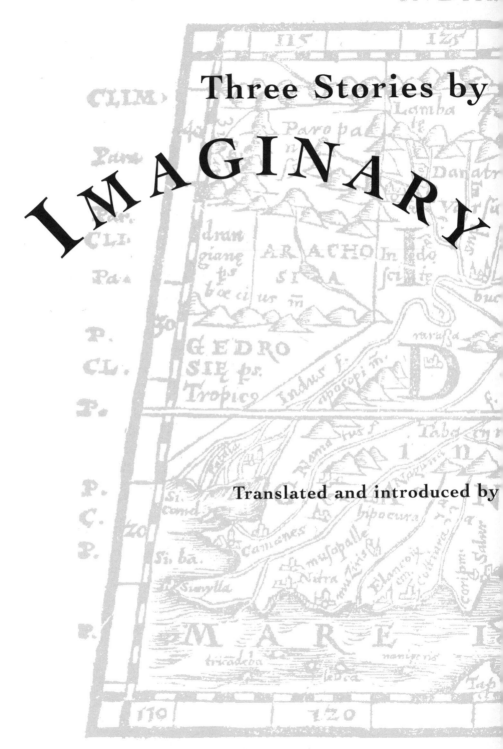

Three Stories by IMAGINARY

Translated and introduced by

Mahasweta Devi

MAPS

Gayatri Chakravorty Spivak

Routledge • New York • London

FOR ALL THE INDIGENOUS PEOPLES OF THE WORLD

Published in 1995 by
Routledge
29 West 35th Street
New York, NY 10001

Published in Great Britain by
Routledge
11 New Fetter Lane
London EC4P 4EE

Copyright © 1995 by Routledge

This edition published by arrangement with Thema Publications.

Printed in the United States of America on acid-free paper.

Library of Congress Cataloging-in-Publication Data

Devi, Mahasweta.
   Imaginary maps / by Mahasweta Devi ; translated by Gayatri
Chakravorty Spivak.
      p.   cm.
   ISBN 0-415-90462-5 (HB). — ISBN 0-415-90463-3 (PB)
   1. Devi, Mahasweta—Interviews.   2. Authors, Bengali
—20th century—Interviews.   3. Short stories, Indic—Trans-
lations into English.   4. Indic literature—20th century—History
and criticism.   5. India in literature.   I. Spivak, Gayatri
Chakravorty.
   II. Title.
   PK1718.D4737Z465   1993
   891'.4437—dc20   93-1284
                                                         CIP

Contents

The Author in Conversation

The following is a lightly edited version of a conversation, originally in English, taped in Calcutta in December, 1991. The questions are mine, the answers hers.   —GCS

History and fact first.

The tribal population of India is about one-sixth of the total population of the country. The tribes are divided into many groups. India belonged to these tribals long before the incursion of the Aryan-speaking peoples. The *Ramayana,* one of India's two ancient epics, seems to contain evidence of how they were oppressed, evicted from their homeland, and then forced to occupy the lower reaches of the mainstream culture. Bits of their old culture can still be glimpsed. In the nineteenth century, for example, mainstream Indian reformers had to struggle to pass a Widow Remarriage Act in caste-Hindu society, the society that is generally called "Indian." Among the Austric and Dravidian tribes of India, on the other hand—in the states of West Bengal and Bihar alone there are Oraons, Mundas, Santals, Lodhas, Kherias, Mahalis, Gonds, and more—widow remarriage has always been the custom. In tribal society, there is no dowry system, only bride-price. It is difficult to discern at this late date who borrowed from whom, especially since the tribals relied upon an oral tradition. Their word for Hindu is Diku—outsider. Remember, Draupadi in the *Mahabharata* is a black woman. She must have been a tribal. In the State of Himachal Pradesh we still find the sort of fraternal polyandry that Draupadi was supposed to have practiced in the *Mahabharata.* The polyandrous tribal women of Himachal Pradesh are said to belong to the Draupadi Gotra or clan. Among the South Indian tribals, Sita, the Queen of King Rama in the *Ramayana,* is not a human being. She is the wind in the grass, she is the flowing river, the fruit-yielding trees, the harvest to be gathered. She is Nature. Glimpses of their history remain in their songs and ballads. They were advanced in agriculture, though some groups were forest dwelling hunters: the Sobors.[1] The modern

es not know the word "orphan," because it is their com-
bligation to bring up a child whose parents are dead.
al pomp and splendor are also unknown.

And communal land holding, the absence of private property?

They had no sense of property. There was communal land
holding because, just like the Native Americans, they also believed
that land and forest and river belong to everyone. Their society has
of course broken under mainstream onslaught. Today in the village
of Kuda only seven families hold 21 acres of land. Now those 21
acres are getting irrigated and the crop will be equally divided
among the entire community. They understood ecology and the
environment in a way we cannot yet imagine. Happily, Native
Americans are trying to resurrect that spirit and place it before the
world. Like them the Sobors (the hunting tribes) will beg forgiveness if they are forced to fell a tree: You are our friend. I do this
because my wife doesn't have any food, my son doesn't have any
food, my daughter starves. Before they killed an animal, they used
to pray to the animal: the bird, the fish, the deer.

The tribals and the mainstream have always been parallel.
There has never been a meeting point. The mainstream simply
doesn't understand the parallel. As long as the forests were there,
the hunting tribes did not suffer so much, because the forests
used to provide them with food, shelter, timber, hunting. But now
that the forests are gone, the tribals are in dire distress. Some, like
the Santals or the Oraons from the Deccan, have advanced
because they took to agriculture long ago.

But the smaller tribes, like the Lodhas and Kherias you have
seen, small hunting tribes all over India, suffer deeply. The government of India has pauperized them. They have to beg for
everything they need. They do not understand mainstream machi-
nation, so although there are safeguarding laws against land-grab-
bing, tribal land is being sold illegally every day, and usurped by
mainstream society all over India, especially in West Bengal. In
North Bengal, extensive lands are being converted into tea gardens, fruit orchards. They can't keep their land; there is no education for them, no health facilities, no roads, no way of generating
income. Nothing is done for them although so much money is
allotted for them. They do not want money; they want facilities;
they want to live the life of an honorable poor Indian, you might
say. But they are denied everything. The tribals of India are

denied everything. All the big dam projects are made to fit the new rich Kulaks.[2] For that the tribals are evicted from their home-land, with no compensation. And yet a lot of their culture sur-vives! Perhaps because no one is interested in them as persons.

Then there are the industrial projects, for example the one in Tatanagar or in Bhilai. The entire Singhbhum district is minerally rich. India makes progress, produces steel, the tribals give up their land and receive nothing. They are suffering spectators of the India that is traveling toward the twenty-first century. That is why they protest, that is why there is Jharkhand, there is Chhattisgarh [place-names associated with ongoing tribal libera-tion movements against political and industrial exploitation]. Although they fought bravely against the British, they have not been treated as part of India's freedom struggle. A tribal girl asked me modestly, "When we go to school, we read about Mahatma Gandhi. Did we have no heroes? Did we always suffer like this?" That is why I started writing about the tribal movements and the tribal heroes. Of course I am involved with them, but it had to be written. I repay them their honor. They want to feel proud that they are tribals.

The tribals, then, paid the price for decolonization? They have not been part of the decolonization of India?

They have not been a part. Yet they have paid the price. I am wary of the West. I do not know my Western readers. In America I found such lack of information about the Native Americans. Why should American readers want to know from me about Indian trib-als, when they have present-day America? How was it built? Only in the names of places the Native American legacy survives. Otherwise entire tribes have been butchered. Their land has been taken away. There is movement, there are protest camps. But I say to my American readers, see what has been done to them, you will understand what has been done to the Indian tribals. Everywhere it is the same story. They reclaimed the forest, converted it into agricultural land, yet they were dispossessed.

And your involvement in the tribal movement?

The tribal movement now?

Yes.

But my involvement started long ago. In 1965, I started going to Palamu. Of course my mental involvement was already there. I was interested in them, but did not know very much. Palamu is still an inaccessible district, the poorest in the state of Bihar, perhaps one of the poorest in India. In such backward, feudally oppressed districts, the bonded labor system survives. The bonded labor system was introduced by the British. They created a new class, which took away tribal land and converted the tribals into debt-bonded slaves. The present government of India had to introduce, in 1976, the Bonded Labor System Abolition Act. You will be surprised to know that, from Kashmir to the Indian Ocean, and from East to West, in every state, there are districts marked as bonded labor districts because there are more than forty thousand bonded laborers in each of them. The Palamu I have depicted in my stories—only a few have been translated—is a mirror of tribal India. I have covered all of the district on foot. I walked miles, stayed somewhere overnight, went from place to place. Thus the bonded labor system, in its naked savagery and its bloody exploitation of women, became clear to me. I started writing about Palamu. I also started getting bonded laborers organized. In 1979, the government of India had supposedly liberated a handful of bonded laborers in Seora village on top of a hill. And, on paper, had given them land. What land? Land on top of the hills, no water level, where nothing could grow. And the people who kept them as bonded slaves were low echelon government officials themselves. It was through their hands that the government gave money to rehabilitate these people. Naturally nothing reached the tribals. They were in desperation. They said: "We will not go back to bondage again." On a broken mud wall of Seora village I wrote with a piece of chalk: Palamu District Bonded Labor Liberation Organization. The next year, for the first time in the heart of Palamu, in its head town of Daltonganj, bonded laborers came in the thousands. I led a procession through the streets of Palamu; we went to the District Commissioner. The women led the procession, shouting slogans: "Bonded System Must End," "The Land Belongs to the Tiller, Not the Absentee Landlord," and many others. The state of Bihar is divided into agricultural and forest areas. About forest Bihar I have written fiction. About agricultural Bihar I have written reports. You know I do a lot of journalism. When I understood that feeling for the tribals and writing about them was not enough, I started living with them. Tried to solve the problem by seeing everything from his or her point of view. That is how my book about Birsa Munda [*Aranyer Adhikar*—the right of/to the forest] came to be written. This book has been translated into almost all the Indian languages but not yet into English. The tribals think it has done justice to the tribals of India for the first time. The day Birsa was killed, Martyr's Day, is now observed by them with massive attendance, oaths and pledges, songs and dances. They understand the necessity of reviving and maintaining their culture.

Tell me about the principles animating your work with the Kheria Sobors of Purulia.

The British had isolated the small tribes. They were afraid to touch the majority tribes for fear of widespread havoc. They branded the small tribes as criminal tribes because they lived in the forest and did not take to cultivation. These tribes had no concept of money. They would come out of the forest, go to the village market, place honey, leaves, roots, flowers, and silently take away whatever they needed: rice, oil, spices. So they were thieves! With the felling of the forests, these tribes were exposed to the current savagery. They did not know where to go, they did not have any land. In the 1950s, the government of India "denotified" these tribes. The society immediately adjacent to where they now live—the police and the administration—still see them as thieves, robbers, criminals. And definitely use them in criminal activities. And on their backs grow rich. In West Bengal there are only two such denotified tribes, the Lodhas of Medinipur, and the Sobors. Kheria is also a Sobor or hunter tribe. That is how it was discovered that between 1979 and 1982, about forty Lodhas were lynched. In 1978, I formed the Lodha Organization which started protests. I investigated when a Lodha killing took place, and I wrote . . . My state government finally had to recognize that Lodhas were human beings after all. Purulia is the most neglected and the poorest district in West Bengal. The tribes and the non-tribal poor are equally neglected. There was a person there, Gopiballabh Singh Deo, you have seen him, he fought their cases, he fought for them when the police restricted them, and eventually Gopi and I joined hands there. Within ten years we have formed the Purulia Kheria Sobor Organization. I have gone to Delhi, fought and fought, and demanded schemes [projects] so that we could implement them, not through government agencies, not through their officers. The tribals can now plant forests, and fantastic forestation has been done. In a drought prone district like Purulia, out of one lakh trees, ... What is one lakh?

A hundred thousand.

Out of a hundred thousand trees, eighty thousand have survived. Eighty thousand trees have survived. And they are fairly well grown; mostly fruit trees, timber and leaf-giving trees, trees for silkworm. They have dug wells. They are building on their tradition of silk-weaving and trying to find markets without middlemen. The most incredible thing is their handicrafts. The Kheria tribal never did handicraft work before. But now with date palm leaves and wild grass they are earning money with the handicrafts they are producing. Their women are opening small savings accounts. We have started schools which they have started to attend. I should not say that we have done this. Gopi and I could have done nothing if they had not come forward. You have seen with your own eyes how responsible and good they are. You saw those two Kheria boys who went to take training in Ranchi. Now they are operating lift-irrigation in the fields and water is rising where it had never been before.

And in the literacy movement, the teachers are tribals or the so-called scheduled castes—the untouchables.

Yes.

The women who are being trained in primary health care are tribals. The moment they were given some recognition as human beings they took their own improvement and development in their own hands.

That's what our aim was. It is their work. They are responsible, sensitive people. They are civilized people. Only they have never been approached, they have never been given any responsibility by the rulers. You will be surprised to see how these tribals have gone and made extensive surveys of villages. Handmade surveys of sixty villages—population, school-going population, nearest school, need for a literacy center. Their traditional midwives are taking midwifery training. Now we have schools running for adults and children. Through the schools we can generate awareness. After they finish literacy and numeracy, we will give them books written in easy language by me to let them know their rights under the Indian Constitution. Let them know their rights, and let them stand up and fight for them. Their involvement is an amazing experience. All over India I have said to people, if you want to rehabilitate a denotified tribe, just giving some money to a broker is not enough. You have to go there, you have to love and trust them. Once you give trust, they give you back trust, Gayatri. This time you were not there. On the second and third of November, seven thousand Kheria Sobors came for their annual gathering. Before the conference began, they asked the local liquor shop owner to close his shop. "Come and join our festival," they said. "What if my shop gets looted," said he. The Kherias looked him in the eye and said, "What if we looted just now, and set fire to it? Can you do anything?" So seven thousand tribals in the winter night, men and women, did not drink a drop. The police could not charge intoxication and unruly behavior. Liquor is a great problem because the government encourages round-the-clock hours at illegally distilled liquor shops. And now? The women walk maybe fifteen kilometers a day with children tied to their backs to take midwifery training and health work training, and now infant mortality has gone down. Their service has been recognized.

And their interest in a sustained income all year round for the possibility of a sustained literacy program? Their own interest in changing their life pattern?

They have always wanted to change their life pattern. But they were never given any help. They now choose their own trees. And they tell us themselves, because the trees take time, in between them we will grow vegetables. We are digging water tanks, and we culture fish there. On the Arjun tree they cultivate silkworms. Formerly all the poor tribes and the scheduled castes migrated to other areas after harvest. Now they are not migrant workers anymore. We will do it with the Oraons as well, because they were the first big field peasants. Twenty-three Oraon tribal villages are making bricks. We are going to establish a brick-makers' cooperative. And the Kherias who had never made bricks before are making better bricks than the traditional brick makers.

You are also useful to the tribals because of the journalistic exposure that you immediately give to every act of exploitation and discrimination that they have to suffer. Their case gets known in Calcutta [the state capital], in Delhi [the capital of the country], as soon as something happens.

Gayatri, I've been doing this for many years. I write these days for *Frontier* [Calcutta-based], and even for *Economic and Political Weekly* [national circulation], and I have been doing a regular column contribution to Bengali dailies since 1982. Wherever there is exploitation, I report it immediately. I write directly to the pertinent ministerial department. I send a copy to the area, they make a mass-signature effort and go to the local authority. Each minister has one or two hundred of my letters. I think a creative writer should have a social conscience. I have a duty toward society. Yet I don't really know why I do these things. This sense of duty is an obsession, and I must remain accountable to myself. I ask myself this question a thousand times: have I done what I could have done? My house is full of them, they write to me, they come and stay with me, I go and stay with them. And this journalistic exposure is very necessary. The government officials admit that they are afraid of me. What will I write next?

And the tribals know this. You are also interested in undoing the divisions among the tribes, so that they think of themselves as a united community in India.

I'm very happy that you have referred to this. With the passage of time, sharp divisions have arisen among the tribes. When it comes to Lodha killing or the killing of denotified tribes for example, other tribes have participated. In 1986, I formed the *Adim Jati Aikya Parishad* [Tribal Unity Forum] in desperation. Now the Santal will not kill a Lodha anymore. The government is angry at this, at the uniting of the tribes. I have to hammer and hammer upon this. All the time, all the time. I want you to go to Bernard Bagwar [a Christian tribal]. You know Bernard Bagwar.

Yes, I've met him.

Bernard Bagwar is the General Secretary of this Tribal Unity Forum. If anything happens to tribals anywhere, our people will go there, they will write to me, and I will harp upon this—tribal unity, tribal unity. You see, the integrated man of the large Santal tribe may think, "I am in good clothes, I have a government office job, I am educated, I am very different from the village Santal, who is plowing land. As for the other tribes, these Lodhas, these Kherias, these Mahalis, they are inferior to us." I must hammer upon that pride, break that pride. I tell such a man, "To the gov-

ernment all of you are tribals. All of you belong to that con-
temptible category of the 'scheduled tribe.' Disunity among the
tribals is something the system wants. The system is just exploiting you, creating this disunity, so that you remain divided."
Wherever there is a movement now, they join hands, they are no
longer disunited. You will still find disunity where there is no
movement. The movement should start everywhere. It's such a
pity that Shankar Guha Niyogi was killed in such a brutal manner.[3] How much that one person achieved! I have seen his work.
Wherever there is someone fighting for the tribal cause, I am fortunate enough to be linked with it, directly or indirectly. Bernard
is carrying on a glorious fight.

Will it be right then to say that you are not trying to keep
their separate ethnicities alive . . .

No, no, no.

. . . but a general tribal identity as Indian.

General tribal as Indian, not only that. They are Indians who
belong to the rest of India. Mainstream India had better recognize
that. Pay them the honor that they deserve. Pay them the respect
that they deserve. There are no dowry deaths among the tribals.
And when they are called criminal tribes, I say, there is crime all
over the state of Bihar. All over India. All over the world. Do these
tribes commit all these crimes? They are your easy victims, they
are your prey, you hunt them. The system hunts them. And wants
to brand them. The system which hunts them and uses them as a
target is the criminal.

From this demand for the recognition of the tribal as a citizen
of independent India with an advanced cultural heritage, we can
turn to the three stories in this book. The relationship among the
stories as you perceive them, the place of the central character in
the first two. And then, what is it that you are trying to achieve in
"Pterodactyl"?

Is what I have said enough?

Enough I think for this introduction. You'll look at it when I
edit it. And now we go to the stories.

Let us first take up "Shikar" ["The Hunt"]. I know that area
like the palm of my hand. I have seen the person I have called

Mary Oraon. The tribals have this animal hunting festival in Bihar. It used to be the Festival of Justice. After the hunt, the elders would bring offenders to justice. They would not go to the police. In Santali language it was the Law-bir. Law is the Law, and *bir* is forest. And every twelfth year it is Jani Parab, the women's hunting festival in Bihar. Every event narrated within that story is true. What Mary did that day has been done in that area again and again. Among the tribals, insulting or raping a woman is the greatest crime. Rape is unknown to them. Women have a place of honor in tribal society. When I went to Lapra I would see this light-skinned girl in a yellow sari worn in the village way, on the back of a big old buffalo, sitting in the most relaxed manner, chewing sugar-cane. Maybe chewing popcorn. I see her in Tohri market, bargaining for fruit and other produce, chewing *pan* [spiced betel leaf], smoking *bidis* [tobacco-leaf cigarettes], arguing and always getting the upper hand. Such a personality. Then I learned what she had done on Jani Parab day in order to marry the Muslim boy. I learned this through songs. Every event that the tribals come to know they transfer to song, they do not write. They have retained the memories of their fights, of natural calamities, in this way. Some collections are being made. Sitting around the fire on a winter night, under the open sky, I came to know her story. And that man was just like a Lakra, a wolf, that had been killed. The real point is, Gayatri, that it was Jani Parab, the women's hunting festival day. She resurrected the real meaning of the annual hunting festival day by dealing out justice for a crime committed against the entire tribal society. One of the causes of the great Santal Revolt of 1855–56 was the raping of tribal women. People say that in the story I have gone too much for bloodshed, but I think as far as the tribals or the oppressed are concerned, violence is justified. When the system fails in—justice, violence is justified. The system resorts to violence when people rise to redress some grievance, to protest. India is supposed to be a nonviolent country. But in this nonviolent country, how many firings, how many killings by bigots take place every year? When the system fails an individual has a right to take to violence or any other means to get justice. The individual cannot go on suffering in silence. Tehsildar represents the mainstream. He is a contractor, the entire administration is behind him, because this illegal deforestation, which continues all over India, is done with great skill, and always the tribals are condemned. Once a tribal told me, "I need five rupees a day to buy rice.[4] Ask me to fell a tree, I'll do it unwillingly, but I'll do it. Ask me to chop off a head, I'll do it, because I need five rupees at the end of the day." So that the hands that fell the tree are not the hands responsible for the deforestation all over India. Big money is involved in the furniture that you see in Delhi, or Hyderabad, or Calcutta. The local political worthies, local police, local administration are bribed. The railways cooperate by carrying this illegally felled timber. Illegal sawmills come up everywhere. There are bosses in the cities felling the sandalwood in Karnataka. All over the world governments protecting the environment is nonsense. Thus through Mary Oraon I have narrated events that are true of India today. I consider myself an Indian writer, not a Bengali writer. I am proud of this.

Now we come to "Douloti." I told you about my travels all over Palamu district. "Douloti" is situated in Palamu. The fight of the Naxalites in Palamu, as in the entire states of Bihar and Andhra, for minimum wages for forest workers, plantation workers, agricultural workers, is of course the only solution to the bonded labor problem.[5] What I have written about in "Douloti" is how a woman, how women especially, were exploited.

I wrote about the central problem in "Douloti" in the *Business Standard* and am still fighting with the government of India. They have apparently abolished the bonded labor system. But the bonded labor system is no longer confined to the agricultural sector. Contractor's laborers, brought in from out-of-state to work as casual labor for any industrial project, are also bonded labor. This is for example extremely common in the Himalayan district of Uttar Kashi. Women after or before marriage are taken away when husband or father has borrowed money from the money-lending upper caste. They are taken straight to brothels in the big cities to work out that sum. And the sum is never repaid because the account is calculated on compound interest. I wrote three stories on bonded laborers. "Douloti" is the first story. In "Palamu" the formation of organized bonded labor is again seen through the experiences of a woman. In the third, "Gohumni" [forthcoming in translation], the woman retaliates. She punishes the moneylender who comes to take her away. Incidentally, Gohumni means female cobra. I saw Crook Nagesia with my own eyes in the month of June, just before the rainy season. Palamu has very little rainfall. Under the burning sun the landlord loads the bullock cart with paddy and tells the man to pull the cart to the local market.

He could not do it. He fell under it. He was crushed. He became twisted and crooked for the rest of his life. I asked the landlord why he did it. In order to approach the landlords of Palamu you have to say you are a superior government officer taking notes, and that's what I was. The landlord offered me a glass of milk with sugar-cane crystals. He was trying to please me. "You are an upper-caste person," he said. "These bullocks are costly. if I send a bullock, it will suffer in the heat and it might collapse. But these bonded laborers don't count for much. A man can be wasted, a bullock cannot." This was his argument, the perennial argument, after all, for sweating "cheap labor" rather than using costly machines. Out of this argument, and seeing a skeletal girl in the local hospital who could only pronounce the name of her village and nothing else, I made the story. I have named the village Seora. But there are such villages everywhere in Palamu. Now they cannot do this anymore wherever there is a movement against bonded labor. But the sale of girls for rape still goes on. "Douloti" is still true, and true for the rest of India.

That is why I have ended the story like that. Douloti's bleeding, rotting carcass covers the entire Indian peninsula. In Hyderabad, there is a special area where buyers from the Middle East buy women in the name of marriage. Parents flock there because they are so poor, they cannot give their daughters food and clothing. The basic reason is poverty. *Times of India* did a very good series of stories on this. As long as eighty percent of the Indian population lives below poverty lines, this cannot stop. Decolonization has not reached the poor. That is why these things happen. Women are just merchandise, commodities. In the border districts of West Bengal there are women from Bangladesh being sold in the name of marriage in the bridegroom's house. For the flesh trade all you have to invest is two saris, a bit of food, some trinkets, and a bit of money for the parents. Poverty, poverty, poverty. What we need is mass-based public opinion formation, pressure on the government, vigilance. But what can we expect of the system, when the burning of a Rajput woman becomes a great national issue? When a woman is raped the entire judiciary system is against the woman. The general consensus is: only women of loose character get raped, for India parades that India holds women in great honor. Even women of the left parties in Calcutta have brought that argument in cases of rape.

"Pterodactyl" is an abstract of my entire tribal experience.

Through the Nagesia experience I have explained other tribal experiences as well. I have not kept to the customs of one tribe alone. In the matter of the respect for the dead, for example, I have mixed together the habits of many tribes. If read carefully, "Pterodactyl" will communicate the agony of the tribals, of marginalized people all over the world.

Wherever you see heaped boulders in Ranchi district, it is an ancestral burial ground. Once in the remote district of Singhbhum I was walking through forests and rivers. I told the tribals that if I walked twice for twenty miles in the summer heat, I would die. They comforted me by saying, "Don't worry, we will carry big stones from far away to place upon your grave." I said, "What consolation will this be to me when I'm dead?" "Didi [elder sister]," they said, "we have plenty of stones right here. But these stones, though large, will not give you great honor. If we carry stones from far away, *that* will mean honor." But I didn't die there. Actually I don't want to die now. I want twenty working years.

So "Pterodactyl" wants to show what has been done to the entire tribal world of India. We did not know it, it was like a continent. We did not try to know it. It is the same everywhere. I think of the two American continents. We did not try to know them. We did not try to find out what potential has survived in them through all these centuries. What has survived in them? Have you ever seen them, very carefully going very respectfully in file? If a thousand Indian tribals, men, women, and children, sit, how quiet they are? How quietly they listen to people? Mainstream people cannot believe it. They shove and nudge, they hum and sing, they whisper. It is not in us. In their blood there is so much patience, it is like nature. Patience of the hills, of the rivers, the tribal contains everything. Each tribe is like a continent. But we never tried to know them. Never tried to respect them. This is true of every tribal. And we destroyed them. I found the Nagesia tribals making their leaf huts on the hills. In some forgotten time the Nagesias had been invaded by outsiders. Then they built their huts on the tops of hills so they could watch from which direction the enemy came. But they cannot stop the invaders anymore. As far as the tribal is concerned, the road, the big road, is the enemy. It will take away whatever crop he grows, whatever vegetable he grows, and in times of famine and natural disorders like rain failure or flood they will come in lorries and trucks and take away their children to be sold in other places as bonded labor. Shall I

ever forget that in Palamu, eight boys aged six to ten were scared
out of a carpet making factory where the factory owner had
branded their backs in case they escaped? The parents and state
and national police had gone there. Those boys were rescued. But
what about the thousands of tribal children and scheduled caste
children who are working in Tamil Nadu, in match and fireworks
and metal factories, in Kashmir in carpet workshops, all over
India in various kinds of enterprises? In the capitalist market
there is great demand for children, especially tribal children. You
pay them little; you can starve them; you can kill them; no one
will come for them. The pterodactyl is prehistoric. Modern man,
the journalist, does not know anything about it. There is no point
of communication with the pterodactyl. The pterodactyl cannot
say what message it has brought. The journalist, the representative of the mainstream people, has no point of contact with the
tribals. Their roads have run parallel. He does not know what the
tribal wants, what the tribal holds most dear to the heart. The tribals want to stay in the place which they know as their own. They
want the respect that they hold for their dead ancestors.
Whatever has come in the name of development has spelled disaster for the tribes. And they do not know how to dishonor others.

Our double task is to resist "development" actively and to
learn to love.

Translator's Preface

I thank Mahasweta Devi not only for the interview but also for her meticulous reading of the manuscript of the translation. She made many suggestions, noted omitted passages, corrected occasional mistranslations, and supplied names for government agencies. This is indeed an authorized translation. Any faults that remain are of course mine.

Constraints on Method

This book is going to be published in both India and the United States. As such it faces in two directions, encounters two readerships with a strong exchange in various enclaves. As a translator and a commentator, I must imagine them as I write. Indeed, much of what I write will be produced by these two-faced imaginings, even as it will no doubt produce the difference, yet once again. But the "imaginary" in our title—"imaginary maps"—points at other kinds of divisions as well. "India" is not an undivided perspective, much as both conservatives and radicals in the United States would strive to represent it as such. And the divisions within the United States are there for deconstructive pedagogic use, although both politicians and ideologues on both sides in India would like to convince us otherwise. In what interest or interests does the necessity to keep up this game of difference—India is "India" and the US is the "US," and the two are as different as can be—emerge, today? The stories translated in this collection can help us imagine that interest or those interests. I am convinced that the multiculturalist US reader can at least be made to *see* this difference at work, and it is the expatriate critic who *can* make the effort. I also remain convinced that the urban radical academic Indian reader can be made to question his or her complicity with keeping the US as demonized other while reaping or attempting to reap the benefits of its "be-littling be-friending." But then Mahasweta must not be commodified as a "national cultural artifact," *only* accessible to "Indians," a seam-

xxiii

whose interest is served by the distinction?

less national identity after all, when her entire effort focuses on what has been left out of such a definition; for that feeds that transnational US multiculturalist hunger on both right and left. Add to this the fact that Cultural Studies in the United States today is also fed by the migrant academic's desire to museumize a culture left behind, gaining thus an alibi for the profound Eurocentrism of academic migrancy.

This myth of pure difference is the displacement of an old slogan, after all: "East is East ... " et cetera. Or is the "imagination" of new maps in the name of decolonization or the New World Order too crucial an enterprise for it to be exposed to serious intellectual investigation?

I want to use the risky word "deconstruction" again, to keep at bay the easy rewards of inspirational prose. In the particular context that I have described generally above, where both the "US" and "India" are interested in claiming sometimes the place of the "same" (or self, or knower) and sometimes the "other," it is the following deconstructive formula that I find myself acting out:

The same, precisely, is *différance* ... as the displaced and equivocal passage of one different thing to another, from one term of an opposition [here "India" and "US"] to the other. Thus one could reconsider all the pairs of opposites ... on which our discourse lives [precisely to include the subaltern, here the Indian tribal], not in order to see opposition [between "India" and "US"] erased but to see what indicates that each of the terms *must* appear as the *différance* of the other, as the other different and deferred in the economy of the same ...[6]

In this traffic of same-and-othering, the groups that do receive some attention in the cultural sphere are the new immigrants (sometimes unjustifiably conflated with exiles, refugees, diasporics, and post-colonials *in* the former colonies), old minorities in the North, urban radicals sponsoring organized protests or the historical or contemporary ethnographic other in the South, and sometimes the indigenous organic intellectual of the South, this last celebrated as *the* "subaltern" in the North.[7] In the Afterword to this volume, I will try my best to show how the figures in Mahasweta's fiction do not belong to this catalogue.[8] Here let me say that no amount of raised consciousness field-work can ever approach the painstaking labor to establish ethical singularity with the subaltern.[9]

"Ethical singularity" is neither "mass contact" nor engagement with "the common sense of the people." We all know that when we engage profoundly with one person, the responses come from both sides: this is responsibility and accountability. We also know that in such engagements we want to reveal and reveal, conceal nothing. Yet on both sides there is always a sense that something has not got across. This we call the "secret," not something that one wants to conceal, but something that one wants to reveal. In this sense the effort of "ethical singularity" may be called a "secret encounter." Please note that I am not speaking of meeting in secret. In this secret singularity, the object of ethical action is not an object of benevolence, for here responses flow from both sides. It is not identical with the frank and open exchange between radicals and the oppressed in times of crisis, or the intimacy that anthropologists often claim with their informant groups, although the importance of at least the former should not be minimized. This encounter can only happen when the respondents inhabit something like normality. Most political movements fail in the long run because of the absence of this engagement. In fact, it is impossible for all leaders (subaltern or otherwise) to engage every subaltern in this way, especially across the gender divide. This is why ethics is the experience of the impossible. Please note that I am not saying that ethics are impossible, but rather that ethics is the experience of the impossible. This understanding only sharpens the sense of the crucial and continuing need for collective political struggle. For a collective struggle *supplemented* by the impossibility of full ethical engagement—not in the rationalist sense of "doing the right thing," but in this more familiar sense of the impossibility of "love" in the one-on-one way for each human being—the future is always around the corner, there is no victory, but only victories that are also warnings.

The initial attempt in the Bandung Conference (1955) to establish a third way—neither with the Eastern nor within the Western bloc—in the world system, in response to the seemingly new world order established after the Second World War, was not accompanied by a commensurate intellectual effort. The only idioms deployed for the nurturing of this nascent Third World in the cultural field belonged then to positions emerging from resistance within the supposedly "old" world order—anti-imperialism and/or nationalism. The idioms that are coming in to fill that space in *this* new world order, to ascertain, perhaps, that the cultural lobby be of no help in producing an appropriate subject, are: national origin, sub-nationalism, nationalism, cultural nativism, religion, and/or hybridism.[10] I have written extensively about these problems elsewhere. In the Afterword I will attempt to show how Mahasweta's fiction resonates with the possibility of constructing a new type of responsibility for the cultural worker. It has always fascinated me that, although her writing and her activism reflect one another, they are precisely that—"a folding back upon" one another—re-flection in the root sense. The Afterword will therefore also concentrate upon the difference between the literary text and the textile of activism. Indeed, if one reads carefully, one may be seen as the other's *différance*.

The Organic Intellectual

I want to clear up a few confusions by way of conclusion. Reading merely "Douloti," a migrant academic dismissed it as an exercise by the pessimistic and jaded post-colonial middle class. Reading my commentaries on the guardians of the horizon—such as the pterodactyl in the final novella—my friend Sara Suleri has unaccountably diagnosed a case of exoticization.[11] And there is also a feeling that perhaps this is a denial of voice to "the subaltern," so that she can only be spoken for. Sujit Mukherjee, the prominent intellectual of the publishing world particularly concerned with the quality of translations, has called me a *dwārpālika* (female doorkeeper) of Mahasweta in the West.[12] There is some truth in this and I want to perform the doorkeeper's obligation by commenting briefly on these misapprehensions, part of the risk taken by work such as Mahasweta's. If these comments are seen as "too theoretical," I will remind the readers of this translation, with respect, that the migrant in the North, a species of "wild anthropologist," at least knows the points of rejection or contempt hidden behind the mask of untheorized solidarity, without liabilities.

When the subaltern "speaks" in order to be heard and gets into the structure of responsible (responding and being responded to) resistance, he or she is or is on the way to becoming an organic intellectual. By way of Mahasweta's political generosity, I have had the good fortune of encountering a handful of contemporary tribal intellectuals among whom two have seemed to me to have perhaps traversed the hardest road: Chuni Kotal and

Jaladhar Sabar. Chuni, as a woman daring to breach the general "intellectual" establishment, took her own life under the weight of social prejudice.[13] I had initially thought to include some documents of ground-level intervention produced by Jaladhar Sabar in this Introduction. But now, because of my double-edged feeling about the *type* and *area of effectiveness* of testimonial work, I hesitate to commodify them here. They were not produced for this sort of exchange, and I obtained them through my archival interest.[14] Mahasweta has published what amounts to politically interventionist and informative testimonials in her journal *Bartika* for years, without making a noticeable mark upon the general reading public in West Bengal, let alone enthusiasts of multiculturalism and Cultural Studies in the United States. The misguided and uninvolved benevolence that sometimes stands for political pedagogy in the United States might find in this particular documentation as interesting a research novelty as Madonna. (I have tried to bypass this by always insisting upon the sheer difficulty of teaching Mahasweta, in her turn, as an Indian cultural exhibit.)

The point I am trying to make is that there is no lack of the celebration of the organic intellectual in Mahasweta's work and writing-work. In the present collection of stories, Mary Oraon in "The Hunt" is one of those figures. Yet in her case, a share of violent imperialist blood and her consequent singularity are emphasized. I look for post-colonial woman writers cognizant of the aporias or ethico-historical dilemmas in women's decolonization.[15] It is in this spirit that Assia Djebar of Algeria claims that the ancestress of the Algerian *mujahidat* or women freedom-fighters is Pauline Rolland, the French revolutionary of 1848 whom France banished to Anaba.[16]

In my estimation, in the case of "Douloti," Mahasweta confronts a much more severe truth: that one of the bases in women's subalternity (and indeed in unequal gendering on other levels of society) is internalized constraints seen as responsibility, and therefore the very basis of gender-ethics. Here woman's separation from organic intellectuality is a complicity with gendering that cannot not be perceived by many as sweetness, virtue, innocence, simplicity. If in the case of Bhubaneswari ("Can the Subaltern Speak?") and Jashoda in Mahasweta's "Stanadayini," it is parts of the sexed body—menstruation, lactation—that are invested with meaning and yet are not heard and not read, in "Douloti" it is the bonded prostitute's body that Mahasweta makes visible as graphic comment on the entire map of India. It is a mistake to think that this fierce love is the jaded pessimism of the bourgeoisie.

Yet sweet, innocent, responsible Douloti is not a subject of resistance. Mahasweta dramatizes that difficult truth: internalized gendering perceived as ethical choice is the hardest roadblock for women the world over. The recognition of male exploitation must be supplemented with this acknowledgment.[17] And the only way to break it is by establishing an ethical singularity with the woman in question, itself a necessary supplement to a collective action to which the woman might offer resistance, passive or active. Douloti as a subject is a site of this acknowledgment.[18]

Sujit Mukherjee has also complained—and this is particularly important for US readers who are looking for either local flavor or Indian endorsement—that the English of my translation is not "sufficiently accessible to readers in this country [India]."[19] This may indeed be true, but may not be sufficient grounds for complaint. I am aware that the English of my translations belongs more to the rootless American-based academic prose than the more subcontinental idiom of my youth. This is an interesting question, unique to India: should Indian texts be translated into the English of the subcontinent? I think Sri Mukherjee is begging rather than considering this question.

Let me end with the South African writer J. M. Coetzee's comments on his translation of the Dutch poet Achterberg. (It should be noted that Coetzee's relationship to both English—his is an Afrikaans name—and Dutch is askew, as is mine to English and to Bengali, though in a different way):

> It is in the nature of the literary work to present its translator with problems for which the perfect solution is impossible ... There is never enough closeness of fit between languages for formal features of a work to be mapped across from one language to another without shift of value ... Something must be "lost"; that is, features embodying certain complexes of values must be replaced with features embodying different complexes of values in the target language. At such moments the translator chooses in accordance with his [*sic*] conception of the whole—there is no way of simply translating the words. These choices are based, literally, on preconceptions, pre-judgement, prejudice.[20]

Upon this acknowledgment of prejudice (not derived from the possibility of an unprejudiced translation, even in reading), bequeathed by a writer who responds to the compromised position of "white writing" in South Africa (a much greater compromise than translating Mahasweta into "American"), I invite you to acknowledge your own and turn now to the text.

Translator's Note

All words in English in the original have been italicized. This makes the English page difficult to read. The difficulty is a reminder of the intimacy of the colonial encounter. Mahasweta's stories are *post*colonial. They must operate *with* the resources of a history shaped by colonization *against* the legacy of colonialism. This "deconstructive embrace" is not only her message, but also her medium (assuming that there is ever a neat split between the two.) The language of the practical everyday life of all classes (including the subaltern), profoundly marked by English, mimes the historical sedimentation of colonialism by the degree to which the words and phrases have been lexicalized, and the degree to which, therefore, they exist "independently" in Bengali. By contrast, the culturalist intellectual—a group addressed in the "Translator's Preface"—and the State can affect a "pure" idiom, which disguises *neo*colonialist collaboration. (Since Bengali is not the national language of India, state interference is less noticeable. For that, one must turn to neighboring Bangladesh—whose national language *is* Bengali— or to Hindi, which is the national language of India.)

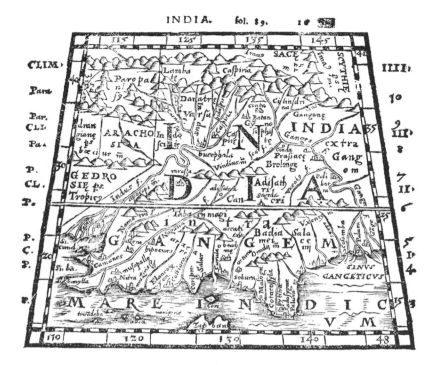

The Hunt

I

The place is on the Gomo-Daltonganj line. *Trains* stopped at this *station* once upon a time. The expense of having *trains* stop was perhaps too much. Now one sees a stray cow or a goat in the *station* room, in the residential *quarters* and the porters' shanties. The *billboard* says "Kuruda *Outstation, Abandoned.*" Arrived here, the *train* slows. It gasps as it climbs. It climbs Kuruda Hill bit by bit right from here. It is a low hill. After a while the *train* enters a ravine. On both sides of the half-mile ravine there are *blasted* stones. There's a bamboo thicket on the hill, and occasionally the bamboo bends in the wind and hits the *train.* Then the *train*

1

descends and it gathers speed. Now the *station* is Tohri. The busiest *station* in this area. The *junction* of many *bus* routes. Tohri is also a *coal halt*. The *train* picks up coal. There are *surface collieries* all around. In these parts low-grade coal is to be found almost above ground. But Tohri's real benefactors are the timber brokers. It is a Sal growing area. Sal logs arrive night and day by *truck*. They are split in sawmills and sent in every direction. Tohri's bustle is an experience after the silence of Kuruda.

It is an experience to watch the *train* move on the hilltop from distant villages. The villagers see this every day, yet their amazement never ends. The *train* goes on, the *engine* gasps; now the ravine swallows the *train*. If you run you can see where it will spit it out. There were some elephants seen one day at the top of the hill. The elephants stopped as they ate the bamboo. From a distance they looked like toy elephants. After the *train* passed on they ran off trumpeting, trunks raised.

The village of Kuruda is a good way behind the *station*. There are two hills, one beyond the wide meadow. If it had been a bit closer the villagers might have started living in the abandoned brick built house.

For people who live in villages like Kuruda, life holds few breaks other than annual festivals. So their eyes are charmed by the scenes on top of Kuruda Hill.

When Mary Oraon comes up, she looks at the *train,* as the passengers look at her if they see her. Eighteen years old, tall, flat-featured, light copper skin. Usually she wears a print sari. At a distance she looks most seductive, but close up you see a strong message of rejection in her glance.

You wouldn't call her a tribal at first sight. Yet she is a tribal. Once upon a time whites had *timber plantations* in Kuruda. They left gradually after Independence. Mary's mother looked after the Dixons' bungalow and household. Dixon's son came back in 1959 and sold the house, the forest, everything else. He put Mary in Bhikni's womb before he left. He went to Australia. The padre at the local church christened her Mary. Bhikni was still a *Christian*. But when Prasadji from Ranchi came to live in the Dixon bungalow and refused to employ Bhikni, she gave up *Christianity*. Mary pastures the Prasads' cattle. She is a most capable cowherd. She also sells custard apple and guava from the Prasads' orchards, driving terrifically hard bargains with the Kunjaras, the wholesale fruit buyers. She takes the *train* to Tohri with vegetables from the field.

Everyone says Prasadji is most fortunate. He pays Bhikni a wage. With Mary the agreement is for board and lodging, clothing and sundries. The Dixon bungalow was built as a residence for whites. Bhikni says the whites kept twelve ayahs—servants—sweepers. Under Prasadji Mary alone keeps the huge bungalow clean.

Mary has countless admirers at Tohri market. She gets down at the *station* like a queen. She sits in her own rightful place at the market. She gets smokes from the other marketeers, drinks tea and chews betel leaf at their expense, but encourages no one. Jalim, the leader of the marketeers and a sharp lad, is her chosen mate. They will marry when either's savings reach a hundred rupees.

She has let Jalim approach her on the promise of marriage. Daughter of an Oraon mother, she looks different, and she is also exceptionally tall. So she couldn't find a boy of her own kind. The color of Mary's skin is a resistant barrier to young Oraon men. Mrs. Prasad had looked for a match. Their gardener's son. She had said, You can stay on the compound.

Bhikni was ecstatic. Mary said, "No. Mistress Mother has said it to keep her worker captive."

— She will give shelter.

— A shack.

— He's a good boy.

— No. Living in a shack, eating mush, the man drinking, no soap or oil, no clean clothes. I don't want such a life.

Mary was unwilling. She is accepted in the village society. The women are her friends, she is the best dancer at the feasts. But that doesn't mean she wants to live their life.

Many men had wanted to be her lover. Mary had lifted her machete. They are outsiders. Who can tell that they wouldn't leave her, like Bhikni was left with a baby in her belly?

There was a fight over her once in Tohri market. Ratan Singh, the *driver* of a *timber truck,* had got drunk and tried to carry her off. It was then that Jalim had cut in and hit Ratan Singh. After that Mary was seen selling vegetables or peanuts or corn sitting beside Jalim. She has never been to his room. No, marriage first. Jalim respects this greatly. Yes, there is something true in Mary, the power of Australian blood.

There is distrust in Mary somewhere. She doesn't trust even Jalim fully. Even the marketeers of Tohri know that they'll marry as soon as there is a hundred rupees. Jalim's version is that he himself will save those hundred rupees. It will be good if Mary brings something herself. So she has left to Jalim the responsibility of saving money. It's not easy for Jalim. He has his parents, brothers, and sisters in the village. Here he'll have to rent a place, buy pots and pans. He won't be able to carry all the expenses. And he wants to give Mary clothes, the odd cake of soap.

Mary gave him the first present. A colored cotton vest.

— Your gift? Jalim is delighted.

— No. Your brother's wife sent it, Mary says sarcastically.

After that Jalim gave her presents now and then. Mary doesn't wear those clothes. She'll wear them after the wedding.

Mary understands that Jalim is taking many pains to save money. Even so she says nothing, for she has saved ninety-two if not a hundred rupees.

She has earned that money. At the Prasad establishment. By government regulation, if there are mahua trees on anyone's land in the forest areas, the right to the fruit goes to the picker. Mahua is a *cash* fruit. You get liquor from mahua, you cook with the oil of the black seed of the mahua fruit, the skin goes to make washing soap. It is Mary who picks the fruit of the four mahua trees on the Prasad property. No villager has been able to touch the fruit even in jest. Mary has instantly raised her machete. This is hers by right. This is why she works so hard for no wages at the Prasad house.

Mrs. Prasad doesn't like it much, but Lachhman Prasad says, "Take no notice. Who will clean so well, pasture the cows so well? Sell fruit and vegetables and nuts at a profit in Tohri?"

Mary works like a dog but does not tolerate familiarity from Prasadji.

— So Mary, how much did you make on your sale of mahua?

— What's it to you?

— Open a moneylending business.

— Yes, I will.

— It's good of me to let you pick the mahua. It is government property. I could hire people and have the fruit picked and I don't do it.

— Let the hired people come and see. I have my machete. Mary's voice is harsh and grim.

Prasadji says, It figures. White blood.

Mrs. Prasad has Mary give her an oil rubdown. Out of her lardy body she looks at Mary's hard perfect frame. She says, "So, what about your marriage? What does Jalim say?"

— What do you want with poor folks' talk? Will you organize my marriage?

— God be praised! With a Muslim? I run such a marriage?

— Why not? The Muslim says he'll marry. Your brother wanted only to keep me.

The mistress swallows the slap and says nothing. You have to take words from a girl who works like an animal, carries a forty-pound bag on her back and boards the *train*, cleans the whole house in half an hour.

Everyone is afraid of Mary. Mary cleans house and pastures cattle with her inviolate constitution, her infinite energy, and her razor-sharp mind. On the field she *lunches* on fried corn. She stands and picks fruit and oversees picking. She weighs the stuff herself for the buyers. She puts the fruit bitten by bats and birds into a sack, and feeds it to her mother's chickens. When the rains come she replants the seedlings carefully. She watches out for everything. She buys rice, oil, butter, and spices for the Prasads at Tohri market. She says herself, "The money I save you, and the money I make for you, how much do you put together out of it yearly, Mistress Mother? Why should I take a cheap sari? I'll dress well, use soap and oil, give me everything."

Mrs. Prasad is obliged to dress her well.

Sometimes Mary goes to the village to gossip. When she can. Then she puts her sari around her belly and becomes Mrs. Prasad, limps and becomes Prasadji, makes everyone laugh. There she is easy. When the young men say, "Hey Mussulman's chick, why here?"

— Would any of you marry me?

— Would you?

— Why aren't you tall and white like me?

— You are a white man's daughter.

— Big white chief! Puts a child in a woman's belly and runs like a rat. My mother is bad news. When you see a white daughter, you kill her right away. Then there are no problems!

— What about you if she'd killed?

— I wouldn't have been.

— Stop that talk. Be a Mussulman if you like. Before that, for us . . .

— What?

— Rice-chicken-mutton and booze?

— Sure, I'll throw a fan-tas-tic feast. When have I not fed you? Tell me?

— Yes, true, you do give.

The same Mary who pulls hundreds of pounds, fights the Kunjaras over fruit, doesn't hand out a single peanut to keep Prasadji's profits intact, also steals peanut oil, flour, molasses from the house. Salt and spices.

She sits at any Oraon house in the village, fries wheatcakes on a clay stove, eats with everyone. Just as she knows she'll marry Jalim, she also knows that if she had resembled any Oraon girl—if her father had been Somra or Budhna or Mangla Oraon—the Oraons would not have let this marriage happen.

Because she is the illegitimate daughter of a white father the Oraons don't think of her as their blood and do not place the harsh injunctions of their own society upon her.

She would have rebelled if they had. She is unhappy that they don't. In her inmost heart there is somewhere a longing to be part of the Oraons. She would have been very glad if, when she was thirteen or fourteen, some brave Oraon lad had pulled her into marriage. Mary has seen two or three Hindi films in Tohri. At harvest time itinerant *film* people come to Tohri. They show *moving pictures* in the open field. Not only the girls, but even the boys of Kuruda village have hardly ever been to the *movies*. They haven't been to the *movies*, haven't worn good clothes, haven't eaten a full meal. Mary has a certain sympathy for them as well.

So goes Mary's life. Suddenly one day, stopping the *train,* Tehsildar Singh descends with Prasadji's son, and Mary's life is troubled. A storm gathers in Kuruda's quiet and impoverished existence.

II

Seventy-five acres or two hundred and twenty-five bighas of land are attached to Prasadji's bungalow. Nobody around here obeys the land *ceiling* laws. All the far-flung bungalows of the old *timber planters* have large tracts of attached land. Mr. Dixon had planted Sal on fifty acres. Not the dwarf Sal of the area but *giant* Sal. In time they've grown immense and ready for *felling*. Prasadji used to lament about all that he could have done with this land if there had been no Sal. Now that he knows the price of Sal, his one goal is to sell the trees at the highest price. Lalchand and Mulniji, the two other forest proprietors of the area, are also happy at this news. Prasad's son Banwari takes the initiative and starts looking around in Daltonganj and Chhipador. The fruit of his labors is Tehsildar Singh.

The first thing Tehsildar Singh looks at is trees to be felled. Then they start negotiating prices. Prasad says, "Such Sal wood! How can I sell at such a price?"

— Why sell? You'll sell where you can make a profit.

— Name a proper price.

— Prasadji! Banwari is a real friend. He does *service* in Chhipador, and I'm a broker. Why tell a lie, the trees are *mature,* and the wood solid.

— The whites planted the stuff.

— Yes. But here I'll have them cut, in pieces! *Trucks* won't come here. This is not the white man's rule when I could have brought elephants from the *Forest Department* and pulled the timber to Tohri. I'll have to take it to Murhai. Flat *tires* on the dirt roads. I'll have to cut the trees before that, think of the expense!

— But you'll make a profit!

— Sure. Who works without profit? Still your profit is higher. Bought the bungalow dirt cheap, got a ready-made Sal forest! Whatever you get is your profit. Because you had no *investment* for it. No corn that buffaloes pulled the plow, and fieldhands reaped. No custard apple or guava that you chased birds and bats. *Forest area,* Sal *area,* have trees, sell straight off.

Lalchand and Mulni also said, "Don't make so much trouble, brother. What do we do if he leaves? When the wind's in the Sal and you hear the sea, will he hear? Do you want to watch the flowers of a tree that bears no fruit? He wants to buy, we'll sell."

The broker wants the same thing. What trees the whites had planted. The tops break the sky, the trunks are as big as *railway engines.* Why buy only Prasadji's trees? He'll buy all the trees of the area.

— Every five years or so some trees will be ready and I'll buy. One two three. This is still a *virgin area,* and I'll take the tree *felling monopoly.*

That was the decision. Prasadji realized later that the argument about the expense of carrying the trees was not altogether correct. For the *trucks* came past Murhai, close to Kuruda. That side is flat and stony. No problem with the arrival of *trucks.* The broker pitched his tent there. Two experts came to fell trees.

The broker started planning the deployment of *manpower.*

Oraon and Munda men and women came from six villages—Kuruda, Murhai, Seeho, Thapari, Dhuma, Chinadoha. Unbelievable. Money at home. Others will fell the trees, twelve annas daily for men, eight annas for women for trimming branches and carrying the *pieced* timber to the *trucks*. And a *tiffin* of cornmeal in the afternoon. Unbelievable! Salt and cayenne with the meal. The village priest and elders will bring the men and women. A sack of salt weekly for each village. The elders said, How about the women's honor if they work?

The contractor said, They are everybody's mothers and sisters! Whoever forgets will be sacked.

The elders' heads turned with the *trucks'* speed and the efficiency of fast work. So they couldn't think that the contractor's words were untrue. Everyone can't be brothers and sisters. After the final agreement the contractor gave six bottles of *number* one country liquor to the six elders. The elders of Kuruda told the others, "Go to the village, tell the chief, and offer prayers at the shrine. Good times are coming."

The contractor had a word with the driver of the *train* as well. The *train* stops at Murhai. There could be a deal so that the *train* would stop at Kuruda if needed. They'll get a container car. The contractor gave the *driver* a bottle. He's offering fifteen rupees for a full-grown Sal. No expense will block his tremendous profits. He'll sell by the *cubic foot*. He gave Banwari a *transistor*. If Banwari hadn't told him, he wouldn't have known that one could get Sal of this *quality* in this area of dwarf Sals. The entire venture is highly profitable. The contractor praised the uninstructed ignorance of his caste-brothers Prasad, Mulni, and Lalchand. The idiots don't even know what goods they are abandoning. He has given Banwari a rupee per tree in secret. This too leaves him a wide margin of profit. Countless trees will be ready for felling in a few years. Prasad must be kept happy. Soon these parts will be joined to Tohri at that end and Nirlaghat at this. Roads are under construction. Once there are roads, future *transportation* expenses will be saved.

In a little while, the contractor comes to Prasad's house with a box of sweets and a pot of clarified butter. Prasad says, "Mary! Here's our guest. Bring a bit of tea."

Mary has had a bath today. So her body is clean and smooth, her hair oiled and braided. A printed sari worn with the end spread in front of her breasts, brass ornaments on wrist and ear.

Mary enters with tea and snacks on a *tray*, Tehsildar Singh sits up. Wow! what a dish! In these woods?

Prasadji saw it happening. As soon as Mary left he said, My maidservant's daughter. When her mother was as young as she, then . . .

He explained the secret of Mary's beauty and said in conclusion, My wife thinks of her as daughter, she respects us as her parents.

"Of course." Tehsildar Singh says, "Otherwise why do people call you a big man? A big man has a big heart." He thought, the business of felling trees in this forest is most profitable. Mary can make his stay profitable in the other sense as well. Mary is the regular contact and bridge between the outside world of Tohri and Kuruda. At night when she brought Prasadji warm water for his medicine she said, "The bastard tricked you. He took all the profit. Everyone from Tohri to Chhipador is laughing."

Prasadji took off his false teeth and put them in a bowl of water. Then he took his medicine. In a while he said, "What to do, Mary? With no *road*, have I the power to sell at profit to anyone? This happens if you live in the forest. Banwari brought him. Banwari is pig-headed and takes after his mother I first said 'no,' then Lalchand and Mulni got angry. There were many objections at home."

— Banwari's taken his cut.

— You know this?

— I am aware of it.

— What a shame.

Prasadji sighed and gave her a rupee. He gives her like this from time to time. "You take such trouble so I don't get tricked over a piece of fruit, a grain of corn," he said. "My own son understands nothing. What shall I do? Don't I know that he'll sell everything and take off when I die?"

— When you sell trees later, there will be a *road*, don't give it to him. Go yourself to Chhipador. Talk to the big *companies* and do your business. Don't be soft then.

— You're right.

Mary told the Kuruda elders as well, "Twelve annas and eight annas! No porter carries gentlemen's *cases* for this price."

The elders said, "What to do, Mary? If I said 'no' the villagers would go wild. They would say, Who gives us this kind of money?"

Mary said, "He's greedy now. He'll come again in five years.

Then we'll bargain for three or two rupees. And he'll have to give. Otherwise how will he get an outsider here?"

— No *road*, no jobs, you know how it is.

Mary thought, in return for the broker's glance she had shrewdly revealed the man's true nature to everyone.

But Tehsildar Singh didn't forget her. A few days later, when Mary was returning on a water-buffalo's back herding other cattle, the contractor came up to her. How pretty, he said. You look like Hema Malini.

— What?

— You look like Hema Malini.

— You look like a monkey.

Tehsildar Singh felt much encouraged by such a remark and came up close. Mary didn't stop her water-buffalo. As she moved on she took out a sharp machete and said in a lazy voice, "Brokers like you, with tight *pants* and dark glasses, are ten a rupee on the streets of Tohri, and to them I show this machete. Go ask if you don't believe me."

Tehsildar found her way of speaking most beguiling.

Banwari said at the evening meal, "Mary has insulted my friend."

He was speaking to his father, but it was Mary who replied, "How did I insult your friend?"

— You spoke to him rudely.

— This time I let him go with words. If he comes to fuck with me again I'll cut off his nose.

Banwari was scared as well. He said, "What, did he do something crazy?"

— It's crazy talk to me. It may be good talk to you.

Prasadji said, "Ask him not to. These problems don't go with buying trees."

— And Mary shouldn't talk about selling Sal trees at Tohri market. It is illegal to sell Sal trees if they are on your own land. The Sal belongs to the Government.

— Ah, keep your laws. Who keeps land legally here, who doesn't sell Sal in these parts?

Mary said straight to Banwari, "Have I spoken about your tree sale in Tohri market?"

— Have I said you've said? I just asked you not to.

— Don't try to set me straight.

Mary left. Prasadji said, "This is not correct. Tell your friend.

Lives in the house, like a daughter, I am insulted if she's accosted."

Banwari said to Tehsildar, "She's a real bitch, a rude girl, doesn't give a damn for anyone."

— Who wants a damn?

— Besides, her marriage is fixed.

— Where?

— A Muslim's house.

— Dear God! Isn't there a man in her tribe?

— Her choice.

Tehsildar didn't believe that a Mary Oraon from a wild village like Kuruda could blow him away. He stuck to Mary through marking and felling the trees, cutting and transporting them. That Mary wouldn't look at him and would rather marry a Muslim increased his anger.

Then he brings a *nylon* sari for Mary from Daltonganj, sweets for Prasadji. He says to Prasadji, "I come and go, she feeds me tea, I give her a sari." Prasadji didn't accept it, but Tehsildar insisted. Mary had gone to Tohri. She heard about the sari when she got back. First she gave Prasadji the accounts for Tohri market. Then she had tea and toast in the kitchen. Then she went out with the sari.

Tehsildar was sitting in the tent paying the men and women. Lots of people. Mary enters and throws the sari at him. She says, "You think I'm a city whore? You want to grab me with a sari? If you bother me again I'll cut off your nose." She goes off proudly swinging her arms.

Tehsildar loses face in everyone's eyes. He wants to say, I gave something in good faith . . .

The elders say, "Don't give again."

— What?

— Don't give again.

— Is she a good character? Would a good one marry a Muslim?

— Don't say that again.

Suddenly Tehsildar understands, he and his men are in a minority, the others are greater in number. Everyone has a spear or a machete. He shuts up.

At night the *driver* tells him as well, "Don't make trouble with all this. These tribals are a bloodyminded lot. Be problems if they tell the police."

The *driver* knows Tehsildar has a wife and children. He knows that Tehsildar still lusts after women. Mary is indeed an eyeful, but it would be stupid to provoke the tribals and create a *police* case on her account. If Mary was willing, there would have been no problem. Mary is unwilling. Tehsildar must accept that.

Now Prasadji gets serious as well. It is Bhikni who brings tea these days. Tehsildar stops going to the house. But he doesn't give up chasing Mary.

When Mary returns from pasturing cattle, returns from Tohri, or goes the three miles to Murhai *station* to go to Tohri, or goes marketing to Dhuma, Tehsildar keeps his distance and follows her.

The girls say, "Mary, that broker loves you."

— Because he can't catch me. If he does his love will vanish. The white man also loved my mother.

— He'll marry you.

— He has a wife.

— So what?

— Let it go.

The felling goes on. Slowly the weather warms. There are *miles* and *miles* of the flamboyant plant in bloom all around here. New buds appear. Then the gong sounds one day in the priest's house. It is revealed that the ritual of the hunt that the tribes celebrate at the spring festival is for the women to perform this year. For twelve years men run the hunt. Then comes the women's turn. It's Jani Parab. Like the men they too go out with bow and arrow. They run in forest and hill. They kill hedgehogs, rabbits, birds, whatever they can get. Then they picnic together, drink liquor, sing, and return home at evening. They do exactly what the men do. Once in twelve years. Then they light the fire of the spring festival and start talking. Budhni tells stories. That time we killed a leopard. I was young then.

The old women listen, the aging women cook, the young women sing.

They don't know why they hunt. The men know. They have been playing the hunt for a thousand million moons on this day.

Once there were animals in the forest, life was wild, the hunt game had meaning. Now the forest is empty, life wasted and drained, the hunt game meaningless. Only the day's joy is real.

Mary was getting tired of Tehsildar's tireless single-minded pursuit. Jalim might get to know. He'd be wild if she let him know. He might go to Tohri market to kill Tehsildar if he got the chance. Tehsildar has a lot of money, a lot of men. A city bastard. He can destroy Jalim by setting up a larceny case against him.

Tehsildar too was losing patience. The felling would soon be over, they would have to pull up stakes and then what?

Tehsildar caught Mary's hand one day.

The timing was good. No hunt for the men this year. The men will drink and make up new songs for the Spring festival, dress up as clowns and go out to sing for money. Tehsildar has promised them liquor for the festival.

Returning from the felling there is singing every day. In a droning monotone. Mary was listening. On the way back from market. Dusk fell as she listened. She started home.

Tehsildar knew she would come. Tehsildar caught her hand. He said, "I won't let you go today."

At first Mary was scared. Struggling she lost her machete. With great effort, after a good deal of struggling, Mary was able to spring out of his grasp. Both of them stood up. Tehsildar did not have his dark glasses on. Long sideburns, long hair, *polyester trousers*, pointed shoes, a dark red shirt on his back. Against the background of the spring songs Mary thought he was an animal. A-ni-mal. The syllables beat on her mind. Suddenly Mary smiled.

— Mary!

— Stop, stop right there. Don't move up.

— What are you looking at?

— You.

— I, you—

— You want me a lot, no?

— A lot.

— Good.

— What's good?

— I see that you really want me.

— Really want. I've never seen a woman like you. You are worth a million. How will that marketeer know your worth? That Muslim?

— Will you?

— Sure. I'll give you clothes, jewels—

—- Really?

— Everything.

Mary took a deep breath. Then said, "Not today. Today I'm unclean."

— When Mary, when?

Mary's eye and face softened. She said, "On the day of the

feast. Stay near that rock. The women will go far to play the hunt.
I will come to you. You know which rock! You look for me from
behind that stone."

— All right.

— Then that's our pact?

— Yes, Mary.

— But don't tell anyone! A man can do no wrong, but a
woman is soiled. As it is I am illegitimate, and then I was going to
marry a Muslim.

— Tell me you won't.

— Why anymore? Have a bit of patience. Don't follow me
around like that.

— I took so much trouble over you . . .

— I'll make up for everything. On the day of the spring festival.

Mary patted his cheek. She said, "You are nice, dear! I didn't
see at first." She took off sinuously. She knew Tehsildar wouldn't
clasp her from behind a second time.

III

The fire burned last night and tonight as well. Last night the
spring festival fire burned very high and reddened the sky for
quite some time. Today from first light the men are wild with drink
and songs and color. The very old women are looking after the
children.

The women are all in the forest. Each woman has stood
excited in front of her own door armed with machetes and the
men's bows and arrows. As soon as the priest struck the gong they
burst the sky with sharp halloos and ran forward. Bhikni is running in Prasadji's *shirt* and Mrs. Prasad's petticoat.

Budhni, Mungri, Somari, Sanichari—their running days are
over. They have gone to the abandoned Bomfield bungalow with
bottles of liquor, food for cooking, pots, snacks, fried corn, onion-
chili. There is water in the well there. The men too cook and eat
there after the hunt. Budhni had said to the women, "In our time
we never returned without something, a hedgehog, a hare, a par-
tridge. Let's see what you do. How you hunt."

Mary is wearing a new sari today. Jalim's gift. There are beads
around her neck. Dancing she clasps Budhni and says, "I'll marry
you after I play the hunt. Then I am the husband, you the wife."

— Good.

— I'll make you dance.

— I'll dance.

Mary is running over with joy today. She has put ten rupees into her mother's hands and bought four of her mother's chickens. The chickens are now in Sanichari's hands. Mary has also contributed two bottles of liquor. This is over and above. The women have already asked and received liquor from Tehsildar. Tehsildar has given the men a goat plus the liquor. He has promised to demonstrate the *twist* dance of the city in the evening. He will drink bottle after bottle. His tree-felling is done, just small pieces are left. Many bits. With great generosity he has given them to the people of Kuruda as firewood. He has said, I'll come again, I'll hire only you to fell trees. I'll keep you pickled in liquor then.

Joking with Budhni's group Mary also ran along. Sanichari said, "Look how Mary is looking today. As if she's Mulniji's daughter-in-law."

Budhni said, "When she leaves after marriage Kuruda will lose an eye."

Mungri said, "She has never come to the village empty-handed. You see her now, you've forgotten how pretty Bhikni was as a young woman?"

Somri was half-asleep as she walked. Suddenly she sang out with eyes almost closed:

Fire in the Spring   Fire at the feast

Look and come home   Not to forget—

The others took up the refrain. Four elderly decrepit women long past their youth singing songs of love, the sun warming, the mood thickening, and the sound of gong and horn in the distance.

Mary ran on. The women are all going up Kuruda Hill, entering the forest, going to the side of the cut. Mary is laughing. They won't find a kill. Like all games the hunt game has its rules. Why kill hedgehogs or hares or partridges? You get the big beast with bait.

In her colored sari and red blouse Mary is now like the flamboyant tree in motion. As if a bunch of flowers from that flamboyant tree is running in the wind. Red flowers on all sides. Everything is red. A hare ran past. Mary laughed. She knows where the hare lives. Go back! No fear! Mary said laughing. In her drunken abandon. A great thirst dances in her blood. Tehsildar, Tehsildar, I'm almost there. Tehsildar wants her a lot. Now Jalim is nothing to her. With how much violence can

Tehsildar want her? How many *degrees Fahrenheit*? Is his blood as wild as Mary's? As daring?

A hedgehog. Go, go away! If it hadn't been today Mary would have killed it, eaten the flesh. Today a small thing cannot please her. She wants to hunt the big beast! A man, Tehsildar. She sees the rock from a distance. Straight, steep stone. Stone jutting out from the top like a *ledge*. Gitginda vines have come down in a dense mat. On it the yellow flower of the gitginda. Behind the creeper is concealment. Mary's blood burst up at the thought. Forward behind the creeper is the ravine, loose stones on its sides. No one knows how deep the ravine is. No one has gone all the way down. If one could go down into that bottomless cold darkness? She and Tehsildar! She noticed Tehsildar's red *shirt*.

Imported liquor, *cigarettes*, Tehsildar.

— Come inside, dear.

— Where is inside? Inside you?

— Yes dear, yes.

— By the ravine. Behind the creeper.

— First have a drink?

— Why just a drink? Give me a *cigarette*.

— How does it taste?

— Great.

— Not so fast.

— I want to get drunk.

— How drunk?

— I want to get very very drunk.

More booze. She's getting drunk. Stars are strobing in her head. Ah, the stuff is putting spangles in front of her eyes. Shining spangles. Behind them is Tehsildar's face. More liquor. The bottle rolls off. Into the depths of the ravine. Not even a sound. How deep is the ravine? Yes, the face is beginning to look like the hunted animal's.

Mary caresses Tehsildar's face, gives him love bites on the lips. There's fire in Tehsildar's eyes, his mouth is open, his lips wet with spittle, his teeth glistening. Mary is watching, watching, the face changes and changes into? Now? Yes, becomes an animal.

— Now take me?

Mary laughed and held him, laid him on the ground. Tehsildar is laughing, Mary lifts the machete, lowers it, lifts, lowers.

A few million moons pass. Mary stands up. Blood? On her clothes? She'll wash in the cut. With great deftness she takes the *wallet* from Tehsildar's *pocket*. A lot of money. A lot of money. She undoes the fold in the cloth at her waist and puts the money with her own savings.

Then first she throws Tehsildar in the ravine, his *wallet, ciga-rettes,* his handkerchief. Stone after stone. Hyenas and leopards will come at night, smelling blood. Or they won't.

Mary comes out. Walks naked to the cut. Bathing naked in the cut her face fills with deep satisfaction. As if she has been infi-nitely satisfied in a sexual embrace.

In the women's gathering Mary drank the most wine, sang, danced, ate the meat and rice with the greatest relish. At first everyone mocked her for not having made a kill. Then Budhni said, "Look how she's eating? As if she has made the biggest kill."

Mary kissed Budhni with her unwashed mouth. Then she started dancing, beating two empty bottles together. The night air is cool. Sanichari lights the fire.

Drink and song, drink and dance. When everyone is dancing around the fire and singing,

Ooh Haramdeo our god
Let there be a Spring feast like this every year—
Let us hunt this way every year—
We'll give you wine
We'll give you wine—

Then Mary moves back as she dances. Backing in the dark. They are dancing, dancing hard. Mary runs fast in the dark. She knows the way by heart. She will walk seven *miles* tonight by way of Kuruda Hill and reach Tohri. She will awaken Jalim. From Tohri there are *buses, trucks.* They will go away somewhere. Ranchi, Hazaribagh, Gomo, Patna. Now, after the big kill, she wants Jalim.

The spring festival fires are scattered in the distance. Mary is not afraid, she fears no animal as she walks, watching the *railway line* in the dark, by starlight. Today all the mundane blood-condi-tioned fears of the wild quadruped are gone because she has killed the biggest beast.

Douloti the Bountiful

I

These days everyone calls Ganori Nagesia Crook Nagesia. He wasn't always Crook, crooked and broken, that is. He was firm and straight like everybody else. How he did get up in the morning, and go off to the field with his can of water, chewing on his tooth twig. Back from the field he would say to his wife, Give me something love?

Oh yes, rice-lentils-puffed bread-stuffed bread.

No Nagesia gets such a menu from a wife of a morning. This is the talk of their deep despair. Or the talk of the dream that does not come true. The wives of the Nagesias give them cornmeal, or

19

kurthi porridge. Ganori's wife gave him the same fare. Having fed, and drunk a deal of water, with a pinch of tobacco in his mouth, Ganori would run to the Master's house. He would slave from morning to night, carry sacks of paddy and wheat on his back.

How blemished his fortune, that he broke into a crooked mis-shape.

He is a Nagesia by birth, their community is small. In Palamu, the communities of Nagesias and Parhaias are small. The bigger communities are Bhuyians, Dusads, Dhobis, Ganjus, Oraons, Mundas. The village is called Seora. Its owner is Munabar Singh, a Chandela Rajput. Crook's job is to look after Munabar's plow steer. Everything is his job. Crook can't reckon what is and is not his job.

Sometimes Crook imagines some bespectacled town gentle-man who has come by car, and listening to him, is writing down everything. Actually these people have heard that the government is going to abolish the bonded labor [kamyouti] system. Then bespectacled gentry will come from the towns and write every-thing down on paper. This too is a dream.

Crook talks to such a gentleman in his mind.

— All work in the owner's house is yours?
— Why not, sir?
— Why must you do all the work in Munabar's house?
— How can I not have to do it all?
 O learned town gentleman with glasses
 All Munabar's work is Crook's work
 I am his bondslave [kamiya].
— You are his kamiya?
— I am his bonded laborer [seokia].
— His seokia?
— I am his bonded worker [beth-begar].
— Hey, what are you? kamiya, seokia, or beth-begar?
— I am everything, I am his chattel slave. Come come, write everything down. Write and get in your car, buzz off to town, and I stay behind in the jungle. Each in his own place.
— You and I are men of two different worlds.

No such conversation has taken place. Crook has thought it all up. If such a thing had happened, if some bespectacled gentle-man had come, words like this are what he would have heard from Crook Nagesia.

Crook Nagesia is Munabar Singh Chandela's kamiya. Who

reckons how long the Crook Nagesias have been their servant-kamiya-seokia? It's a matter of hundreds of years. When did the Rajput brahman from outside come to this land of jungle and mountain? When did all the land slide into their hands? Then cheap field labor became necessary. That was the beginning of making slaves on hire purchase.

Crook Nagesia is Munabar's kamiya. Munabar Chandela is a big man. You must cross four villages. His huge house is on the bus route, in the market area, with an extensive garden. Munabar's son lives there. The son is very smart. An important government servant. Now times are different. There is a need to keep one's own man in a government department to hang on to the land. His son is an important government servant. Munabar's footing has become much firmer as a result.

Munabar Singh Chandela has built the house. But he doesn't live in the house. He lives in the village of Seora. He keeps Dusad, Ghasi, Nagesia, Munda, Lohar, Oraon, Bhuyian, Chamar, Parhaia as kamiya. There is no end to the people he has lent money to, and made into kamiyas. By what strength? Where is his strength?

That all kamiya women know. On winter nights old kamiya women light fires to warm their limbs. Then they say,
By the strength of loans, by the strength of loans.
Two rupees ten rupees hundred rupees
Ten seers of wheat, five of rice
Munabar lends us.
We don't know what to do
We gape like fools
His pet wolves catch our hands
Smear ink on our left thumbs
Take our mark on white paper
Put the paper in the safe
He has thousands of sheets of paper like this
He is king by the strength of loans
He is the government by the strength of loans
He is the patwari, he is the jungle *officer*
He is the police station, he is the *policeman,*
He the judge the verdict the court.
If he wants to go to town
The *train* stops at Chowkipura *Halt* that day
If he invites
The Minister comes to Seora village

He has become the government by lending money
And we have become kamiyas
We will never be free.

When Crook Nagesia's name was Ganori, then he gave his
thumbprint to Munabar and took three hundred rupees. How
daring he had become that he took three hundred rupees, he feels
faint to think. He really needed it then. Quite a few of them had
gone to *jail* on charges of stealing water-buffaloes from the market. If you go to *jail* and do time you have to feed your community when you return. This is such a rule that you can't get
around it.

At this time his eldest daughter and his eldest son were both
married. And he had to feast the folks again and again. He also
had to do the purification for returning from *jail*. Had to give a
goat to the son-in-law. Ganori borrowed all that money for many
reasons. Some flour was left over even after everything was over.
They could eat flour and water for some days. Ganori became a
kamiya when he took that money.

At first Ganori didn't think becoming a kamiya was a special
misfortune. He's been seeing kamiyas all over since birth. It's
fate's decree to become a kamiya. Our Lord Fate comes to write
fate on the forehead of the newborn in the dress of a head-shaved
brahman. No one can evade what he writes down.

On the high-caste boy's forehead he writes property, land, cattle, trade. Education, job, contract. On the outcaste's forehead he
writes bondslavery. The sun and the moon move in the sky by
Fate's rule. The poor boys of Seora village become kamiyas of the
Munabars, Fate's rule.

Who will change this rule?

Ganori Nagesia is not that man. He did a million things for
the master, watched the plow-cattle. His work was over at evening
when he put expensive oxen and water-buffaloes back into the
pen. Then he returned to his shanty. They never had or will have
a home better than a shanty. Bono Nagesia wanted to build a
good home, and he suffered much thereafter.

The Nagesias know well that when a Nagesia child is six days
old, that day our lord Fate will lower from the sky a yellow
turmeric-dyed string. Lord Fate will come down to earth on that
string. He will look like a head-shaved brahman.

He will never enter the room with the Nagesia mother and
child. He stands outside the shanty and writes with a thick pen in

high-Hindi in the clothbound ledger, You will spend your life as you are born. You will never build a home better than a shanty.

Bono Nagesia from Seora village did not keep this in mind. His feet always had wheels. He went here and there. They say money flies in the Bihar air. High-caste folks know this. I am only a Nagesia, a negligible person. Yet shouldn't I try and see? I don't hold with work fixed by birth.

Bono went to Dhanbad to dig for coal. A contractor called him. I'm taking some Mundas to Ranchi district to quarry coal. Let me write your name also as Munda, like them. Let me write your address as Station Duranda. Come on, come on. Raise a lot of cash at a coal quarry.

Bono cut coal and returned with cold cash. The cash turned his head. Tell me why it shouldn't. What Nagesia in Seora village has seen real cash? Cold cash?

And what Nagesia has come back with news of the underworld? You see the world above ground, below is the underworld. Bono would say, "O my god. I saw the sky dark. I saw the darkness of hell in the coal mine. *Double* darkness. How far down we went, it was like the underworld."

— What did you see?

— What was there to see? I saw darkness.

Bono wanted to build a home with the money from Dhanbad. An adobe structure. Very firm, very strong.

He built a fine adobe cabin. All the money he brought from Dhanbad he poured into the hut. The other Nagesias sighed.

Not in envy. The Nagesias of Seora village do not sigh in envy. They are not Munabar's wife that they will sigh in envy. Munabar's wife can't bear others' good luck. A simple soul, she gasps with her fat body. She smokes a water-pipe. She can't hide anything. She says all the time, "I can't bear other people's good fortune, dear!"

She goes to her son's house from time to time. She says, "I'll stay here a month." She comes back after four days.

— O mistress, why did you come back?

— I couldn't stay.

— Why mistress, why?

— Daughter-in-law didn't let me stay.

— What did she do?

— Nothing. What will she do to me? She will cook a pudding, she puts in this much butter. She tears her dress, she gives it to the maid. The holy man begs, she gives away a rupee. I am filled with envy. My chest burns.

— So you came back?

— I saw more, new rooms, new cows. I can't see other people's good fortune, dear, I'm filled with envy.

— They are not other people, he's your own son.

— Listen, everyone but yourself is other people.

Munabar's wife is an openhearted person. She suffers only when she sees other people flourishing. So she doesn't go and look. She gasps with her fat body at home, and curses.

Munabar is a bad man.

The Nagesias of Seora sighed when they saw Bono's house go up. What is Bono doing? A Nagesia doesn't do this. Raise a house because he has two hundred rupees in hand?

First, a Nagesia shouldn't have money. If he does, he shouldn't raise a roof. If you raise a roof, or buy a water-buffalo, the master will notice. If you buy land, the master will grab it. If you buy cattle, the master will snatch them. If you buy an umbrella for your head, or shoes for your feet, he'll have you tied to the post in the yard and beaten. That's why the other Nagesias sighed when they saw him build a hut. What sort of thing is Bono doing? Munabar Singh Chandela will consider this a dreadful impertinence. He will punish Bono in whatever way.

Old Bhuneswar had said, "There's only aunt, wife, and son in your family. How much better it would have been if you had taken the money and gone somewhere else with them."

— Where would I have gone?

— Again to Dhanbad.

— What would I have done?

— Worked at the mine.

— Mine! Work!

— Well, didn't you bring back money with that work? My word! So much money!

— I did not want to spill all this. Now I see that I must speak. I was the contractor's *laborer*. People brought by the contractor work in the mine. They don't get much money.

— What?

— Yes. The contractors cheat you hard. When I told the unine [union] bosses they agreed in word. But they did nothing. Contractor and unine are friends under cover. The government took the mine. But how many workers are permanent? The contractor brings *labor*. The unine is there for permanent *labor*. No unine will say make contract *labor* permanent.

— What does that mean?

— What am I telling you? Government—unine—contractor—slum landlord—market-trader—shopkeeper—post office, each is the other's friend. Down in the mine! How dark down there! And at week's end, *double* darkness above the mine as well. The contractor's hoods stood with guns. They snatched the money. We got it only after they took their cut.

— You had a hard time.

— The unine didn't do a thing. Talk to the government *officer*, he laughs. The slumlord takes out rent. The trader and the shopkeeper will zoom down like a hungry wolf. They will falsify your account. Everyone sucks the coolie's blood. If a note comes from home, the postman doesn't give it without money. Send money home, the mail clerk says, "Give me a cut."

— Then how did you bring money? Your aunt cried a lot for you. I'd reason, why are you bringing Bono bad luck with your crying? He is all right.

— No uncle, I wasn't all right.

— How did you bring money?

— Much suffering. You think people mortgage their lives in exchange for a loan only in Seora? At the mine too they borrow and are mortgaged to the moneylender.

— Tell us about your money.

— A hood used to come to the coolie shanties. He had a liquor store as well. He walked around in the area. He had a lot of money. Pockets always heavy. He'd take out a 100-rupee note to buy *cigarettes*. A man with so much money is hard to find.

— Why did he go to the shanties?

— Lusting after women. He wouldn't leave a woman alone. Then he'd sleep in our rooms. It was very late that night. He was very drunk. Finally he passed out and fell asleep in our room. There are many men who look like babies when they sleep. When you look at them you think this is some mother's child, and you feel some compassion. When a hood sleeps there is no compassion. He doesn't look like a mother's son either. This guy was like that.

— You took his money?

— You feel no compassion. When a muscleman sleeps you think it's a devil asleep.

— You killed him?

— I didn't kill him, uncle. I was watching him and thinking, you've opened a liquor business in the ghetto to suck the coolies' money. You're also taking the honor of their daughters and wives. You are a real devil. And then ...

— What happened?

— It was as if my two hands did a dance. My hands said, Let's wring his neck. I reasoned with them a lot. My hands didn't listen. They said, We cut coal in the mine. We'll do what we like.

— Then?

— Then my hands did their dance. They ran up. A sleeping drunk is heavy. Dead he's heavier. See how much strength my hands had? My body has no strength. I am thin and slight. I myself dragged him in the middle of the night and took him very far. Far away I threw him near a drainage ditch. I rolled him into the ditch. Then there was only one thought in my mind, the coolies will suffer if his body is found in the slum.

— You took his money?

— No, Bono didn't kill for cash. When I got home I saw the *wallet* lying there. I saw a lot of money when I opened it.

— Won't the *police* get you?

— Uncle, there are many murders in Dhanbad *town,* which one is solved? Who'd they catch? Do they know my name and address? They knew I am Bono Munda, from Ranchi District. If they look, they'll look for Bono Munda, Duranda Precinct, district Ranchi.

— Good, you did fine.

— Not me, my two hands.

— Tell me why you're building a house.

— What else? The master will snatch pots and pans, cattle, whatever I buy. He can't take my house.

— You're building such a fine place, won't the master object?

— No no. I went to the master. I asked for permission at his feet.

— And the master gave permission?

— Yes, he did.

— He did!

Bhuneswar knitted his brow. Suspicion appeared in his mind. Bono Nagesia will raise a roof on adobe, and the master gave him permission? Why? The suspicion in his mind is at a great depth.

Behind it is a narrative that is as immemorial as the Ganga River or the Himalayas.

The bespectacled town gentlemen will never understand these things. Among the Nagesias of Seora village, Bono went to Dhanbad, and Bhuneswar went to Daltonganj once. The school-*master* from the next village called him. There a bespectacled gentleman had asked him so many things. Bhuneswar hadn't been able to give all the answers. But many questions were awakened in his mind. These he put to the school*master*. The school*master* was Chamar by caste, from Patna district. All the proprietors like Munabar were enraged because a man from the Chamar caste had come as the school*master*. It was they who'd maneuvered him out. The school*master* had told Bhuneswar to come with him when he left for Daltonganj. Bhuneswar told him many things later.

— Sir! The gentleman with glasses came from town. There's electric light in town, and so many cars. No one speaks of caste there. He told us we were independent, and there was no difference in castes any more.

— That's true, uncle.

— If so, why don't the rules change? Why doesn't Nagesia-Dusad-Ganju kill a brahman or Rajput with a gun?

— All this has happened for ever, but it can't happen any more. This too is true.

— Sir, the ways that are in force are the ways of before. All I see is my lord the Sun rising in the east, the birds eating acorns, and the Koel River flowing.

— Bravo Bhuneswar, you say it well, you know?

— I see also that the old rules are in force. I want to build my place with my money, I need my master's permission. I'll buy pots and pans with my money, the master must say yes. I can't eat on metal plates, can't use umbrella or shoe, can't send my boy to government school, even if I have money, for I don't have the master's order.

— These rules don't exist no more.

— These are the rules that go on, sir. Rajput or brahman doesn't put his offerings at the feet of Chamar or Ghasi, they don't say, Orders please, sir! I'll arrange my son's marriage, my daughter will come home after her wedding, my mother dies, I must mourn her the right way. Everyone is equal? How so?

— Why didn't you tell the gentleman?

— Dear me, wouldn't he have thickened his eyes and

scolded me then? The high-caste town gentleman would have heard these words from the low-caste villager and torn up his paper and left.

Bhuneswar didn't say all this to Bono. The statement that the master had given permission raised a suspicion in his mind that kept needling him.

Bono Nagesia built his house. The walls were whitewashed. The roof was thatched. His aunt mixed colors and painted monkeys, elephants, horses, birds, flowers on the white walls. Everyone came to see. Everyone said it was wonderful.

Munabar Singh Chandela got some men to surround the place and burn Bono's house. They trussed up Bono like a pig and carried him hanging to Munabar's office. It was quite dark. Munabar's face couldn't be seen. But Bono could feel that even at the sight of Munabar's face no compassion would come. Nor the thought that Munabar was some mother's darling.

When the hood was sleeping, then Bono's two hands had told him many things. Now both his hands are tied with new rope. So the hands couldn't speak. Munabar kept him locked up in a room all night. In the morning he undid the ropes and made him put his thumbprint on a sheet of white paper.

— Take these twenty-five rupees. You are borrowing this because your house burnt down. From now on you are my bondslave. You will repay by the body's labor. I could have made your aunt, wife, and son my bondslaves too. But they have no strength in their bodies, they won't be able to work hard. I won't ever get back the cost of giving them snacks and their breakfast of thin gruel.

Bono had stood up.

— If you work with concentration, you will repay twenty-five rupees. You'll go to Dhanbad again, you'll bring money again.

Bono had said nothing.

— Go, build a brick house. Munabar laughed when he said this. Encouraged, the men around him laughed as well. Bono left the room. The blood in his body was throbbing hard.

Bhuneswar had taken his aunt, wife, and son. The aunt cried out when she saw Bono. Bhuneswar stopped her. What's there to weep for? Has the master never burnt down a new house put up by a poor Nagesia before this? Did a poor Nagesia never become a bondslave before this? It had happened before, and would happen again. It would go on in this way for as long as my lord the Sun would rise from the Eastern Hills and set in the Western Hills.

Bhuneswar had spoken in profound compassion, "Bono! Don't worry. We will all bring bamboo from the forest, we will give labor, we will put up your place again."

— Do you have Moua [a drink made from a local fruit]?

— To drink?

— To massage on my body.

— I'll give you the burnt oil from a lamp.

Bhuneswar massaged burnt oil on Bono's body with great care. He had said to Bono's aunt and wife, "Stay with me now. You'll go when you have a new place."

Bono gave Ganori ten rupees. "Buy some rice at the open market, Ganori. Let's cook some starchy rice, let's all eat together. Don't buy in the village. The master will know. True. The village store will also cheat on the weight."

Bono sat down to eat with everyone. After the meal he doesn't leave the leaf. Hey Bono, get up. The rice on your fingers is crackling dry. How long will you sit?

Bono says, "What will happen to auntie?"

— What do you mean?

— This is something to think about.

— What nonsense are you saying?

— I took money to build my place, and became a bondslave. I will arrange a marriage between Dhano and Ganori's daughter Douloti. Thus Dhano has borrowed money, he too is a bondslave. Douloti will come to live, I'll have a feast. Thus my wife has borrowed, she too is a bondslave.

— What are you saying?

— I am right. Then see, father-mother-son are all Munabar's bondslaves. But no one reckoned for auntie. She is dead. She must be burnt, must have a funeral, will she become a bonded worker herself to supply those expenses? There is no one else to become a bondslave? I can see Aunt dying, and then becoming Munabar's bonded worker. The living and the dead are both his bondslaves.

Bono foamed at the mouth and fainted as he said this. Then everyone poured water on his head, brought him to his senses. Then Bono sighed and lay down under a tree. He did not speak again.

That night there was a knock on Ganori Nagesia's door. Ganori opened the door.

— Is it Bono?

— Yes, Ganori?

— Come, come in.

— No, Ganori.

— Where are you going?

— I am leaving.

— Where?

— I don't know. But I'm not going to slave for his bond. I will go anywhere I can.

— If the master catches you?

— I will escape by *train*.

— Where?

— Do I know? There are many places like Dhanbad and Patna. Calcutta is also a very big city. No untouching problems there. When I was in Dhanbad, I heard a lot about Calcutta.

—You'll leave?

— Yes. I really wanted to make a marriage between your daughter and Dhano. It's not to happen. Give my wife these ten rupees. I am going with five. There is a brass dish buried under the foundation of the house. Uncle Bhuneswar should dig it up and take it.

That was Bono's final departure from Seora village. So many things happened in Seora village. Munabar's white horse died. The lightning-struck tree suddenly fell over one night and suddenly the bear-players came to the village. Although Munabar made the bears dance in front of his own house, the whole village could after all see.

Munabar stampeded after Bono in vain. He cross-examined the Nagesias most thoroughly. The Nagesias had no clue. The villagers themselves did not talk about this but cutting wheat in Munabar's fields they would look at each other and think, We could not escape the master's clutches. However, one of us has. Bono has escaped.

The women started up the harvesting song whenever they remembered Bono:

Down in the wheat field a yellow bird has come

O his beak is red.

Their small children would pick the fallen grains of wheat. They would pick them up quite like birds.

Munabar did not give any work to Bono's aunt, wife, and son. They too left the village one day. Whether they left following news from Bono is unknown. In this way the name "Bono" was erased from Seora village.

II

So many things came up as I tried to tell you how Ganori Nagesia became Crook Nagesia. These things must be said. In the world of Seora village, Bono is just as true as Ganori.

After Bono left, Munabar became extremely ruthless about his bonded workers. Whenever the Nagesias, the Dusads, Ghasis, the various tribes of bonded laborers met, this is what they discussed.

There are landowners and moneylenders in every village. They are not all so ruthless. Bonded labor is sown into the soil of this district. Every house has a bonded laborer. Not all masters are so ruthless. No one has seen what a good master is like. But they have heard that there are good masters.

At this point, unsettling everyone, arrived the body count or census of 1961. Mohan Dusad knows the various disasters that can happen if human beings are counted like cows and sheep. Weaving grass mats is a way of assuring extra income for people of this area. Suddenly, weaving a mat, Mohan started speaking. Mohan has a very particular way of speaking. He says everything in a quarreling tone. As if people had been quarreling for some time and words are leading to words. He suddenly burst out as he went on weaving.

— It is most unnatural to count human beings.

— Why?

— You count people, you are asking for famine. There was a census at the time of my father's father. And right away a big Hunger, a real famine. All the new babies were deaf and dumb.

— Yes, I've heard.

— Did they count your mother?

— Mother wasn't born yet.

— If your mother had been born, if she'd been counted then, you too would have been born deaf and dumb. And we wouldn't have had to listen to all this.

— No joking matter. You think a census is an easy thing.

— Not at all.

The census was a hard thing in Seora village. The government people were out of their minds. At first Nagesia, Dusad, Dhobi,

Ganju neither opened their mouths, nor spoke. And when they did it was hard to stop them.

— What sort of thing is this? You won't write the names of the children who are dead? Dead or alive they are my children. Their names won't be in the government books?

— Listen sir! Write my mother's brother's name first. Uncle stole my goat and ran off to his daughter's in-laws. You are government people. If you write it up, I will surely get it back.

— You'll write my age? Write, write, maybe ten, maybe twenty, eh? What? I have grandchildren, I can't have so few years? How old are people when they have grandchildren? Fifty, sixty? No, no, how can I be sixty? I have heard that our brave master is fifty. I am Ghasi by caste, and poor. How can I have more age than he? The master has more land, more money, everything more than me. How can he have less age? No, sir, write ten or twenty.

The 1961 census took place in this way.

In 1962 was the *vote*. What *vote*, why *vote*, tell me what the people of Seora village know about this. They will *vote* for whomever Munabar tells them to *vote* for. They don't know what the vote or the election signifies. But Munabar is a Rajput and Jayvant Singh is also a Rajput. Munabar has told them that they must *vote* for his caste brother. Then that's what they'll do. You can't say "no" to the master.

Munabar Chandela said to the opposition candidates before the *Elections*, "Why are you wasting your pains? They will *vote* for the candidate we specify. They will vote for the group of candidates we mark out. Jayvant Singh is our candidate, everyone will vote for him. This time around. Why are you spending so much breath? When they come to your speeches, they come for the fun."

Jayvant Singh depends on Munabar Singh as well. Will they *vote* for him? he asks.

— Why not?

— Who knows what they'll do? Shall I give them a rupee per head? Whatever you say.

— Brother, they too are giving a rupee.

— Shall I feed them puffed bread and stuffed bread?

— That may be better.

Much later gun and muscleman enter the voting game. In 1962 the picture was clearer. Jayvant Singh leaves everything to Munabar. Money he has to spend. He gives all the money to

Munabar and Munabar tells everyone, Put your vote on Jayvant's symbol, otherwise things will go bad.

Even after all this there is a festival in the air on *Election* Day. As if it's a Fair or a Holiday. People excitedly get in groups and go *vote*. But they find the appearance of the *voting* center most suspicious.

Omniscient Mohan Dusad starts whispering and muttering. "What sort of thing is this, that each person is put into an empty pigeonhole? How shall I put the mark on the paper or on my hand?" The *election officer* explains. Bhuneswar cannot understand at all. The *officer* scolds him loudly. So Mohan Dusad says, "Now run away. No doubt there will be fighting."

Everyone runs for their life. The representatives of the candidates run to catch the *voters*. The *police* run to help them. When the *police* run, then Mohan Dusad says, breathing hard, "The government doesn't mean well."

In such glory do the Third General Elections come to an end. After the counting Jayvant Singh disappears from the Voting Center, relieved for the next five years. The roots of the wood apple tree in front of Munabar's office were hollow. Suddenly it crashed down in a storm. Word got around that the Baram-Spirit lived in the tree, and he left in anger. Everyone had thought it was a summer storm. Baram-Spirit left in a cloud of dust.

Munabar was in pain after the tree fell. Perhaps there will be *cholera* or smallpox in the village now. He will arrange for a penance service. An educated *sadhu* comes as priest. He tells everyone, we must worship the Mother Cow and we must unite to protect Hinduism.

Seora village remains highly unstable for these reasons. It is at this time that Ganori Nagesia's carelessness sends Munabar's plow steer into the tiger's belly. All the jungle has not yet been cleared. Leopards still turn up. Drunk on moua, Ganori had forgotten to fetch the animal from the field at day's end. The jungle is a good way off from the field. The steer was independent spirited. It was probably going to take a look at the moon. Otherwise there's no reason why it went toward the forest.

The fall of the sacred wood apple tree. Then the untimely death of the steer. Munabar is furious. If the steer's gone you fill the cart. Take the yoke on your shoulders. Lift, lift. Pull the cart. Do you know how much a head of steer costs? I'll straighten you out with the whip.

The scene is delightful. The big *officer's* Dad, the big land-owner of the area, Munabar Singh Chandela has put the axle of the carriage on the shoulders of a human being and is screaming his abuse, shaking his whip in the air. Ganori tries to lift the cart by the strength of his shoulders. Trying, he falls on his face. The axle sits hard on him.

Tohri hospital is eleven miles away. Bhuneswar and others take him there on a wood-and-rope cot. After three months he returns with his body broken and becomes Crook Nagesia. His back is stooped, and he has to limp on his right foot when he walks. You cannot expect a better repair job at the Tohri hospital. Is his head all right? He sees his little daughter Douloti and says, "Who is this girl?"

His wife said, "God save me! That is Douloti."

— Is that it? Where is the goat?

— I sold it.

— Did you sell it or did Kalia's mother sell it?

— I sold it myself. Take this, here's a smoke. It's a nice blanket around your shoulders. Did they give it to you at the hospital?

— No, no. Bono bought it.

— Bono? Which Bono?

— There is only one Bono. Bono Nagesia.

— Where did you get him?

— He came. Listen, if there is a real human being in Seora, it is Bono. We are all animals. It's good that the master beat me and made me crooked. What should he do with an animal but beat it? Bono is human and we are all animals. This is the thing.

— Shut up, people will hear.

— What do you mean "people will hear"? Everybody knows this.

— Where did you find him?

— They put me in hospital. Bhuneswar, Jhari Munar and Jakan were gassing away outside the hospital. They are thinking that I will die. There's a *truck* waiting outside the hospital. The *driver* is drinking tea. What a surprise! Who gets out of the *truck?* Our Bono.

— O Lord Mahabir the great. What an astonishing thing! We had taken it for granted that the bastard was dead. No, no, the son of a bitch is not dead. He asked Bhuneswar and the others, What are you doing here? You bond workers of Munabar Chandela, why are you here? How very well he speaks now, eh.

— How does he look?

— Different. A red and blue shirt on his back, a band around his head, and a drum around his neck.

— Why?

— He travels about in far market towns, gets people together with his drum, and tells stories as he sings. I feel amazed to think where he learnt stories, and where he learnt to sing. He sits on a *truck* if he gets one.

— Really amazing stuff.

— After Seora he has really been around. He went to Ramgarh at the time of the famine. Someone gave him that shirt there.

— You saw yourself?

— I did.

— I can't believe this.

— Do you think I believed it? I opened my eyes in hospital and saw Bono standing. Then I thought, dear oh dear! Bono is dead, and so am I. No one gave him a proper funeral so he's wandering about as a demon and a ghost, and he has come to take me. But he said to me, You asshole bondslave! He put you in the shafts instead of a beast and you pulled the cart? Then I realized that it was truly our Bono.

— His wife, Dhano, aunt?

— They are all digging a pond in Boroto.

— What, Bono is getting a pond dug?

— Don't talk nonsense like townsfolk, Douloti's mother. There is a huge *mission* at Boroto. The *Father* there is having a big pond cut after the famine. Bono's wife and they are doing the digging work. Bono is wandering in the market towns. He's right. He's seen the world. How brave he is. Not an animal like us.

— He gave you this blanket?

— Bono gave it to me. Gave it to me one day in hospital. He said, They gave it to me at the *Mission*, I give it to you, don't sell it, wear it.

— Nice blanket. Keeps the cold out.

— Douloti is wearing a nice cloth?

— I'll tell you everything.

— What, wife?

Crook's throat is dry. What will the wife say? What will he hear? When he's not home, where does his daughter get a good cloth? They beat up the father and sent him to hospital. Did the master abduct the girl? Munabar never does such a thing. His lust is for mature women, after all. His children are born in the houses of Mukami Dusadin and Rajbi Dhobin. Those boys are also Munabar's bonded laborers. Did Munabar lose his mind over Douloti?

Douloti's mother kept sighing. "What shall I tell you? You're not expected to live, I was half-crazed. I went to Tahar with the daughter."

— Why?

— Misraji [Mr. Misra] is a barambhon [brahman], a god. I went to take consecrated flowers and leaves from him.

— What happened there?

— Another god was sitting there. Some relative of Misraji's. Big strong man. The father of three sons. He felt a lot of pity for Douloti. What's the matter with you, how did it happen, asked the lot. How much talk, what can I tell you!

— You didn't say anything, did you?

— No no, what do you think? Munabar Singh always goes to Misraji. If I say a word, master will know everything.

— That's the thing.

— But that god fed Douloti a lot of puffed and stuffed bread, found out everything. The more he heard the more he shook his head, clicked his tongue, and said, What a pity, how unfortunate.

— O god! Douloti told everything?

— Told everything. Then the god bought us two pounds of flour. I tied up the flour at the end of my cloth and came home. Ate very well for two days.

— Very good. Then what happened?

— Let's say this was a month ago. Then Douloti was going to cut matting grass with Bhuneswar. There too the same god. Saw them.

— Oh my god!

— He was talking with Bhuneswar and looking at Douloti. Douloti came home running. That god gave Bhuneswar this cloth for Douloti. He said, Give her this. I feel sorry for the girl.

— So he gave. Why did Douloti wear that cloth?

— She always wears torn stuff. If she gets a new cloth can she be patient, or hold herself?

— Why did Douloti tell him everything? Is she a child? If she were married she would be a mother now. She told everything about the master, this will go to the master and he'll take off my hide.

— A god after all! She told him everything because she was afraid.

— She was very wrong.

— The master was looking for you.

— I'll go, definitely.

Bhuneswar, Mohan Munar, Jakam, and Jhari came to Crook's place. They are very curious. Ganori Nagesia fell on his face as he tried to pull Munabar's cart. His body broke and he became Crook. He will never be able to stand straight in this life. They are all very sorry at his misfortune.

But this is also true that he has been in a hospital in a market town like Tohri. Electric light burns there. *Buses* run, the *train* stops, the market sits three times a week, the *circus* plays in a tent. Occasionally there are *movies*. Tohri is a little town. It is not Munabar's empire like Seora. Is it to be minimized that Ganori has stayed in such a place?

Everybody has arrived, Crook felt highly honored. Then tears sprang in his eyes.

— I will not be able to walk without a stick.

— Yes, yes, that is so.

— And will I be able to work?

— Some.

— What's in my future?

— Brother, don't go on about the future. The way you were hurt, you should be dead.

— It would have been better if I had died.

— Stop that noise. Now tell us, did they keep you in the bed where they put you, or did they put you on the floor?

— I stayed in bed. Nice mattress and pillow, and at night they would even put up a mosquito net.

— You couldn't walk. How did you go to the field to take a shit in the morning? Did they give you a toothbrushing twig in your hand, a mug to wash your ass, did they go with you?

At this Crook's face falls. He shakes his head in great sorrow. No no, why go to the field? There was an attached lavatory, there too he couldn't go at first. They would make him shit and piss in the kind of shiny pot or pan that you would find in the house of Master or Moneylender. Who has heard anything stranger? To piss and shit in pots and pans? Pots and pans that he'll never be able to eat off in his lifetime, to have to do his business in such costly things, this sorrow will remain in his mind.

— Did they give you enough to eat?

— Yes, yes, why not? They gave rice, lentils, vegetable, tea, wheaten bread, bread, milk.

— You lived well.

— The hospital is a good place?

— It's good. But there's one problem. They won't let you smoke and they won't let you spit on the floor.

— You can't have everything.

— Now tell me your news.

— We too have news.

— What news?

— Let uncle Bhuneswar speak!

Bhuneswar loves to speak properly. Now he amazed Crook and told him a fairy tale. At the end of this fairy tale Cinderella doesn't become queen, and the shepherd boy king. But in 1962 in the District of Palamu, the precinct of Tohri, the village of Seora, this event is a fairy tale.

Hanuman Misra, the priest at the Shiva temple in Tahar, is a man of name and substance. His relative is a compassionate god.

He felt much compassion when he saw Douloti. Fed on puffed and stuffed bread, Douloti told him everything. Hearing about Munabar Chandela that god said many times, "Oh! How long will the caste-Hindus continue this torture on outcastes and tribals? When will this regime of inequity come to an end?" It was that god who sent a new cloth for Douloti. A really fine cloth, fast color, ten arms length. Must have cost ten or fifteen rupees.

Munabar's son is a top officer of the district's Lac Development *Corporation*. He has worked it so well that he lives in his own house, and also picks the government's *pocket* and takes rent money. An important holy man came to Palamu from the Gandhi *Mission* from Delhi. Munabar's son came to Tahar with him. That compassionate god was sitting there then.

— Munabar's son Kamaljit Chandela?

— Yes yes, who else?

— Where was he going in Tahar?

— To Hanumanji's temple.

— Then what happened?

— The holy man from Delhi said, "Gandhi *Mission* will establish a center in Palamu. All oppression of outcastes and tribals will stop. Tahar Hanumanji will have to help him."

— But this is strange news, uncle Bhuneswar?

— Listen carefully. That compassionate god did not know Kamaljit Chandela. He said to the Delhi holy man, "these are just words, nothing will be done. This Palamu is a great scene of oppression. Here all the brahmans are good and all the Rajputs are scoundrels. Real scoundrels."

— He said this, in front of Kamaljit?

— What else? Kamaljit said, "My lord, don't bring up caste." The god said, "Why not? Munabar Chandela from Seora village was drawing his ox-cart with his bondslave Ganori Nagesia. The man is badly hurt, lying in hospital. Munabar is such a monster that he has made no provisions for Ganori's wife and daughter."

— What did Kamaljit say?

— He was very angry. He said, "Everything that you hear is not true. Low caste people habitually lie about the upper castes."

— Lies?

— Listen, all the shopkeepers at the Tahar temple said, "No, no, this is absolutely true. Ganori Nagesia is lying in hospital, go and see."

— They didn't come to the hospital, did they?

— No no. Then there was a fight between the Delhi holy man and Hanumanji from Tahar. I was in the crowd. When I went to see you, I would sit in the temple courtyard. I sat and saw the fun.

Bhuneswar had seen everything and told Crook everything with many hand movements. A true fairy tale.

— The Delhi holy man said, "I'll go to Seora. I will see for myself if the high caste landowner-moneylender oppresses the outcaste tribal or not."

— Hanumanji said, "This is the townsman's bluster. If you go to see Seora you will stay in Munabar Chandela's house, there you'll be fed and served, and you'll see the suffering poor. I've seen many holy men like that."

— I'm not such a holy man.

— Where will you stay?

— I'll stay in the outcastes' slum in Seora. If the incident is true, I'll sit in prayer with that proprietor and those bonded workers. For seven days we will praise Rama. The name of Rama cleanses the soul. Gandhi took the name of Rama to the very end.

— Gandhi was truly a great soul, he called the outcastes God's children [harijan]. He also thought about their welfare. But his work was all wrong.

— How?

— He went to the infidel country England, and in Africa during the Boer War he also carried infidel corpses. Should one do such things?

— Is this all wrong?

— Sure it's wrong. He died so terribly because he made these mistakes. He did not get a house in old age, served by his son, cared for by his wife. Finally he died dreadfully.

— This you're not saying right. He tried to end the caste system and all these differences.

— The caste system and its differences are rules. You are taking the name of Rama the king of the Raghus, but didn't he kill Shambuk? Shambuk was a Shudra. He killed him after all. Caste differences, untouchability—these are God's rules. You can pray, you can praise Rama, but this will not change. Proprietor—bond laborer—caste difference. Everything will be as before. Delhi's rules will not work in Palamu.

— Then what is to be done?

— These untouchable tribals are great sinners. Give the money for a grand penance festival in my temple, everything will be all right.

— How?

— Well, first you have to raise the cry that the Seora bond laborers are mortal sinners and great sins are happening because of their sinfulness.

— Is that possible?

— Why not, trust me, everything can happen. If I set up a penance festival in Seora, then Munabar Chandela will raise and give money. The untouchables will surely bring rice and molasses, and the Ahirs—the dairy castes—will give milk and butter.

— But this is exploiting the poor.

— The untouchables' back will be broken. They will no longer say to the master, "You terrorize us." They will bear everything in silence. The strong oppresses, the weak suffers, this after all is the rule. Are you trying to overturn this working rule?

At this the Delhi holy man covered his ears. Then Munabar's son came to Seora Village with that holy man. The Delhi holy man did as he said. He stayed a week in Rajbi the washerwoman's yard. A marquee was set up.

Hearing all this Crook said, "What a lot of fun in the village, and I couldn't see a thing."

Jhari said, "Brother, it was all because of you. If you hadn't become Munabar's ox and pulled his cart, you wouldn't have been hurt. You were hurt, went to hospital, so word got around." Then hearing all the Delhi holy man sat in Seora village.

So for seven days Rama's name was sung under the marquee. The holy man sang, spun thread on a wheel, and explained good things to everyone. You are not untouchable. You, me, Munabar Chandela, are offspring of the same mother.

Hearing all this the washerwoman Rajbi said, "How can that be, *Sadhuji* [Mr. Holy Man]?"

— Yes, sister, quite true.

— Why, what happened?

— We are all offspring of the same mother.

— No Sadhuji, untrue untrue.

— Why?

— If the offspring of the same mother, we are all brothers and sisters, yes?

— Should be.

— But Munabar doesn't know that. Munabar's children in my room, Munabar's children in Mukami Dusadin's place as well, and all these boys are bonded labor. Tell me how this can be.

— Sister, not that kind of mother, Mother India.

— Who is that?

— Our country, India.

— This is our country?

— Of course.

— Oh Sadhuji, my place is Seora village. What do you call a country? I know *tahsil* [a pre-independence revenue-collecting unit], I know station, I don't know country. India is not the country.

— Hey, you are all independent India's free people, do you understand?

— No, Sadhuji.

Bhuneswar and the others look around and shut up. Jhari says to Rajbi, "Over the hill, you're old now, making like a tease. Listen to everything Sadhuji says. They will never understand what we say, and we will never understand what they say."

Rama's praise was sung for seven days. And all the villagers ate rice-and-lentils at Sadhuji's expense for seven days.

Meanwhile Munabar's son explained many things to his father: "Pa! It's not good that you are still using the old rules with the kamiyas."

— So you'll say. You are a government officer, I am a house-holder, a cattleman.

— Look, this man has come from Delhi. If the newspapers print stuff with your name and my name our name will be ruined.

— How?

— Listen, the Patna newspapers will bring out that the *officer's* father terrorizes his kamiyas. If some scoundrel raises questions in the State Assembly about this, then there will be an uproar. The greatest problem is *Father* Bomfuller of the *Mission.* He is collecting information about kamiyas, touring the district, do you understand? You understand nothing.

Munabar is respectful toward his *officer* son, speaks in a soft voice.

— Son, who is Bomfuller?

— The *Mission Father.*

— What's that to me?

— How to explain? If he makes a report, everyone will accept it.

— Look! The land is forever. Offsuri is wage-work. I've never worked for a wage. You as an offsur, do you live well? When your mother goes to the field with her mug, two maids go with her and pull her up when she's finished, she is so heavy. Your wife is thin as a rail, like the wind can blow her away.

— Pa, are these useful topics?

— I still drink and digest three quarts of milk. You can't even drink a quart. Well, you strayed with your mother's people and got learning, you've forgotten country ways. Your father did something to a kamiya, and you bring this Delhi Sadhuji to the village. Listen son! don't let the West Wind into your home. When that wind rises, you have to keep your windows shut.

— You won't understand.

Munabar kept shaking his head. "You have to keep your windows shut when the West Wind rises. Otherwise straw and chaff blow in and destroy order." How will Kamaljit understand this? "Look son! When you were a little baby, India was not yet independent. I lived then in Ranchi. I lived in *town,* and traveled to the areas. I reclaimed jungle areas and gave the tribals wages in those areas. Then the police came from the station and took away Dudharam Misra. A young boy, his mother's darling, he went to fight the British."

— I've heard all this.

— So hear again. He came to the village, and brought in the West Wind! All kinds of killer thoughts came blowing in the wind like the straw blowing in.

— The West Wind entered the jungle district?

— Sure. The tribals started doing Satyagraha as well. Salt wages are not enough, give us money. Give us a share of the produce of the ground we till. There was a lot of trouble with that, I remember very clearly. What a West Wind, O god! It took a long time to bring the tribals under control. Bono Nagesia also came as the West Wind into this village, he's out and now the village is peaceful. Now you my son bring the West Wind into the village! Now let's see what happens. It's best to go by set rules. Rule breaking is not good.

— What will happen Pa? Sadhuji stayed seven days, Rama's praise was sung. You gave support, I gave support. Now there will be no more trouble.

Crook heard all this with great care. Then said, "Now I've heard it all, fellows. But what's the good for me? My body is broken up. Shall I be able to work like before? I am startled if a human shadow falls on the yard. I think that the boss has sent a trooper or a constable to catch me."

— Don't think so much.

— Thoughts come.

— Your wife is now doing worship like the bosses. She seems to have learned the gods.

Crook's wife said, "Why not? When I can weave I can sell. When I can't, I starve. Then I say, today I have to worship Samkatnarayan, the troubleshooting god, today I have to starve."

— What god is Samkatnarayan?

— Do I know? There's a new tax-collector at the market. He is organizing a worship-service for Samkatnarayan every Friday.

Bhuneswar said, "How much cash he's pulling in! Raising it at the market, money at the ceremony, the swine's looks have changed totally."

— Should we set up a worship ceremony?

Jhari is young, his way of talking is sharp. He beat his belly and said, "Yeah, great idea. Our bellies are called Samkatnarayan. Feed it. The gods will be pleased."

Bhuneswar said, "That's true too. What a pissant thing the Delhi Sadhuji did. He fed us a lot for seven days. We got used to eating full meals. Then he split. Now it takes time to lose the habit. Before it wasn't so hard to go hungry. Now it's very painful."

Jhari said, "He used to say Rama Rama, and he did a Rama-pissant thing. However, we ate a lot."

One day Samkatnarayan took human form and came to

Ganori Nagesia's shack. That brahman god, Hanuman Misra's relative. A shortish man, very strong, very dark. Iron-grey hair cut short, also a long tail of hair in back. No eyelids to speak of. Shining and piercing his glance.

— My name is Paramananda Mishir [a variant of Misra]. You are Ganori Nagesia? You were in hospital all this while?

— Yes, god, at your feet, god.

Not touching him Ganori bowed to the ground. Didn't ask the god to sit. He's nervous. Something is moving in his belly, sweat prickles his skin. Never has such a thing happened to him. Never has a Paramananda Mishir stood in the yard of a Crook Nagesia in Palamu district.

If it had happened even once before, then Crook Nagesia would have known what to do in such a situation. He doesn't know. So he leans on his stick, mutters "at your feet, god," stumbles down to bow, and then just stands.

III

Paramananda Mishir did not sit down on the rush mat in Crook's shack. He said, "There's no fault in the earth as seat. The earth is everyone's mother. Our birth and our life are on this soil."

He sat under the barren olive tree in the courtyard. He said, "Sit, I have to talk to you."

— No, god. I will be in the wrong.

— There will be no wrong.

— The boss will be angry.

— Your boss is Rajput. I am a brahman. What I say is right.

— It hurts me to sit on the ground.

— Sit on the stoop. Listen, Ganori. How many years have you been Munabar Singh Chandela's kamiya?

— A long time.

— How long?

— I can't reckon.

— Was Douloti born then?

— Yes, Douloti was tiny then.

— How old is she?

— When there was independence for you and the bosses, the boss fed everyone puffed bread and stuffed bread, had a big show, went to town. Douloti was born the year after that. The paddy was ripe then.

— How much did you take?

— Three hundred rupees.

— Did you give a thumbprint?

— Yes, god.

— Can you walk?

— Yes, god.

— Walk with me a bit?

— Where will I go?

— I have to talk.

Paramananda walked ahead, Crook behind. All the villagers watched amazed. Such a thing had never happened in this village, in the district of Palamu. A brahman is calling forth a Nagesia. Paramananda said, "Ganori! I will go with you to your master and repay the money."

— What did you say, god?

— Repay the money.

— I am Crook Nagesia, god, untouchable, very poor, god. I eat rice only on feast days.

— Hey! What happened?

— I never harmed you, god.

— What are you talking about?

— I am not worth your fun.

— I don't make fun.

— Then why are you wanting to give money? Three hundred rupees? Hey, after harvesting for a month the Parhaiyas had wanted three rupees wage, the boss shot them. Who gives whom three hundred rupees, god? This is not a joking matter.

— Listen fellow, I have more to say.

— What, god? If you give him money, I will be your kamiya, no? How? By what labor will I repay the loan? My body has become spoilt now.

— Eh! I see he doesn't understand.

— You are an outsider, and you will leave. How will I go to foreign parts with you? I don't have the courage to go away either. Only Bono Nagesia has the courage among us. He is not here, he has left.

Then Paramananda roared at him, "Idiot, pig, old goat! Who wants to make you kamiya? Do I believe in bonded labor?

I really dislike bonded labor

I am compassionate, most compassionate.

My forefathers left kamiyas.

I have freed them
I am compassionate after all, most compassionate
I have farm property in Joukhan village
I have given everything to my wife and children
I am compassionate, carrying money bags
I free kamiyas
In the present age the brahman is the liberator of the
    untouchable
I am that brahman, Samkatnarayan."

Crook didn't understand anything. He wept himself into a state. Then what Paramananda said was most astonishing. No one has ever heard such a thing except in old mothers' tales. Paramananda said, "I have got down to this work as the god Narayana, I must have a goddess Lakshmi with me. I will marry your daughter Douloti."

Hearing this, Crook said, "O Rama, I'm caught by a madman"—and started to run with his crooked body.

How can he keep up running with Paramananda? These events of Crook's life are like stories after all. He caught up with Crook. Crook said, "Let me go, god, let me go home."

— Why you dumb beast?

Paramananda gripped Crook hard. Crook filled the sky with his screams, "Truth is being destroyed, the Law is being destroyed! This brahman, this god, is holding me, please! He must be plumb crazy."

— You ignorant fool, why are you screaming?

— Oh Rama, oh god!

Crook screamed loudly indeed. He had eaten well for some months at the hospital, his body was strong. And, he was most nervous at Paramananda's chatter. Fear for his life made his voice strong.

Both of them were shouting away, when a third voice shouted even more loudly, "Hey! What's this?" Munabar Chandela. Munabar never walks alone on the village paths before sundown. His status is hurt if people don't run before and behind him. After dark he walks alone. Munabar's people separated the two.

— What's up, Ganori?

— Boss! This god ... Crook started sobbing loudly, "This god is saying, he'll end my bonded labor with money, he's saying, he'll marry Douloti."

— What?

— Yes.

Munabar then took a good look. After that, he made Crook totally nervous.

— It's Paramananda Misra from Joukhan, no? Releases fathers of daughters from bonded labor, marries the daughters.

Munabar roared with laughter, "Hey! What fun talk! Come come, god, come. You are the son-in-law of the village, let me give you the wherewithals, you brahman cook your meal clean [according to caste laws], be served. Will the marriage take place in my residence?"

Paramananda started chewing betel nuts with a loud noise.

He said nothing. Munabar said, "Crook, go home lad. I'll talk to the god."

Crook said, "I'll be off, boss."

— Go without fear. This god plays this game from village to village. He has so many wives, and he has built so many nice homes and kept them in such happiness.

Crook returned to his place.

Paramananda and Munabar must have talked at length. And he must have been served and fed at his house, since he didn't turn up at all in the afternoon. Late in the afternoon Munabar's man came to call Crook.

Munabar and Paramananda were sitting in the office-room. Munabar said without preamble, "This god has ended your bonded labor with the payment of three hundred rupees. You took three hundred rupees thirteen years ago. You don't have to hear how much it had become with the increase of interest. I could have made you work another thirteen years with no trouble at all.

But that I can't do, my body is made of compassion.

And! God has made my body and mind

With all the world's compassionate and kind cream-double
    cream and caramel scrapings

Each year on the day of Rama's celebration

I cannot not give a whole rupee to the poor,

I must, I must, a body made of compassion!

My body is made of compassion, otherwise just see,

Ganori Bhuyian from Seora village,

Yes, Yes, he too is a Ganori, he too is a Ganori—

Took five hundred rupees for his own wedding

From Joala Pandey

Oh dear, he's doing bonded labor for thirty-eight years Ganori
    is now seventy-eight—

Bond-labor loans are the troops of blood-seeding

One rupee gives birth to thousands of rupees.
The debt won't be repaid—
Ganori will put that debt on his son's shoulders
And blow death's bugle—tara ra, tara ra, tara ra.

Do you know Pujari Bhuiyan from Kelkar Village?
Took seventy rupees from Bhola Sau
To fill his belly, burning up with belly-fire
Boom, that money is not repaid in twenty years
Will it be repaid in the coming twenty years?
Bond-labor loans are surely the troops of blood-seeding
One rupee gives birth to thousands of rupees
The debt won't be repaid—
Even Piyari's brother has become Bhola Sau's kamiya.
Tapeswar Manjhi from Simri Village is a Dusad by birth
Baram Pandit loaned him eighty rupees
Tapeswar was fifteen then
And when his father was sick Baram Pandit loaned him
    money, boom!
For twenty-five years Tapeswar gives free bonded labor
Giving and giving—giving and giving—
Tapeswar's age? About forty.
Bond-labor loans are, yes, the troops of blood-seeding,
Increases by the thousands.
I could make you toil a much longer time
As long as you live, I can keep you as my kamiya.
Bond-labor loans never end
But, didn't I say it?
Did He make me with all the last drops
Of the world's compassionate and kind cream-double cream
    and caramel scrapings?
I just can't be cruel and dispassionate.
In mango season I *must* give a mango to a beggar—
I throw in a bit of corn and millet with your water for your
    breakfast and—
I find myself giving you water from the Panchayati well—
It is compassion and empathy that have brought me to this
    pass—
If it were a market town—
They would name a street after me—a street.
But Crook! Listen to everything the god says. He is not an

ordinary man. Hanumanji is his relative; if you don't obey this man he'll be angry. And if Hanumanji is angry even the landed Rajputs are scared. And you only a Nagesia!"

Crook said, "Yes, sir."

What word, what he should listen to, he didn't think at all. He said "yes" to whatever he heard. Because if the Master says something the machine in Crook's head stops working out of fear. He hears the Master's bellows, but grasps nothing. To say "Yes Sir" to the proprietor is a very long-standing habit. Why everyone—the people in the office-room, Munabar, Paramananda—laughed loud as soon as he said "Yes Sir," this Crook didn't understand at all. He only saw that Paramananda carelessly took out a wad of bank notes and Munabar, counting them, said, "I'll get my wool jacket made now."

Inside Munabar's safe were many many labor bonds bound in red baize. Taking Crook's bond receipt he threw it in Crook's direction. And said, "What will you eat now?"

Crook held up his palm and inclined his head and thus explained his helplessness. "What will you eat now?" is not a question one puts to Crook Nagesias, this Munabar doesn't know. Crooks don't eat, they are used to not eating. Yet their hunger doesn't disappear, this is the problem.

And thus a strange fairy tale was created. How the brahman Paramananda tried to show compassion to Crook Nagesia the kamiya. And what compassion in Munabar Chandela. The kingdom of Heaven descended on this sinful earth, on this cursed jungle district Palamu. Where the human beings, who are Nagesia-Parhaia-Oraon, Munda, Bhuyian-Dusad-Ganju-Dhobi-Chamar by birth, are all people who are enslaved by their burning hunger at very low wages, for very little grain, by the so-called upper castes. And the sociologists travel around Palamu and write in their files, every sonofabitch is becoming kamiya because of weddings-funerals-religious ceremonies. That the peasant is becoming the Kulak's kamiya, this the sociologists avoid rather skillfully.

    These savants want government support
    The government wants the Kulak's support
    Land-lender, this new agri-capitalist caste
    This caste is created by the independent government of India
    The government wants the support of the Kulak and the agri-
       capitalist
    Because of nothing, nothing, nothing

Bhilai-Bokaro-Jamshedpur
Plowed land supplies tax-revenue
These are the king-emperors of that land.
And Kulak, agri-capitalist, the king-emperors
Want free labor, free land—
So they recruit kamiya-seokia-haroaha
One mustn't know this, or write this, because—

Everything would have remained a fairy tale, but the conclusion of the fairy tale is life, bloody, pain-filled life.

So Paramananda took away Crook's fourteen-year-old daughter Douloti one day. Crook protested greatly. But Munabar said with menace, "Didn't he give you money? Didn't he make you free?"

— Why will I give my daughter, my lord?

— It's your great good luck that he said he'll marry your daughter.

— If he hadn't said anything but I'm taking her away to make her a kamiya?

Crook came back. Douloti understood nothing. When does a brahman marry a Nagesia girl? Bhuneswar's wife said, "I knew there was some problem the moment he gave cloth and flour."

All the women crowded into Douloti's house, the men were talking in the yard.

Everyone shook their heads repeatedly. No, no one had ever heard such a thing. There is some other thing here, some profound conspiracy of the Master society. They'll be greatly relieved to know what the conspiracy is, Crook will go to cut grass, Crook's wife will go to pick up the fallen grain.

Bhuneswar said, "Send news to your older son."

Crook shook his head. One of the many reasons he took the three hundred rupees was this son's wedding. He said, "Older or younger, I have the one son. Where is he? Does he ever ask for our news? He doesn't even live in Latihar any more, I don't know where he is."

— He says he'll marry, he won't keep caste. He has a grown son at home. What's up?

Of course Jhari said, "Jokhan is not that far. Where will he go with her? We'll certainly go get news."

Douloti and her mother were two stones clasping each other. The mother was running her hand gently and constantly over her daughter's body. A split broken hand. Running her fingers she was weeping and humming, What is this, my mother, I never heard such a thing? The Boss-moneylender always takes away our daughters-in-law from field and barn. When does a brahman marry a daughter of ours? They take them to bed and that with the lamp snuffed out. It'll be a sin if they see the face. Marriage! This is a great wonder, my mother!

Douloti put on her whole cloth. Paramananda said, "You don't have to take your torn rags and remnants. I will buy you everything. Leave that stuff behind."

Leaving everything behind, Douloti left Seora village behind Paramananda. What on earth happened? Fairy tale.

Washerwoman Rajbi pulled on her water-pipe and said, "You can take a look at his eyes and see that the guy's a devil. We will surely know what his trick is."

Mukami Dusadin said, "Who knows what Douloti ate, what she rubbed on her body. Her looks were so lusty, that's why she caught his eye. When the bloom comes to a girl of our kind the vultures will surely fly overhead. I've seen so much."

IV

Douloti's legs hurt with walking. As much curiosity as fear. But she is a quiet girl. She sits under a tree and rests a bit. Paramananda had opened his bundle and given her a paper bag of molasses candy and sun-dried rice.

Douloti drank water at the tea-shop when she got to the bus route. Paramananda drank tea.

This is Douloti's first experience of going somewhere by bus. She became drowsy as she kept vomiting with the stink of *diesel*. Then they left Tohri *bus junction* and got off at a market town. Paramananda had undoubtedly been to that place many times. Since he seemed to have a room already rented in this very place, in Madhpura, for Douloti. He unlocked the door, and threw down a mat on the floor. He said, Lie down a bit. You'll feel better. Douloti lies down and immediately goes to sleep. She sleeps a lot. She awoke after dark. Paramananda said, "Go—take a piss there, wash your face and hands."

Douloti had never seen such an arrangement for urinating and defecating. A courtyard with a very high wall, in a corner a place for relieving yourself, that too surrounded by a *tin* wall. Not a kitchen, not a stoop. On one side of the yard a well, and in the room rope and bucket. The room was middle-sized.

Douloti came back and sat down in the room. Paramananda has lit a paraffin lamp. He said, "I've kept food in a clay bowl in that corner, eat. Drink some water. Sleep again. I'll lock the door and go out for a bit."

Paramananda left. How closed, how pressing-in. In a big clay bowl some puffed bread-vegetables-sweet balls. Douloti's eyes were bursting with tears. Her father, her mother, had never eaten such good food. But of course you can no longer compare Douloti to them. Douloti is going to be the bride of a brahman god.

It's hard to understand this god's plans. Will he keep Douloti here after marriage? In this kind of room with brick walls all around and clay tiles on the roof? Douloti's own place is much better. You can see trees and sky if you stand at its door. The latrine is by the door. O how much better it is to "go" in the fields. When one of Douloti's uncles went to the field as a child, a tiger took him. Douloti has seen wolf, hyena, and fox. She has never seen a tiger.

When she was a child and Mother was cross, Mother would say, "Come, I'll put you in the tiger's hole."

Douloti's father has seen tigers many times. And what does great-uncle Bhuneswar say? He says, "Even if you haven't seen the tiger, the tiger has certainly seen you."

When she got up the next morning she realized that the god had slept in the bed as well. But he hadn't touched her. After a while a one-eyed man came. To talk to Paramananda.

— Got only one this time Mishirji?

— Yes.

— Someone's wife?

— No no, unmarried, and—Paramananda winked—still a virgin.

— What are you saying?

— Listen, I'm telling the truth.

— With you here she remained a virgin?

— What can I do, fellow? I've taken cash.

— Whose?

— Mr. Babu Latia's.

— Yes, yes, Latiaji has been ordering for some time, yes, untouchable girl wanted virgin wanted. True he spoke to me too, but a girl in full bloom, and yet still a virgin, how can one get everything? They are all married in childhood and as soon as they are a little grown the man at home and the boss-moneylender out-side—do they let them stay virgin? I was in a real bind.

— I heard that.

— Then Latiaji sought you out?

— Yes yes.

— What did you say?

— Look, I too am "in a bind," but I'm not the person who gives up, saying "I'm having trouble." The harder the job, the greater my stubbornness to do it. Staying on the lookout I found the real thing.

— Not all that eye-catching though.

— Let Latiaji's need be fulfilled. Rampiyari will make her eye-catching.

— What's the use of eye-catching?

— Latiaji's ... the story of that girl ...

— Who? Hey, why bring that up?

— What Latiaji does with those girls. Even an elephant would die to suffer such manhood.

— These are the Mahatma's children of God [*harijan*]. Hard-working people. They can lift a forty-pound bag of paddy.

— Well, see. You are a fortunate man.

— A male is a lion. He makes his own fortune. If I sit around, how will I eat?

— You have set up a great bond labor trade. You know where a kamiya has a virgin daughter in full bloom, which girl is a virgin. There will be a change of government and the *police* will get you.

— Who will get me brother? The police *officer*, the railway inspector, who can stay away from Rampiyari's house?

— That's true too.

— Now I must do a little shopping. I must buy some clothes for the girl. *Such* a waste of money. But there's Latiaji, there's the *railway contractor* babu, there are the Punjabis of the *bus* depot—must buy clothes, soap, hair oil.

— This too I really want to know.

— What?

— Will you take payment?

— Sure thing. A thousand times. My right.

— What pays for their clothing, food, cosmetics, medical help?

— What do you do?

— I go to Tohri, at the end of the month I make my reckonings and take two rupees, one rupee, half a rupee from everyone, whatever they owe, that's it. Whatever is left over, that's theirs.

— They'll eat, pay the rent, everything?

— I pay the rent after all. They eat at their own expense.

— You have a cycle-rickshaw business in Dhanbad, you've kept to the same rules in this work too? But these are my bonded laborers and my slaves. The house is mine, the food costs are mine. If you can seduce your client into giving you the money for clothes and cosmetics, all the better. If not, borrow. And that loan you'll add to the principal? Is that what you're getting at?

— So should I give charity?

— Paramanandaji, you'll surely get the Padmasri.

— Yes? What is that?

— A rare thing.

— What?

— A government title. Talented people get it.

— Who knows about us, tell me? In this jungle area, procuring goods on foot and running a shop, how hard that is—how hard and painful it is, how can I make people understand? The government will surely know. And then they will make you Padmasri as well. Well, I must go. In Rama's name, Paramanandaji. God keep you.

— I'll visit you one day. I'll come and see you in Tohri.

— Do.

This conversation takes place in front of Douloti and she doesn't understand a bit of it, but some perhaps she grasps. What she doesn't understand makes her afraid, but also what she does.

The man leaves. Almost immediately a dreadful, hugely fat woman enters. She wears a printed sari and, Douloti is astonished to see, she is wearing anklets as well as shoes.

— At your feet, god.

— Come, Rampiyari.

— When will you leave?

— Late afternoon.

— It seemed like Kishanji had come?

— Yes yes. Bastard devil, he smells it out, and immediately comes along. Now that he's been here, I know what he'll do. As long as he sees the goods are drawing customers, he'll buzz like a dung-fly and try to spoil trade.

— Don't worry, I am here.

— I rely on you.

— So I'm off now. I'll go by the market.

— Go. And look here, don't clean me out with food bills. The market is bad, do you understand?

— Whatever you say. If you like I'll feed them air. One can get that free and without cost.

— Listen sweetie, that's not what I said.

— So how much more will I have to understand, tell me that? I am not seeing you for the first time today, and I've never heard you say the market is good. Even now a rupee's worth of squash and eggplants fill a small sack in Madhpura. So many people will eat, you won't buy five rupees' worth? Your look is such that you buy the calf, in five years she is an old cow, barren. And no care, no medicine in ill-health, so they die quick. Then you weep and wail, and say what a pity.

— Look, do what you think is right.

— How about what I told you?

— What?

— The nose ring?

— Oh ho! I forgot to bring that even this time.

— You haven't forgotten, why tell a lie? OK. Words lead to words, so I'm off. Go to Tohri and take a look at Kishanji's whorehouse. Brickbuilt rooms, two wells, rates off for those who have no work, a different enterprise.

— Let him be.

— And you know what he says! Now everybody does unine, in Dhanbad my cycle-rickshaw drivers do unine—so these people need a little comfort when work is over, they must have something in hand. If I don't think of this, they too will set up a unine.

— Yes, yes, everyone has made unines, extorted rights, now these people are left.

— I'm off, god.

— The Tohri whorehouse, the Dhanbad cycle-rickshaws, the Dhanbad house, are all his father-in-law's gift. He has no children, and therefore no compassion or kindness. His case is different.

Rampiyari really got up this time, she's so fat that it's very hard for her to get up. Douloti smiled and looked away. Rampiyari said, Smiling? Smile now. I'm getting so fat everyone laughs. My body is half water.

Rampiyari left.

Paramananda went out. When he returned, he had a colored

tin box in his hand. Lowering the box on the floor he said, "Take a look."

— Yeh, cutthroat prices.

— Two new saris. One printed, one *silk* and cotton mixed. Underskirt, *blouse,* red dye for the feet, kohl, hair ribbon, comb and mirror, zinc bangle and anklet, bead necklace, glass earrings, dots for the forehead. One soap. One washcloth.

— All this is mine?

— Everything yours. Use this soap and have a bath. Wash out the cloth you're wearing. Put on this underskirt and this printed sari after your bath. When your hair dries oil it and dress it.

Much sorrow can be forgotten if so many new things are received. Douloti had her bath, dried her hair and then rubbed oil into her hair and braided it. She darkened her eyes, dotted her forehead.

A man brought in rice-and-vegetables, unsweetened yogurt. Eating her fill, Douloti thought that what was happening was all a dream. Rice is something to be eaten on feast days. At Karam Puja, at Sohrai, and at the Festival of Lights. Douloti's kind eats rice on these few days of the year. Rice is a luxury you get in dreams.

After she finished the rice, the warmth of the rice poured sleep all over her limbs. This is the last sleep of Douloti's life that will not be nightmare-ridden, but Douloti doesn't know that yet.

Paramananda awakened her in the afternoon. "Not here, we'll have to go somewhere else."

— Where, god?

— To another place.

— By *bus*?

— No no, close by.

The man has given her food and clothing, some trinkets. Fed her a lot, yet hasn't touched her. Douloti will be married to him as well. So Douloti says as she walks with her tin box on her head, "Going for marriage?"

— Yes, yes, that's it.

— To another place?

Why does she chatter so much? She messed up my reckoning, I gave three hundred rupees to Munabar, fifty for her clothes et cetera? Or fifty-two? The box ... how costly everything has become! Chattering away they reached a strange house, a long alleyway with a very high wall lined on one side by a row of rooms, with thin clay-tiled roofs. Lights in every room, people.

Rampiyari came forward, Let's go Douloti. I am walking in and out now since when.

Paramananda said, Go with her. She will dress you. Dress her nicely, hear?

Rampiyari sat her down in a room. Closed the door from inside. Then said, "Put down your box. Sit on the bed. Eh, dusty feet!"

Opened the door and took her to the wellside. Douloti washed her hands-feet-face. Then Rampiyari said, "You have taken a bath with soap, no?"

— I have.

— All the better. Came from home, wild smell in your body, why would the god be pleased?

Rampiyari sighed. Then said, "Take your hair down, I'll put it up nicely."

Her hair was gathered up in a knot, some white stuff was rubbed on her face, on her hands, and feet designs with red dye, finally that fine sari, fine blouse. After her toilette, Rampiyari gave a looking-glass in her hand. Douloti didn't know herself.

— Sit on the bed, drink this juice. Stay sitting. I'm closing the door.

— Don't shut it, I feel afraid.

— No, I'm not shutting it.

Still Rampiyari remained standing with the empty juice glass in her hand. Then she said suddenly, "Feel afraid. If you feel afraid, why did you come with him?"

Douloti didn't respond. Suddenly her blood seemed to tingle, then she felt weak. She lay down. What a big bed, what a soft mattress. Then the wedding will be here. The god must have gone to dress up as a bridegroom. Who knows how a man of such looks looks when he is dressed up as a bridegroom? Who will do the marrying? Will this Rampiyari sing the wedding songs? Does she really know the songs?

But her body is feeling dulled.

The door opened with a slam. Douloti wants to sit up in haste, but she can't. Who are these people?

A huge middle-aged man with sideburns. Paramananda with him. Three more men.

Paramananda said, "Take a look, Latiaji, village girl, Harijan, unmarried and is still a virgin."

— Virgin?

— See today, pay tomorrow.

Everyone left. Latia closed the door. Then said, "Here, get up, take off your clothes."

Douloti tried to shout, fear choked her voice. The man pulled her up roughly. Then pulled off her sari. Trying to resist Douloti realized, her body was now very weak. Rampiyari had put something in her drink.

Douloti, Douloti the daughter of Ganori alias Crook Nagesia of Seora village seemed to look upon another Douloti, dressed up in a peacock-blue silk-cotton wedding sari, staring in such dread. Latia pulled off her sari, he has torn off her blouse. He has taken off his own top, is he going to be naked? Lips trembling, tears in her eyes, what is Douloti saying?

— No no lord, no no no lord, let me go lord—

Are the spectator Douloti and the tortured Douloti becoming one?

What is Latia doing now? What is this? The two Doulotis became one and a desperate girl's voice cracked out in terrible pain.

To keep his virility spirited and bestial, Latia takes *aswagandha* root at night, his sexual hunger is boundless. Douloti is bloodied many times all through the night. Finally her sobbing and entreaties could no longer be heard. But the "grunt grunt" of a rooting pig could be heard.

When Paramananda entered in the morning, Douloti was stretched out quite naked. Slack with no sleep ... A completely naked Latia was sitting with a glass of tea in his hand. The door was open. Latia has a lot of money, he is a contractor. He runs up to Patna. This whorehouse is Rampiyari's house. There is no objection here to his sitting around naked. Here everybody fears him. Latia has behaved like this before. This way is natural for him.

Douloti was afraid of Latia's naturalness.

Paramananda has entered this room this way many a time. He has completed exchange with the rapist without glancing once at the violated, naked harijan woman's helpless body. This behavior is natural for him.

Douloti was afraid of Paramananda's naturalness.

Paramananda threw some betel nut into his mouth and said, "In the name of Rama, Latiaji, have you noticed what a cold wind is blowing since last night?"

— How will I get a feel of the cold, you fool? My body is hot with that native medicine. I will throw down even a she-elephant.

You are a scoundrel, you were destroying my manhood by feeding me roots and barks."

— Latiaji! Your manhood increases if you drink raw milk and the root of *aswagandha* at night.

— Let yours increase, motherfucker.

— Well, how was it? Didn't I give you the right goods?

— Yes, that you gave. Give me my shirt.

Latia threw a handful of bank notes at Paramananda. He said, "Tell Rampiyari, this girl is now mine. When I let her go she can take clients."

— Yes yes Latiaji, why not?

— Now send her to be cleaned up, have the room opened up. I'll sleep.

In unlimited boundless audacity Latia walked naked to sleep in the room *reserved* for the valued client. Paramananda took along his clothes.

Rampiyari entered. She sighed and said, "Get up, wrap up. Come have a bath. Your fathers! They blow me away. This animal says marriage, he'll marry a Dusad, Dhobi, Chamar, Parhaiya girl? Brahmans? Who burn harijans? They catch you to make you a kamiya ... wrap up. I'll hold you. They catch you to make you a kamiya ... now they'll eat the fruit of your work ... why are you crying? Don't cry. They caught me one day too ... come, hold me, walk. Later I'll teach you more. You won't be able to go out, you see. This is called bonded labor. I will teach you to live strategically like me. Come, won't you clean your teeth? Come."

Another girl, yet another girl—Rampiyari said, "Reoti, Somni. Look after this one. Let her have a bath, be clean, give her something to eat. I'm going to market. Latia being here means a lot of trouble. He'll eat meat and buttered flat bread."

Douloti said with great effort, "These are all whores?"

— Hey, you too are a whore now. Whore would be better. You are all that Paramananda's kamiya.

These are all Paramananda's kamiyas.

Douloti and Reoti and Somni

Field work, digging soil, cutting wells is work

This one doesn't do it, that one doesn't do it, the other one
    doesn't do it—

The boss has turned them into land

The boss plows and plows their land and raises the crop

They are all Paramananda's kamiya.

They are all some people's *maat*—
Near the foot of the Himalayas in Jaunnar-Bauar
They don't say kamiya, they are called *maat*
Tulsa and Bisla and Kamla
Kolta girls are some people's *maat*
Only field work and shoveling soil is work
This one doesn't do it, that one doesn't do it, the other doesn't
    do it—
The boss has made them land
He plows and plows their bodies' land and raises a crop
They are all some people's *maat*.

V

The harijan woman with the unwounded hymen does not remain a virgin after the first night, Latia's attraction for her is exhausted in a moment. In Douloti's case the attraction lasted three years.

In the very first month Douloti started retching. "Hey Rampiyari, give her medicine."

— Medicine?

— Manhood increases with more care from the native doctor. And this broad seems even more fertile than Somni. She's made herself a belly. Dose her. Such kicks! everything will be spoilt.

— Yes yes sir. But . . .

— I know I know. I won't come for three or four days.

— Give her a week off at least. Otherwise . . . we had such trouble with Kalabati. Giving Douloti medicine Rampiyari said, He's really taken by you.

— Who?

— Latiaji.

— What has been taken?

— His mind.

— Mind?

Douloti was most surprised. The lust-struck animal that digs and tears her every day, he has a mind?

—Yes yes. Otherwise whose belly hasn't he put two or three children into? To all the girls, to each and every one, yearly . . . he has a lot of strength. How much meat and butter he eats every day. He gave you a week off and Kalabati . . .

— What?

Rampiyari sighed and said, "He was much taken by Kalabati. She got a belly in two months. I dosed her. But the medicine was strong. On the third day passing blood like water. I ran to the medicine man. In the meantime Latia, dead drunk, entered Kalabati's room."

— Then?

— The girl died. The police came. Latiaji gave money and arranged everything.

— Died?

— Yes yes. Don't be afraid. Does everyone die?

Douloti said, "I'm not afraid."

Why should Douloti be afraid? If this is her life, she didn't choose this life. She didn't make the bondslavery system. People do not become kamiyas by choice.

In Andhra the people of Matangi, Jaggali, Malajangam, Mahar and other castes become Gothi. In Bihar Chamar, Nagesia, Parhaiya, Dusad become Kamiya or Seokiya. In Gujarat the Chalwaris, Naliyas, Thoris and others become Halpati. In Karnataka the low of birth become Jeetho, in Madhya Pradesh Haroyaha. In Orissa Gothi and in Rajasthan Sagri. The Chetty rayats of Tamil Nadu keep Bhumidases. In Uttar Pradesh the Bhumidas are called Maat or Khandit-Mundit or Sanjayat. The Bhumidases of the Laccadive Islands are Nadapu.

Different names in different regions.

The system is slavery.

The marginal, the harijan, the tribal is its sacrifice.

Who becomes a slave willingly? They do so under loan obligations. The landless agricultural worker or the small peasant becomes a slave. Not willingly, under loan pressure.

The social system that makes Crook Nagesia a kamiya is made by men. Therefore do Douloti, Somni, Reoti have to quench the hunger of male flesh. Otherwise Paramananda does not get money. Why should Douloti be afraid? She has understood now that this is natural. Now she has no fear, no sorrow, no desire. She might have died even with the medicine.

Douloti is shunted to Somni's room. Somni has aged a lot just at thirty. Now she has no clients. Occasionally someone from the village market. Even that just once in a long while. You have to get out if your earnings fall. Even in this life children are born. One gets out *with* them. But Somni is very intelligent. She knows she will go when her body is spent. So she has made herself useful to Rampiyari in other ways.

Rampiyari is really bloated. Somni washes her dishes, cooks, washes her clothes, looks after her.

There are eleven women now. Each one is anxious to cook in her own way. But Paramananda does not approve. Rampiyari will cook and feed them.

Paramananda takes every bit of their earnings monthly. Doesn't give any money in the name of clothing, cosmetics, or medicine. Sometimes ten clients come daily as well. And in Madhpura there is a huge market twice a week, there are three fairs a year. At that time thirty clients enter daily in every woman's room.

The clients pay Rampiyari. Rampiyari counts out that money to the full to Paramananda. There cannot be a problem with the money. Paramananda is greatly cunning.

Rampiyari has spending money. She herself lends these women money for clothing or cosmetics. And she picks up the cash if there are extra clients.

Paramananda doesn't know this. His permanent residence is Madhpura. He says to the women, "Don't I know that human beings need clothing, cosmetics, the odd bit of betel leaf or tobacco? Borrow, borrow."

In the bondslavery trade, the bonded labor system, the recourse to loans is the general regulator.

If this were their homeplace, then the loan taken by the kamiya would have been added to the principal—the original loan that has made the man a kamiya.

Here too all the later loans are added to the principal, and the interest is compounded. The day the kamiya prostitute is evicted from this house, she starts repaying by begging or selling dried cow dung for fuel.

Douloti lay in a heap in Somni's room for seven days. Somni said, "Rampiyari too was a kamiya, but once she got a man to love."

— Here?

— Yes, yes here. Later that man got many *votes* and became a Mye-lay [MLA: Member of the Legislative Assembly], and ended Rampiyari's bonded labor account.

— Then?

— He gave Rampiyari money. Two hundred rupees! Rampiyari would have left with that money. But the god said, Stay. You look after this house.

— Where have you come from, Somni?

— They brought me from Barha village.

— Did they say they would marry you?

— Why should they? I was already married.

— Already married?

— Yes yes. And I have my man at home.

— How did you come?

— Was there another way? My man took two hundred rupees from him, to get land. Hoo, in a year it became four thousand rupees. Then the god said to my man, You won't be able to repay, you are a kamiya. Send your wife. Your debt will be repaid in five years, your wife will return home with money in hand. I kept my son with my husband and came here.

— And the boy?

— He is in Barha. The god has lots of land in Barha.

— How many children do you have here?

— Three.

Somni put her hand to her cheek and said, "See what a strange thing. I was married in childhood, and I stayed with my man for so long. I had only one son. And Latia made me the mother of three sons in a row."

— Those sons?

— They lie around in the marketplace. They beg. They don't let you live with your child, and clients come up to one month before birth. Then I can't for three months.

— Then?

— The god lends money.

— Doesn't he let you keep them?

— No no, would he? When I am burnt up, I go see them. Reoti's son too is Latia's son. And it was Latia's *truck* that hit him and crippled him. As a cripple he gets more begging. He got a shirt too.

— How long will you stay?

— Who knows. As long as it pleases the god.

— Then?

— Then I'll beg. There's nothing in my body anymore. Will I be able to work hard anymore? For four-five years thirty clients a day. I'll beg.

— Won't you return to your village?

— How will I return? My man has brought another wife and they are both the god's kamiya. If I go back, where will these boys go? Why should my man rear Latia's sons? What would he feed them? Is there food in our land?

— No.

Douloti shook her head. Then she said, "The townspeople eat a lot, many times."

— I want a lot to go to Barha.

— Go then.

— The god doesn't even feed us well. If I'd eaten well my body would have kept so much strength.

— Why did your man bring a wife?

— How could he have done without? There's housework. How can he do it alone after his own hard labor? And the son is what they call a halfwit. Not a sharp bright fellow.

— Doesn't the stepmother beat him?

— Oh sure, beats a lot.

Somni frowned for a long time. Then she said, "Latia still likes you, I don't know for how long. The money he will give to Rampiyari. But he has a lot of money. He is a contractor man. Ask for a couple of rupees. Put a little aside from clients. Money is needed."

— Why?

— Otherwise you'll be like me.

Somni, thirty years old, laughed in the broken cackling voice of a seventy-year-old witch. And said, "The stepwife thrashes my man's son, the client's sons beg. I haven't a penny."

— You didn't put some aside?

— I used to, sure. I spent everything feeding Latia's boys. Now worse than a beggar.

Douloti closed her eyes. Lying in Somni's room she is sleepy all the time. She said in a drowsy voice, "Was there bondslavery before? Now that there are kamiyas everywhere?"

— The bosses keep kamiyas. And why not? The fields and gardens belong to them. Keep a kamiya, get all the work done for no more than a morning meal. The gormen [government] is theirs.

— Why is there so much shouting outside? Why is there a crowd?

— Who knows?

The empire of Rampiyari's usury is spread out beyond this house. She trots all over Madhpura and collects interest. Now she returned, put down her shopping and said, "A fighting crowd."

— What fight?

— Do I know?

Somni said, "Auntie, let's go and hear."

— Will you go?

— Why not? It's a circus.

— We'll cook up when we get back.

— Today is market day.

— Go then, let me rest a bit.

Somni returned most troubled from the meeting. "No no, this is not a good circus."

— What's the fight?

— Who knows? They are fighting some China.

— Whose fight?

— Someone called India, his. I didn't understand anything.

Rampiyari said, "Did you see Latia?"

— He is shouting the most.

— That is the contractors' fight. Come, make some tea. Have some yourselves, give me some.

— If there is a fight, I hear the prices will go up.

— Let them. Make some tea.

In the event Douloti gets more than seven days off. For Latia is the only man with many *trucks*. The regional *Congress* party leaders go around in *trucks* abusing the Chinese invasion of India. Latia is a highly trusted government contractor. All the *bridges* that he has built on the Kuruda, Seil, Kora, Rohini, the little rivers in the area, have collapsed about twice.

Latia leaves the scene of action with the money and finally another contractor builds the bridge.

By the same logic he builds roads and the office buildings of the Forestry Department. Nobody has yet been able to blame him for theft, or interfering with government funds.

A certain district magistrate said in desperation, "Why are you here in the jungle with such talents? Go to town." Latia had said, "What an idea! In the jungle area everything is profit. Tribal and outcaste labor is so cheap."

Such a Latia contributes a *truck* and gives a speech himself. Calls out, "Give whatever you have into this shawl."

— Why sir?

— Isn't there a war on?

— Where, I don't know.

— You will never know, bastard motherfucker. China has come to contaminate India's truth.

— Yes, yes? But where is China? Where again is India? Mye-lay or MLA says, "This country is India."

— No, no, Madhpura.

— What! Contradicting the Mye-lay Sir?

Latia jumps into the sea of people with his club in hand and the people run away in every direction.

Then Latia comes again to Douloti's room. Two other people are with him. Government *officers*. Latia doesn't get his contracts if he doesn't soak the government *officers* in oil. It's hard to please the *officers* in such forest areas. Not everybody drinks alcohol, not everyone wants to come to Rampiyari's house.

These two are young, not yet married.

Latia says, "Today I'll show you some real fun. You think all the fun is in town."

Special orders had been given for Douloti, Reoti, Gohumani. Paramananda came by in the morning and told them, "You must do what they ask. Not a two-rupee client. This one is Latiaji." There is meat and buttered flat bread, liquor has come from Ranchi. All three women have had to scrub themselves clean. Latia says, "Shit! Rampiyari?"

— Sir!

— What is this? Why is everything not just right?

— It will soon be, sir.

Rampiyari whispers, "Reoti and Gohumani are, sir, mothers of children. Shouldn't the gentlemen be a little drunk? Their bodies are a bit slack."

— That's true.

— They are not as fresh as Douloti.

— Give me a bottle.

Three women came and stood still after a big bottle was finished. They are quite naked. Reoti and Gohumani sat in the gentlemen's laps. Latia took Douloti in his lap, started kneading her and said, "They are harijans. They work hard, they keep their bodies fresh."

— Great, great!

— Lie down, lie down. Take a look at me.

Three naked women and three men in the raw. The god has ordered, "do what they say." Gohumani keeps getting burnt by cigarettes. The men eat their flesh in a crazed way. At one point the gentlemen fall asleep. Reoti and Gohumani get leave. Douloti doesn't. It goes on, keeps going on.

Towards morning Douloti says, "Sir!"

— Say.

— Will you ... give me something separately?

— Why not? I will.

Latia gave her a rupee, but said in the morning, "Rampiyari! This Nagesia girl is getting clever. She wants money separately. Did you hear that?"

Rampiyari said with a displeased look, "What to do, sir? The town winds touch them."

— Paramananda is a sucking-fly. Doesn't give them anything.

— No no, sir, he lends them money for clothing, cosmetics, whatever they need.

— Lends them? Lends?

Latia laughed out loud. He said, "That's very clever. He'll take the money of the kamiyas' whoring-work, will not give a penny and what he lends will be added to the reckoning of the first loan. That's why your girls dry up like wood. But watch out! No bad stuff with Douloti."

— No no sir, how can I?

One day Latia gave her an entire five-rupee note.

Ordinarily he gives nothing more than small change. Douloti is saving up in a little box. She buries the box in the floor. Now the fair at the end of the first month of the year was at hand. This is the most popular fair in this area. At a certain time this entire area was in the hands of the Rajas of Naoratangarh. It was the Rajas who had established the fair. At one time a pair of swords would come in a palanquin as the Raja's representative. The swords would be put on a high platform. Every visitor to the fair would put in an honor-fee in a brass plate in front of the swords. The great king would gamble with that money at the Light Festival. The fair goes on for three days. These three days Paramananda raises a few rooms in the fairgrounds and brings forty clients on the average to the girls' rooms. At the time of the fair he scolds Somni.

Paramananda hasn't given food and upkeep, Latia has impregnated her time after time. Still was it correct of Somni to let her body get so chewed-up? A client gives even up to five rupees. If Somni were usable Paramananda could have made six hundred in three days. Paramananda said angrily, "Just nine girls are in use. Douloti now belongs to Latiaji. I won't get her, I won't get you. Look Somni, the hundred rupees that your man took is now a lot in seven years. I will reckon it up. Repay the loan and get out."

Rampiyari said, "Huh, what a brain you have!"

— Do you alone have a brain?

— You have taken leave of all your sense and judgment in your craving for money. Tell me, have you thought about it at all? I'll be at the fair. Will Douloti be here alone? If Somni isn't in the house who will watch it?

— You will, now and then.

— I couldn't care less. I can't do it.

Douloti's spirits danced at the thought of seeing the fair.

Gohumani said, "Go see. In our day we saw too."

Gohumani's spirits are low. Her country cousin comes to see his boss in Madhpura once a month. He has brought news that the goat she had bought for her husband with the money begged from clients has died of snakebite. Why this cruelty of fate!

Gohumani wiped her eyes and said, "I am a kamiya-whore, I'll of course be kicked out when my carcass shrivels. Then, with a goat at home I would have sold kids, sold milk, I'd put a lot of hope in that."

Reoti said, "Why do they have fairs? They bring in client after client to me, don't even give me the time to have a drink of water."

Rampiyari will take them to the fair. An accident took place before they left. The woman Jhalo speaks very little. Quite a big sturdy woman with a strong bony frame.

Just before going Jhalo came and sat on the stoop, lit a tobacco leaf cigarette and said to Somni, "I want to go too. Take my flour ration, make up the lumps for bread making."

Rampiyari said, "What is this you're saying, Jhalo?"

— You heard me.

— I heard, but what does it mean?

Douloti realized that Rampiyari's voice was quite soft.

Even perhaps a bit of a wheedling tone.

— You don't know what it's about?

— That's between you and me.

— No, make a clean breast of it.

Somni now put on a silly face and said, "No Auntie! You know how much trouble the god will make if we're late. Why don't you say it quickly?"

Rampiyari heaved a few deep sighs. And said, "Right then. Let's go."

Jhalo is unforgiving. She said in a hard voice, "Own up before everyone that I know you. If things are not said openly with you—so, Gohumani, why are you silent?"

Gohumani said, "I open my mouth and get beaten up again?"

Jhalo said, "Let 'em beat me? Let 'em take a try. I will sit in this room and cast a spell, and our so-called Auntie, that bloody buffalo, will not live three nights. She'll spit blood and die." Rampiyari spoke up in pain, "No no Jhalo. I'm owning up that I'm not owning up. Oh Rama! Why have you put me in such a bind? What's happening to me?"

Jhalo put poison in her voice and said, "You feel very bad, eh? And the fact that you pocket one or two client's money for so long from the fair? So you say 'Oh Rama'?"

— I'll break faith with the god?

— You break faith a hundred times from morning till night. Bloated cunt, stupid buffalo!

— "Oh Rama!"—Rampiyari was almost in tears. Her mountainous bulk started trembling with passion in her arms, her cheeks, her belly. Then she said, "Don't put the poison-arrow spell on me. I was not so fat, who did this to me with the poison-arrow? I swear now that in the three days of the fair five clients belong to Jhalo alone. That earning I don't want to know or take."

— Why?

— What is our fault?

— Why should we be left out?

Rampiyari was going to say something, but Kishanchand got in. He laughed and said, "Great stuff here! Are the kamiya whores making a *union?*"

Rampiyari smiled toothily, "Kishanbabu! Why are you here and not at the fair?"

— I just came for a cup of tea.

— Somni, give him a seat. Make him some tea. Come, girls. I am for you, you are for me, why make trouble for nothing? Why me? Why put me in trouble? I do so much for you.

Jhalo said, "Yes yes you do a lot. That's how Kalabati was murdered. When her father came, waited and waited and went back, you didn't give him a single rupee. You and your god, and who is who, that's all you know. Come now."

Kishan says, "Hey Jhalo? You never went to town, Paramananda didn't become the master, this whorehouse became the factory. Rampiyari is Paramananda's *overseer* and you are all *labor.*

— Again that nonsense.

— You'd know if you went to Dhanbad.

— I know, now we are nine, give us a bit of spending money for the fair, we will mention your name.

— Yes yes, say my name.

Kishanbabu gave a rupee to everyone. Also to Rampiyari, Somni, and Douloti. Then he said, "At the fair I'll ride the merry-go-round with all of you."

They went to the fair. Before going Rampiyari said, "Don't sit long Kishanbabu, god will be angry."

— No no, god is now on the way to the Padmasri, walking about in the fair, looking for girls.

— I'm off.

Kishan drank tea. Somni said, "What about that matter, sir?"

— What matter?

— You said you'd put the boys in the *Mission*? In the *Mission*!

Kishan thought something and then said, "Famine's on the way. Take the three boys and put them at the door of the *Mission*, that's it."

— O dear! Won't they chase them off?

— They don't chase off. They'll surely keep them.

Kishan didn't say a word to Douloti. After he left Somni said, "Hoo! Who isn't afraid of Latia? He didn't say anything because Latia is your client. Now he doesn't take away girls from here. He tried before."

Douloti said, "Take away? How? Can a kamiya woman leave?" Never.

— Why did Auntie accept Jhalo's word?

— O dear! Jhalo knows spells. Knows how to do poison-arrow, knows how to get rid of pain-poison, she is a woman of quality.

— Knowing all this a kamiya-whore?

— Yes she is a kamiya-whore but Jhalo doesn't talk.

— No, she also has a lot of brains. She came here and made medicine. She has had no children here, she has a husband at home and will arrange her daughter's marriage. So Jhalo saves money. She says one thing, My husband's kamiya. I am a kamiya, but I don't want my children to be kamiyas. And even Auntie is silenced by her.

— Will your sons go to the *Mission*?

— Who knows? I say, if they survive I'll make them god's kamiyas. At least they'll have food in the morning.

— Won't we see the fair?

— We'll go at some point.

In the event neither Somni nor Douloti could go. When the others returned from the fair then Somni and Douloti went to see the dismantled fair. There had been many shops, of which they saw nothing. In the broken-up fair Somni's sons were looking for food, grubbing around among the broken clay pots and Sal leaf cones of the tea-shops. Douloti said to Somni, "Buy them some sliced bread. Here is change. Let me look around a bit."

A wiry elderly man with a headband was drinking tea in a tea-shop. Seeing him the bottom of Douloti's chest gave a great shudder. Bono! Bono Nagesia!

— Uncle Bono!

— Douloti?

— Yes, Uncle Bono.

Douloti's tears flowed, she sobbed out loud. Not like a whore but like a country girl. If they come to the fair from their husband's house and see someone from their father's house the country girl gets her weeping done first. This is the rule. If you don't weep everyone will fault you—you're so happy in your husband's house that you don't think about your father's house? They cry by rote, but they also cry with emotion, and Douloti cried for emotion.

— Sit, calm yourself. I came to the fair and looked for you all over. You didn't come to see the fair?

— No uncle.

— I know everything. Your father came to Tohri to the hospital. I learnt everything from him.

— Is Father well? Is Mother well?

— As always. They are weaving mats, now they'll get a permit to gather wood. So it's been six months since you came.

— Yes uncle.

— Here look at Dhano.

— Oh my, look how Dhano has grown.

— He put up a shop at the fair. Betel leaf shop. Dhano now runs a betel leaf shop in Latehar.

— Is he married?

— Yes, he is married.

— What are you doing?

— Work, Douloti, I'm traveling with *Father* Bomfuller.

—You have entered the *Mission,* Uncle?

— No no. This *Father* is traveling constantly in Palamu and finding out where there are kamiya and seokias.

— Why? He wants to keep kamiyas?

— No, no, he'll ask gormen [the government] to stop the bondslavery system. And this is Mohan Srivastava. He is the school*master* in Tohri. He too is supporting the *Father*.

— What do you do?

— The kamiya knows the kamiya's score. And before I had left Seora I didn't know how large our kamiya society was. How can I tell you how many kamiyas there are in Chiroa, Chatakpur, Ramkanda, Daho, Palda, Chandoa, Banari? I saw everything touring with the *Father*. Oh, I didn't know before how large my society was.

— What is it that you do?

— I talk. The kamiyas are very afraid when they see a White, a gentleman—they fear what the boss will say. I talk, the White Man writes. Also I fetch water, I cook.

— What will come of this?

— Gormen will abolish bonded labor.

— Can that be?

— Let's see what happens. This I've told the White man. Sir! What will come of the gormen abolishing bonded labor? Without land, without food, hunger will drive the people of this society to become kamiyas again. The White shakes his head, says you're right. So it goes, let's see.

— The day bondslavery is over, the sun will rise in the West, and the rivers will flow against the current.

— I've spoken of you women too.

— O Bono Uncle, what have you said?

— Of the kamiya-whore trade.

— What good did that do?

Douloti said this lightly. She knows that Uncle Bono has taken up a new fancy and she is just keeping time with him. Does Uncle Bono know that there is a storm blowing in her chest because she's met someone she knows? Dhano has heard everything. Wasn't Douloti to be married to Dhano? If she'd stayed in Seora the marriage would surely have happened. Uncle Bono is a man of his own fancy. He is a kamiya but he certainly made a fool out of Munabar and escaped into a free life.

Ganori couldn't do it. He stumbled on his face when he tried to pull the cart at Munabar's command with the ox yoke on his shoulders. His broken body gave him the name Crook. And Douloti has taken the yoke of Crook's bondslavery on her shoulders. Now Latia is her client, her body is tight. Then going down and down Douloti will be as skeletal as Somni. She will repay the bondslavery loan as a beggar.

But what is Uncle Bono saying?

— Your problems will be solved.

— What will happen?

— You'll be free.

Douloti shook her head. Said, "Uncle Bono, if a kamiya woman becomes a whore the boss makes a lot of profit. No clothing, no cosmetics, no medicine. You have to borrow for everything and the boss adds all the loans to the first loan. No whore can repay that debt in her lifetime."

— When the working years are over?

— They kick you out. Beg to pay interest. Who gives up such a profitable business?

— This must be stopped.

— Who will stop it? Big contractors, government officers, they all come. They all help the god.

— Still this is illegal.

— Then why do the lawmakers come?

Somni called her. Douloti said, "I must be going, Uncle. You don't go to Seora. If you see him in Tohri, give my father my news. Please do."

Mohan Srivastava said, "Sister, listen."

— Calling me, lord?

— Don't say "lord." Yes, I'm talking to you. Where do you live? Where is your house?

— Rampiyari's whorehouse. I must go, Uncle. Let me see you when you come again.

— Who is that woman? And those children?

— That is Somni, a kamiya-whore like me, those are her children, they don't let her keep them, so she has to come out and see them. Great suffering, oh my, great sorrow. Dhano, I must go. Come to the Shiva-festival fair, bring your wife.

Douloti left. Mohan Srivastava said, "A girl from your village, Bono?"

— Yes, Mohanji.

— At the village kamiyas of the bosses, and here too the whore will work and give the boss money.

— Worse than that.

Bono wiped his eyes. His eyes are bloodshot. He said, "You're a gentleman, a good man, will you still understand? The boss can grab our women's honor twice a day, virgin or wife or mother, he doesn't give a damn. Their children must be borne. And here they've brought kamiya women and made them whores. Who keeps them? A brahman. If the whore has a child it must wander the streets. And the whore must go on giving the boss money."

— Everything will end if bondslavery ends.

— Bondslavery will end.

— The struggle must go on.

Dhano said with profound conviction, "How can that be, Babuji? The boss-moneylender keeps kamiyas. Gormen will anger the boss-moneylender? Never will it anger them. Taking away our land by force they put us in such a state that we must borrow and become kamiyas. All that land the boss gets written in his own name. And the clerks and officers of the gormen give the boss-moneylender support in that move. As long as this goes on how can bonded labor be over?"

Dhano said, "Mohanji! You don't get a single seed from the arable land for your own belly, people become kamiyas for reason of hunger."

— No, no Dhano, we are doing this work. People become kamiyas because they borrow for weddings, funerals, festivals. It's written in the books.

Bono said, "That is both true and false. Yes, you see that Bhikhari Sudas borrows eighty rupees for a wedding and becomes Lalchand Baniya's kamiya. But weddings and festivals come and go in life. Who borrows for them? The person who borrows is without land, without resources. Why is there no land? Why is there not a cracked penny in the house?"

— Wait, what did you say?

— Only the person who has no land and not a cracked penny in the house borrows for a social function. You think I don't know? Didn't my father have an acre and a half of land? He only became a kamiya when Munabar took that land, and left bonded labor on my neck when he died. When we borrow, one hundred rupees become ten thousand rupees in one generation. Gormen doesn't know? You say doesn't know.

— It must come to know.

— Look what you can do. You understand keeping accounts, you write accounts in numbers, but I see Douloti, a girl from our society, selling herself to give money to a brahman. Can't we bring her out?

— No, Bono. You have to do a lot of work for a long time to do that. First you have to end bondslavery.

Dhano said, "You can't end bondslavery this way. Rich people keep kamiyas and the gormen belongs to the rich. Who thinks about us?"

— No Dhano, gormen is everyone's.

— I hear that a lot from you, sir, but it's not true.

— If I go to Tohri, says Bono, I'll also tell Prasad Mahato of the Harijan Welfare Association.

— Prasad Mahato! He is a *Socialist*.

— Do I know that? He is himself a harijan, and a lot of work is done from their Association.

Dhano said, "And what can Prasad Mahato do at all, Father? There are whorehouses in Tohri."

— Where isn't there a red light district? But where else is there a system of catching kamiyas and making them whores?

Mohan Srivastava smiles patiently and says, "In Dehra Dun, in Uttarkashi. In Dehra Dun there is a trade also with Kolta tribal women. The women must be rescued, we must arrange for such occupations for them that they can support themselves and live. A lot of work for a lot of time is still left to be done."

— And bonded labor goes on in other states of the Union as well?

— Sure. It has different names in different areas.

Bono said, "That's why I no longer feel alone. Oh, the society of kamiyas is so large."

— Very large. If you call it a society, there is no accounting for the number of people in it.

VI

Latia beat Douloti up a lot because she went to see the broken fair. Whom Latia chooses for his very own must remain at home. No one must see her.

Paramananda also growled a lot. Is Madhpura a town? Just a market town. How much money do the people who come to whorehouses here spend? Latia pours handfuls of rupees. Angrily

Paramananda couldn't help saying, "He wanted a fresh uncut harijan cunt, and he has given one and a half thousand rupees in six months. You'll act out of line and send him off?"

— A thousand and a half?

Douloti was astounded. How much money is a thousand and a half? Somni said three hundred rupees could be repaid five times by it. A hundred rupees come ten times in thousand rupees.

Douloti lay down near Paramananda's feet. "God! your three hundred rupees have come through five times. Set me free then?" Paramananda had laughed. He had said, "Yes yes, you've seen the principal. But interest? I bought you clothes, those fifty-two rupees? My body is compassionate, your money has now increased by interest to two and a half thousand. And all my accounts are written down. When it's repaid in principal and interest, you will be freed."

— Deota, what do I know what you are calculating? Bond-slavery loans are never repaid.

— Listen, you will be free when the time comes, I'll give Somni her leave now. Her loan is unpaid, but let it be.

Somni got her leave very suddenly. She didn't get it, she gave it to herself. At her seven-year-old son's death after a raging fever and puke full of large tape-worms, the five-year-old son and the three-and-a-half-year-old youngest sat down under the thatch of a shop in the market, but wouldn't get up at all. It was the oldest who had roamed the streets with them, who begged and fed them. And they got the starch at the rice *hotel* of course. They knew Somni much less. It was the oldest they knew.

Even after that Somni washed the dishes, cooked, washed Rampiyari's clothes. Then she took her own share of bread and fried veg in her waist-cloth. Dry-eyed.

— What are you doing? Where are you going?

Somni didn't answer a single question, didn't look back once. She did not look at the whorehouse where she rented out the bloom-time of her life to all the trader-contractors, starting from Latia. She shook her head, and took her leave. Somni walked out, and sat on the wayside with her boys like any other beggar. She walked into the society of the beggars, in the rush shacks by the bus route. Like any other beggar she came to beg one day at Rampiyari's whorehouse.

She came muttering, "Why doesn't famine come, famine? Can no one give me a clue when famine will come?"

Douloti remembered she had wanted to put her sons in the *Mission* during the famine.

Very strange, Paramananda didn't say anything to Somni. He could have said, "Give me your beggar's earnings." Didn't say. Why not, who knows? Bondslavery never ends. And Jhalo said, "This is good. Somni has shown the way."

Douloti remained useful to Latia for a good while after this. But one morning naked Latia started screaming. "Rampiyari! Hey Rampiyari! Call Mishir. Ask him to show me a new harijan girl. I am not having fun in Douloti any more. These goods are threadbare now."

Deoki Dusadin came. And Douloti was shifted to a small room. Jhalo said, "If you get a good client you're saved, otherwise ten-twenty clients a day, you'll become like us."

— Where do all these clients come from, Jhalo?

— New roads are being built around Madhpura, and the *cement* works going up near the river. There are a thousand contractors and workers there.

— Why do they all come here?

— They don't bring their wives, it's a wild area. Day and night they swallow booze and look for women.

Gohumani said, "Ask Auntie for medicine. Now you don't have Latiaji. The body hurts managing ten or twenty clients."

— "What hurts," Jhalo said.

— You won't understand.

— I understand neither pain nor hurt. The drunkard is best. He doesn't give much trouble.

Douloti is lucky. Paramananda himself brought Singhji, another contractor, and said, "Why should you go to Tohri if you want a good woman? To Kishan's whorehouse? Is all my stuff here chaff? I'll give you only fresh country girls."

Singhji said, "But used girls, no?"

— Why sir? If you come, she'll be for you. Look at this. Look at this well, take a look?

Singhji is not a ferocious animal like Latia. He came well dressed. He took Douloti on a jeep. He bought Douloti a ring within a few months.

— Why don't you wear the ring?

— They'll see if I wear it and Auntie will snatch it.

Gave her a sari, perfumed soap. He would give Rampiyari ten rupees before he entered the room, gave Douloti one or two rupees as well. But he drank a lot, that's all.

An unexpected thing happened in the life of Douloti's crowd at this time. Paramananda went to his nephew's wedding in Jokhan and did not return.

Not only did he not return, he did not come back to Madhpura at all. He caught *cholera* and died.

It was the middle of the evening then. The women were finishing getting dressed in Rampiyari's whorehouse. Kishan came at such a time. With him a shaven-headed youth. Kishan said, "Rampiyari!"

— Yes, Kishanbabu.

— Come here, I have something to say.

Taking Rampiyari aside Kishan said, "Paramananda Mishir is dead, Rampiyari. This is his son, Baijnath Mishir. All three sons have inherited their father's landed property but this business Baijnath alone has inherited."

— The man died?

— Yes. And Baijnath is such a devil he shits on his father's shoulder. Talk to him. Then I will talk to you, I have things to say.

Rampiyari took Baijnath to his own room, and said, "Sit here, god."

— Now it's time for clients to come. I'll come tomorrow, during the day.

Baijnath went off busily. Kishan said, "You go, I'll be along. Rampiyari is my old acquaintance. I take a cup of tea when I come to see her."

Rampiyari made tea herself. Then she said, "The god passed along but he had said he'd give me a nose-ring and give me this house."

— He lied.

— This son is a swine?

— A devil, ruthless.

— What did you want to say?

— "If I . . . Deoki and Moti . . ." Kishan kept talking in a very low voice and what could Rampiyari do? He definitely wanted money. Kishan wants Deoki and Moti. Let him take them. Will he keep them as kamiya-whores? Buy them? "But you must make the exchange in secret, Kishanbabu, then don't come this way for six months. I know they'll stay well. What will you do with them? Pass them on outside, do what you think best. No no, not a crow will know. Where will you send them on? O dear. I didn't know country girls were traded in such distant cities."

She heaved a great sigh. A little while later, in the great up-roar at the fair of the full moon of the first month, Deoki Dusadin and Moti Parhaiya got lost, and people looked for them every-where. Latia said, "Well, that rat Kishan was going around, he is certainly in this."

Moti and Deoki were not found, and Baijnath must have sus-pected something, for two days later he came and sat down on a stool. He said, "My father was a fool and a compassionate body. Being kind he was not able to make money. And never said a thing about etiquette and manners, but I am not my father. The boss remains a boss, and the servant stays a servant."

— Of course.

— Now I'll teach you. You will never sit down in front of me, You'll speak to me standing. Don't forget.

Rampiyari is a formidable woman. She stood up with her vast bulk. But her heap of fat was quivering with passion. Even Paramananda had not insulted her so. The women were nervous. The person who can insult Rampiyari will perhaps cut off their heads with his bare hands.

— Tell me their names, tell me who takes how many clients. Why doesn't the number of clients go up? Eh? Why doesn't it go up?

Rampiyari now felt she was with the girls. She is no longer of the boss's party.

— Baijnathji, it's hard to find good clients.

— Why?

— The food you give, their bodies dry up. They can't pull in clients.

— The feeding money will go down more, the number of clients will go up more. Body! Kamiya woman's body! If the body dries up she'll depart. Famine's on the way, is there any shortage of harijan kamiya women? And I'll keep the accounts. Your task is to bring clients, and to do housework. It's profitless to make a pet of a parrot. A body like an elephant, it's very hard to keep up with food money.

Within a month Baijnath brought in new girls. Many plans all around, the tribal-harijan areas are crowded with contractor, bro-ker, *overseer, officer*, clerk. Very cheap *labor*, you can make poor girls disappear by very cheap tricks.

The women at Rampiyari's whorehouse were put in a system

of twenty to thirty clients by the clock. Pick up your cash fast. And when the body is empty?

Baijnath took Gohumani and Reoti to Jaukhan. He said, "Madhpura is a market town. There the client doesn't pay for such old cows. I am putting up rooms for them in the village by the brewery. Let them pull in clients at twelve annas, eight annas. My brothers will watch the trade."

Jhalo said, "In front of their husbands and children in Jokhan!"

Douloti said, "Their children?"

— What arrangements did Baijnathji make?

Rampiyari said, "What will he arrange? He'll sell them. Now I hear even children are bought."

Jhalo said, "Become a village whore, or become a beggar like Somni. Isn't that it? Tell me Auntie how we stay alive?"

Douloti said, "Who will stay alive?"

— I'm talking about myself. You are alive. You are most fortunate. Singhji comes. Latia is a pure animal. Yet Douloti, the body keeps if you have a single client.

— How long will it keep?

— Didn't your countryman tell you a lot of stuff? That bond-slavery will be over?

— Uncle Bono was our storyteller when we were little. He told a story.

— Story? A tale? A yarn?

Douloti, a kamiya-whore, leaned against the wall, closed her eyes with fatigue. She said in a voice filled with sleep, "A story, of course."

— What're you saying?

— Yes, like he said, they'll end bondslavery? Not a story? A beautiful tale. Bondslavery finished.

— The gentleman, the schoolmaster, he also told a story?

— Yes yes. Why shouldn't he? He too told a story.

— Your uncle's son?

— Dhano? No no, Dhano didn't tell a story. Uncle Bono is an old man, he spun a bit of a yarn. The gentleman understands books, not people, he too spun a bit. Dhano was looking at me.

— Bono Nagesia ran away, no?

— Yes yes.

— Then?

— Jhalo, what are you talking about? Uncle Bono ran away from bondslavery, did bondslavery end?

Rampiyari said, "How will it end? Paramanandaji told me that it is written in the great epics Ramayana and Mahabharata that ending bonded labor is against religion."

Jhalo said, "Why should it end? No land, not a handful of wheat, how will people eat without becoming bonded labor?"

— That is what Dhano said.

— You didn't see him again?

— Jhalo! How you talk? How should I see him again? He came to the fair on his travels, that's all. Will he come again? Uncle goes from land to land, he's forgotten about us.

Jhalo was going to say something, but Somni walked in with a stick. She leans on it now as she walks. Standing at the door she said, "Hey Ma! I'm hungry, give me something."

Jhalo said, "What's this now, Somni? Why are you calling us 'Ma'?"

Somni kept looking at them and said, "Give a little, Ma! I'm very hungry."

Rampiyari poured a cup of rice in her bowl with a cross face. Somni said—"Long live Ma"—then said, "Is the famine here? You gave me a cup of rice? Famine?"

Jhalo said, "She's crazed."

Rampiyari said, "Is *that* it? Her head is quite clear. She will bring on the famine with her 'famine famine.' How is she alive?"

The girl called Paro talks a lot. She said, "Perhaps she eats better than what you give us to eat."

Rampiyari said, "Tell that to the boss."

Singhji was not for Douloti for long. In two years Singhji went elsewhere with a contract. At the time he gave Douloti ten rupees and told her many things.

— This is not good work, Douloti, you are a good girl, a country girl, go back home. I don't have much money with me.

— But you've given me money from time to time, why should you give me more?

— Why do you say this? That's why I say you're a very good girl. Whores do this work for the lust of money. You never lust after money.

— My lord, if the market whores have some freedom the kamiya-whore does not. The boss takes the cash.

— You are a very good girl.

— My lord, may I say something?

— Say.

— If you see Bono Nagesia on your tours, the old man trav-els with a White—my village uncle Bono. Will you ask him to come here once?

— I will.

Singhji gave her a new sari, soap, many more things. He said, "You gave me a lot of peace."

Latia wanted fun, Singhji got peace.

When Singhji left, Douloti was already twenty. The charm of her body, and the firmness of her face were not yet broken. Rampiyari said, "Let's look for a rich client for Douloti. You will get money, he will be happy."

Baijnath said, "How much will I get?"

— Easily three hundred rupees a month.

— And she will pull in ten-rupee clients for a year, ten a day. A hundred rupees daily means three thousand rupees monthly, where is the higher profit?

— Ten ten-rupee clients a day in this Madhpura? You can't get that, sir. That's why the god tried to get a good client who'd give a big monthly fee.

— There will surely be a bigger profit in what we get, and if we go by father's rules, I cannot carry on.

— Douloti will then turn into Somni.

— That chewed-up thing? Somni has become a beggar in ten years by father's rules. By my rule Douloti will become a beggar in five years. What's that to me?

— All right.

Rampiyari sighed and said, "The cow gives milk if she's fed. If the human daughter turns kamiya no meal, no water, put riders in the saddle and take the money."

— Your tongue is out of control.

— Yes Baijnathji, I can't go on. Let me go. I am not your kamiya.

— Go. I won't lose an eye if you go. Settle your accounts and go.

— You will settle accounts.

— Why?

— I have two hundred rupees in this business, don't you know?

— Where is it written?

— I'll show you. In front of a witness.

The *bus* depot accountant Nandalai read out the paper. Yes, Paramananda is taking two hundred rupees from Rampiyari. Rampiyari will get one rupee in a hundred from the profits.

Baijnath gave the two hundred rupees but not a part of the profits. He said, "Dad was a total idiot. To write down such a thing? Don't calculate profits, just leave. I'll set the *police* on you if you talk too much. I'll say you're stealing money and running out on me."

Rampiyari kept abusing Baijnath. She showed him the door as she abused him. Then she said, "I am going. I will take a house in Nahara before the month is out. I'll open a business. I knew he wouldn't give me money. How long have I been putting some aside from the profits?"

— Going, Auntie?

— Tell me what to do?

Rampiyari's departure is the end of a chapter. Then Baijnath came to live in the house.

And the number of clients goes up, up, and up in Douloti's room. Douloti starts drying up fast. Now Jhalo is transferred to the village. Baijnath tries to raise the interest money as fast as possible.

No matter how great the effort, how high the number of clients, the interest on a bond labor loan goes up and up. And one day, surprising everyone, Bono Nagesia comes along. With him Mohan Srivastava, Prasad Mahato, *Father* Bomfuller, Puranchand from the Gandhi *Mission*.

Baijnath Misra said, "Who gave you permission to come? This is my house."

Puranchand says, "Your name?"

— Hey who are you?

Prasad Mahato of the Harijan Association is a smart kid. He quickly brings out some Harijan Association forms printed in English and says, "We are government people."

— What do you want here?

Bomfuller growled out in Hindi, "We will ask the questions. And question these women. You leave."

— This is my house.

— The *police* will come if you oppose government work.

— What is this! What work can the government have in a whorehouse?

— This is not just a whorehouse, you have brought kamiya women here and turned them into whores.

— The boss can do what he likes with the person who becomes a bondslave. Yes or no?

— The government will end bondslavery.

— The big government *officers* in Palamu keep kamiyas and seokias. Who will stop bondslavery?

— I'll tell you, the big government. Delhi government.

— It can't be. Bondslavery is an ancient law. That is written in religious books.

— What book?

— I've heard.

Prasad roared out, "That's enough, get out of here." Bomfuller said, "I think the man's a scoundrel. Take him to the police station on the *jeep*."

— No no, I'm going.

Mohan Srivastava was looking all this time for a known face. But until Douloti spoke her own name even Bono Nagesia didn't know her. Douloti's appearance is so changed.

— Say, say your name.

— Douloti.

— Father's name?

— Ganori Nagesia.

— I have heard of you. They've kept you as kamiya for three hundred rupees?

— Not kamiya, kamiya-whore.

— Three hundred rupees?

— Three hundred and fifty-two rupees. God bought clothes for fifty-two rupees, he has added that sum.

— Was there any other loan?

— I sometimes got some money from clients, but I ate it sir. They feed you too little, your hunger doesn't go. And once I borrowed ten rupees to buy clothes. Once when I was sick ... and for soap and hair oil ... I had to borrow another forty.

— And all the money has been added to the first loan?

— That's the rule.

— This money hasn't been repaid?

— Bondslavery loan, sir.

— How much have you earned?

Douloti started telling them the rates.

— Latiaji gave three hundred a month, and gave for three

years, yes gave for three years.

— Ten thousand eight hundred rupees!

— Singhji gave two hundred and fifty rupees monthly.

— How many years?

— Three years as well.

— Nine thousand rupees.

— And since then ... well some days five men, some days ten and twenty at fair times—ten rupees each.

— This for how long?

— Two years have passed already.

— Look Prasad, look Mohan, at the reckoning. If on the average a hundred a month, a thousand rupees monthly, twelve thousand yearly, twenty-four thousand in two years? How is she alive?

Having bonded herself with three hundred rupees in 1962—how much has she raised by 1970? Over forty thousand.

Prasad said, "What is to be done?"

Father Bomfuller's fingers were shaking. He said, "The same history in the society of the Dehru Dun tribal women. They do this work in Delhi or Meerut or Paharpur."

— What is to be done?

— Don't get excited, Prasad. Let me take depositions from the other women? Don't get excited.

Mohan poked Prasad Mahato, "What are your political friends doing in Bihar?"

— They are shooting guns in Bihar to keep the honor of the harijan women in Bhojpur. They are not putting a fresh coat of clay on the *school*yard, painting a *map* of India with *chalk* dust, planting a flag and singing "May the flag remain high," like you.

— Is Palamu not in Bihar?

— Will fire remain in one place?

— Will you stop a bit?

— What is to be done? The other women will say the same thing. We will leave after hearing it all?

Father Bomfuller said, "I have started to make a survey of the "*Incidence of Bonded Labor*" in Palamu district on behalf of a committee of the central government. I personally think, that man is a criminal who deserves capital punishment. But that won't work. Even the government *officers* of Palamu district keep kamiyas and seokias. Perhaps they don't turn kamiya women into whores. But the goal of my work is to build a *case* for abolishing the "*bonded labor*" system legally. On a regional basis. Let us not forget that. Yes, abolition."

Bono said, "Sir? What will they do by passing laws? Who will enforce them?"

Prasad said, "Government *officers.*"

— The brahmans, the kayasthas, the Rajputs. No Prasadji, even if there is a law it will be behind the bosses and the money-lenders. Isn't this the problem?

Mohan said, "Let there be a law. If the law is not obeyed, there's the *police*. The *police* will look out."

Bono said, "This Mohanbabu you have said like a gentleman. *Police* never raise their guns toward the boss or the moneylender. The *police* kill us."

Prasad said, "We want the law! And we want organization. Not an organization like the Harijan Association or the Gandhi *Mission.*"

At last Puranchand opened his mouth, "Try to think by way of peaceful means, Prasadji. You spoke of Bhojpur. But is it the way to a solution to take up arms to keep the honor of harijan women?"

Bono said, "Puranchandji? Is the honor of our women not honor? The boss lifts our wives and daughters, so you are saying 'Peace peace—Shanti Shanti.' If someone lifted daughter and wife from your family, would you have said 'Shanti'?"

— This doesn't happen in our families.

— Say that. If it had then you wouldn't have said "Shanti Shanti."

— I would have explained to the transgressor. I would have explained what a great sin it is to go against the moral law.

— Hey, you're a strange bird? You're explaining religion and by then he destroys the woman's honor? No no, this is very strange talk.

Prasad said, "We need organization. I work with the Harijan Association, and all I see is the harijans and tribals getting beaten. We need new organization. My Association cannot end the pain and the suffering of the tribals."

Father Bomfuller said, "The first job is to abolish this system by law. Then we need to make the law workable by the pressure of public opinion. We need organization to create public opinion. Then these freed kamiyas must have an Association to assure them a living. And, in the case of these women there must be social and economic rehabilitation."

Mohan said, "If there is a law."

Puranchand said, "If there is a law."

Prasad said, "Fire, there will be fire."

Bono said, "You will leave after hearing it all? You won't help these women? How long will it take to get the law passed? What will be their state by then?"

Bomfuller said, "This condition is the result of many years, Bono. Does the sin of long years go in a day?"

Douloti brought tea arranged on a tray. She said, "The boss says to take some tea."

Another woman's deposition was being taken. Douloti sat by Bono and started rubbing his feet softly with great sympathy. Uncle Bono alone knows how overwhelming the darkness of their life is. It is only Uncle Bono's breast that's bursting with an equal pain.

Douloti's fingers said, Why grieve, Uncle Bono? Bondslavery loan is never repaid. A three hundred rupee loan becomes infinite in eight years. The boss has raised more than forty thousand rupees wringing this body of mine. Still I owe. There will be a loan as long as my body is consumable. Then I'll leave as a beggar. Somni has become a beggar and she says ceaselessly, Is famine here? Famine?

Don't grieve, Uncle Bono. Why don't you rather tell me those things silently just as I am speaking to you in silence? Let the gentlemen twitter this way. Those words of yours will be much more precious.

Remember that banyan tree in Seora village? Speak of it. I swung myself on its branches when I went to graze the goats. Father didn't take me to the Chhat festival fair. I had a sore on my leg. You took me on your shoulders.

When winter came to the Nagesia neighborhood we would sit by the fire and mother would put the little balls of flour into the fire. How sweet the smell of warm flour seemed to me. At night you beat on *cans,* made a great uproar to chase away tigers.

Then I didn't know, Bono Uncle, that the world had so much liquor, that it held Baijnath, that it had so many clients. I lost those days long ago. I get all of it back when I see you. You yourself don't know how much you give me.

Bono said, "Your hands are so hot?"

— They stay hot.

— Do you get fever?

— Maybe.

Now Douloti untied the knot at one end of her cloth and took out a rupee. She said, "Uncle Bono? Have a little something to eat with this, yes?"

— Money? You gave me money?

— Yes, Uncle.

— My little mother, you gave me money? Gave me money?

Bono Nagesia wept out loud in lament, "You gave me money!"

Douloti said, with affection, like a mother, "Not to cry, Uncle, why do you cry? Don't cry. Should one cry?"

Prasad shook his head hard and said, "There will be a fire." Bono kept shaking his head, "Who will light that fire, Prasadji? There is no one to light the fire. If there was, would the kamiya society be so large in Palamu? There are people for passing laws, there are people to ride *jeeps,* but no one to light the fire. Can't you see the kamiya society is growing?"

VII

Once Bono Nagesia had thought that Mohan Srivastava and *Father* Bomfuller were his igniters. But Mohan Srivastava with all his sympathy for harijan and tribal kamiya-seokias, remained *schoolmaster* at the Basic Primary *School* in Bira village, Tohri *Block.* His faith in the law, in *officers,* in the *police,* remained unshaken. But in the matter of Prasad Mahato he remained faithful.

So when Prasad started working underground in 1971 after rounding the Palamu Bhumidas Freedom Party, Mohan did not inform the *police.* He would have received a reward if he had done so.

The object of this account is not Prasad's quick transformation. Just as its object is not Bono Nagesia's joining Prasad's party. Bono didn't value Prasad so much before. But the day Prasad, the son of a harijan, left the Gandhi *Mission* and the Harijan Association and joined the Liberation Party, Bono searched him out and mingled with him. He said, "Dhano runs a betel-nut shop, he bought his mother a buffalo! What do I do? So I came to you, got it?"

— There will be no law, Prasadji, but you must explain things to the kamiya-seokia.

— What?

— This rule is the rule of slavery, of bondage.

— What happened to our white friend?

— He went to Delhi. With a hey, phoosh.

Bomfuller's survey report reached Delhi, and was imprisoned in a *file*.

Bono had said, "We are making a claim for the landless laborers' wage, why are we making it?"

Prasad's eyes were grey with memory. He said, "The person with little land is also a kamiya-seokia. And so is the farmworker. The government has laws for farmworkers. But the Labor Department of the state government had never implemented them."

What is the net result of this, can you see?

— If they had been paid at the government rate perhaps they would not have had to become kamiya. Isn't that right? Say.

— Quite right. So you see there's no solution even if there is a law.

— The law is giving you this, so it is your right. Just as I can say this when I go among the farmworkers, if there is the other law I can say bonded labor is illegal, don't do it. Can you help the poor by passing laws? Never. We can fight by quoting the law.

— I am old.

— Old is good. An old man like you.

— A fight for the law, the *police* are there too.

— This is seventy-one. The *police* are everywhere.

Everywhere there were *police, military, paramilitary*.

— Farmworkers! Unite on the demand of government wages. Otherwise you'll become kamiyas.

The farmworkers were stopping bullets when they demanded government wages, the corpses of landed farmers were also falling.

Douloti didn't know this news.

In this way, taking clients, one day Douloti saw that her rate had dropped to one rupee.

One can get a client for a rupee. But no one wants to go to Douloti's room.

Baijnath says, "What's the matter with you?"

— What do I know, Boss?

— What have you smeared on your face? Red dye?

— No boss. There are these red swellings all over the place. I can't take clients. Fiery hot inside the passage. Burns me up to take a piss.

Baijnath's face darkened. He said, "Go to the room on the

other side of the courtyard. Here's some ointment, use it. If it doesn't help, go to the hospital."

— Where is there a hospital here, Boss?

— Go to Tohri.

— How? I can't walk.

— Go by *bus*. Go as you can.

— I'll go.

— Come back when you are cured. Why are you coughing?

— The cough gets me all the time, Boss.

— Go, go to that room.

Baijnath called Harramia and said, "Give her food in a clay dish, and throw it away without holding it tight."

— Why Boss?

— She's got a bad disease.

Fuel—dried cow dung patties and coal—is stored in one corner of the room on the other side of the courtyard. Douloti made room for herself on the side and lay down. Harramia left food on a clay dish and water in a clay cup. Douloti said, "Take this rupee note. To do what?"

Douloti said with closed eyes, "Bring me a candle and matches. A slice of bread and a bit of sugar. I don't feel like eating flat bread and lentils."

— You'll spend everything?

— What do I have! You don't have to give me back the change. Buy me a slice of bread tomorrow.

— Haven't you saved up anything?

Douloti smiled weakly and showed her fever-hot belly. And said, "Dear, this traitor ate up everything."

Douloti couldn't eat the sliced bread. Even after this, the relief of not having to take a client seemed to bring her a consuming fever.

Not as a beggar like Somni, not to become a village-prostitute like Jhalo, but destitute in quite another way, Douloti left the whorehouse. She went to market and sold her last resource, the ring that Singhji had given her. A ring made of gold, she got fifteen rupees for it.

Then she somehow got on the *bus* to Tohri and sat down. Sravan—the fourth month of the year—July-August. Broken clouds in the sky. The rains haven't come this year. She put her bundle in her lap and rested her head against the window.

Oh how fast the *bus* does go. Villages like Seora are running

backwards on both sides from time to time. Two shopkeepers are
sitting beside her and talking non-stop.

— Brother, I am dying of *police* trouble.

— You're quite right. Here's some betel-nut.

— The *police* want money all the time.

— Arrey, *Emergency, Emergency,* they've put down *police*
depots everywhere for the Emergency.

— That's what I'm saying. Do I have a son? Is he grabbing
guns? So why should I give three and four rupees every day for
the *Emergency* police?

— We are nothing but small shopkeepers.

— No savings, brother, I'll die if I have to give hundred two
hundred rupees a month.

— Where was this *Emergency*?

— Who knows? The *police* can't stop a riot. The *police* only
know how to terrorize poor shopkeepers and the village market-
folk.

— I'd never seen so many *police* in the villages and the village markets of Palamu.

— Arrey, we don't know police stations. There is no law-
breaking here, we don't have to go to the *police*.

— We're not having to go. The *police* are coming.

Douloti understood some and didn't understand some.

Everyone got down at Banka and had tea at the shop. Douloti
closed her eyes.

She got down at Tohri and went to hospital shaking. Some
dogs are roaming the hospital veranda in the late afternoon light.
Her body couldn't bear any more when she reached there. She lay
down with her bundle under her head.

The sweeper women took her inside from the hospital
veranda. They understood at first glance that this was a whore.
The sweeper women laid her in bed properly and looked at each
other. One kept her eye on the door. Another took out the money
tied in a handkerchief by putting her hand with practiced skill
inside the blouse. Then they went to call the doctor. Douloti
stayed in hospital about four days, unconscious with fever. The
doctor said, "She's come from Madhpura to Tohri? How did she
come? Amazing."

The *nurse* turned up her lip as well. The body hollow with
tuberculosis, the sores of venereal disease all over her frame, ooz-
ing evil-smelling pus, the whores come to hospital only to die.

Still there are the hospital rules. When her consciousness returned after about four days Douloti understood she was in hospital.

The doctor said, What is your name?

— Douloti Nagesia.

— How old are you?

— I don't know, lord.

The doctor said, "This is a bother, doesn't know her age."

— I was born the year after independence.

Douloti smiled in a timid way like any other country woman. The human smile on the face of the unknown skeleton had the innocence of a field of grain. The doctor was surprised.

— Twenty-seven? Just twenty-seven? I had thought ...

— That'll be it, lord.

— What do you do?

— Kamiya-whore, lord. Baijnath Mishir's.

— I see! Now listen, my dear, this place can't treat you. You have to go to the hospital in Mandar.

— No treatment here?

— No, we don't have the facilities.

— Where are they, lord?

— You'll have to go by *bus.* I'll write it down, take the paper.

— By *bus?* I have no money, lord.

— Not even *bus* fare?

— I had ... someone took it.

— What will you do here? See if they let you travel free sitting on the floor of the *bus.*

— Lord.

— What?

— I won't live, isn't it?

— See, go to Mandar and see.

Douloti closed her eyes. And said, "I'll go tomorrow."

The next day Douloti left the hospital *gates* shaking. If Baijnath had let go when a little health was left! Then she could have raised the fare with whoring. Douloti didn't get leave earlier. And now! Something is going down, finishing her body. Well, and how did she get up and take clients a few days ago in Madhpura?

For fear of Baijnathji.

All day she sat under a tree, in the shade. No. No use going to Mandar any more. Better to go to Seora. Father's there, mother's there. Seora is not even that far from Tohri. She will go to

Seora. Everything is cool at night. She won't be tired if she walks slow. There is after all a way. A broad unpaved road for oxcarts.

In the late afternoon Douloti asked for some water at the food shop. Then she started step by slow step. She had never thought she would get to go to Seora again.

The smell of catkins by the wayside, around the necks of cattle the homecoming bells are chiming. Gradually the fireflies flew in the dark, the stars came out in the sky! People had lit a fire, the smoke was rising.

Walking on, walking on dragging her feet, Douloti came to the front of a large hut. A very big hut, close to Tohri. Douloti felt as she stepped in the front yard that it was very carefully clay-washed. And as she groped to the middle of the yard, Douloti realized this as well, that she would no longer get to Seora. Pain is climbing her entire chest, upward, upward.

Douloti lay down. The pain became cough, the cough became blood, Douloti closed her eyes.

In the morning at six, Mohan Srivastava, the *master* at the Basic Primary *School* in Bira village of Tohri *Block,* heard an uproar as he was fixing the Indian tricolor on a bamboo pole.

He came out with the flag in his hand.

Quite a few people have crowded around the *map* of India that had been carefully drawn, first by cutting the *outline* and then by pouring liquid *chalk* into it. Today is Independence Day, the first day of the month of Bhadra. Children come to raise the flag and elders come to see the fun. It is they who are standing crowded together, pointing with their fingers, speaking fearfully, pausing often.

Mohan Srivastava came down from the room and then, looking front, he closed his eyes. His body jerked again and again, as if his arms and legs were tied and a *machine-gun* was being emptied into him.

Filling the entire Indian peninsula from the oceans to the Himalayas, here lies *bonded labor* spread-eagled, kamiya-whore Douloti Nagesia's tormented corpse, putrefied with venereal disease, having vomited up all the blood in its desiccated lungs.

Today, on the fifteenth of *August,* Douloti has left no room at all in the India of people like Mohan for planting the standard of the Independence flag. What will Mohan do now? Douloti is all over India.

Pterodactyl,
Puran Sahay,
and Pirtha

I

Puran Sahay was sitting at the *Block* Development *office* when he heard the account of this unearthly terror.

His grandfather had named him Prarthana Puran—Prayer Fulfillment—for Puran's mother was producing one girl after another, and Puran's father had just left the *Congress* volunteers and become a Comnis [Communist] and was most unwilling to marry a second time for a son—in those days one could have called it a revolt.

Even Puran's mother had told her husband, "Get another wife. Our line will die without a son." The Father, "As a Comnis I cannot marry again."

— But a daughter will not carry the name.

— Son and daughter are the same to me. I'll send the girls to school, they'll be full human beings. I'm proud to be a father of daughters.

A disobedient son, but one must have a male child to preserve the line. So Grandfather went to the four great sacred places of India and offered his prayer. After all this the grandson was born. That is why he was given the name of Prarthana Puran. Among his father's friends there were journalists and poets who also came to the house. The grand name might owe something to their high-toned conversations as well. Long after Grandfather's demise, when he was himself a journalist, ex-social worker, and independent, he changed his name.

Which half to cut. Which to keep. A great problem. "Prarthana" becomes a woman's name, his wife's name was Archana. So he kept the name "Puran." His wife was very lively. She would say, "If we have a girl we'll call her Prarthana." But Prarthana didn't come into Archana's lap. It was Arjun who came. But just after Arjun arrived Archana died of *eclampsia*. Puran didn't marry again. Arjun spent some time with his mother's brother and then returned to Puran's mother. To him "Mother" means the faded photograph of a smiling Archana on the wall. At fifteen, neither adolescent nor young man, Arjun is a good student at the "Udyog" School. Puran's mother manages the house with a firm hand even at seventy-five. She is protecting the money left by husband and father-in-law and the house at Kadamkuan. She has no confidence about Puran. She will make a marriage for Arjun as soon as he's twenty. Puran is as obstinate as his father. He hasn't married since Archana died. Although, in middle age, he tastes loneliness.

Puran's elder sister lives in the neighborhood, so Puran's mother is not altogether helpless. Puran can thus circulate at will as a reporter for the group of daily, weekly, and monthly papers *Patna Dibasjyoti* (formerly *Patna Daylight*). Now he feels like marrying his sister's unmarried teacher sister-in-law Saraswati. It would have worked out if he had married her a bit before this. Now Arjun is growing up, a certain barrier of diffidence has come between Saraswati and Puran. Puran doesn't know what Arjun will say. Arjun, with his English-medium schooling, his attraction

Puran curiously detached, unable to form relationships

for karate, his hockey-playing, has remained a stranger to him. He has become even less tractable after his wits have sharpened in science and mathematics quizzes.

Puran understands that if he goes here and there no spot is left empty at home, for he has long since not been there when he's there. Mother's household is sufficiently replete with Arjun, with the *Gita,* with her two daughters in Patna. Arjun's personal universe is most important to him. The elder sisters inhabit a distant world. They find it hard to understand that Puran, a male of the species, does not make his masculinity felt in harsh words, in manifestations of heat and light. Saraswati herself understands that no real relationship has grown between herself and Puran. Saraswati considers herself squandered. As if her life has floated away like the fruit-offering at the Chhat festival, unaccepted by the sun. The river doesn't eat it, it is not for human or animal consumption, it only floats, and rots floating.

Saraswati's glance says: it's your failure that there was no room for a fleshly, hungry, thirsty, human relationship to grow. Puran accepts that and considers himself half-human at forty-five. And this moral question arises: how will a person merely floating in the everyday world, who has not attempted to build a human relationship with mother-son-Saraswati, be able to do justice to a subject as a journalist?

Yet as a journalist his reporting of the massacre of the harijans at Arwal has received praise, and he too, like others, has fallen into disfavor with the Government in Patna. He wrote about the killing in Banjhi with a razor-sharp edge: "Red Blood or Spark of Fire in Black Tribal Skin?" And then water scarcity in Nalipura. Enteric fever epidemic in Hataori. The blinding of prisoners in Bhagalpur- the owner of the *Dibasjyoti* group is a Punjabi industrialist. He is untroubled by the maelstrom of political moves in Bihar or the pre-historic warfare of casteism. He gives money to all political parties. He has support everywhere. The newspaper is a business to him. If reporting caste war keeps his paper going, so be it. Nothing will touch him. Industrial set-up in Ranchi, clout in New Delhi and Bihar, newspaper in Patna. The illustrated magazine called *Kamini,* devoted to women and the film world, brings in most money. Right beside a balance-sheet on suicides are recipes on the "For the Home" page. Right beside the world travels of an international Guru the statement of a sex-bomb star: "Motherhood is woman's greatest wealth." This sort of a mixed chow mein dish.

Even in this life Puran felt restless. He sensed that he was getting altogether too professional. First investigative journalism, but then no problem writing "Bihar, A Tourist's Paradise." His father had faith in communist ideals. His life was not adrift. But Puran cannot be happy in himself. He has done as he pleased. Yet where is the sense of achievement fulfilled?

These are his reasons for coming to Pirtha. Before he left, Saraswati startled him by saying, "I'll no longer wait for nothing."

— What will you do?

— I'll go to an ashram with a school.

— Not right away?

— And why not?

Saraswati spoke with a gentle smile. For a long time now, she has worn only white. In her white sari, white blouse, and with her long braid and tired dark eyes she looked like Nutan in the tragic film *Saraswati Chandra* (they'd seen it together). The theme song "O driftwood face, O unquiet mind" played in his mind.

— Saraswati, why an ashram?

— I'm thirty-two, after all.

— Let me come back.

— Your life won't be empty without me.

— Give me a bit more time.

— I've been waiting for you, fighting the family, since I was eighteen. My younger sisters are all married off. Now at last I'm weary too.

— Only this once, Saraswati.

She wears only white, as if already a widow.

— This once.

— I can't give my word.

Puran has come to Pirtha with the worry that Saraswati might leave some day. The district is in Madhya Pradesh, the Block is Pirtha. He must go to the distant villages where the eighty thousand tribals among the one million, one hundred and seven thousand, three hundred and eighty-one people of the district live. For a long time people have been dying in Pirtha. Well, the Chief Minister of the state, who built himself a luxurious residence after the Bhopal Union Carbide disaster, is certainly not about to declare Pirtha a "famine area." But Puran's old friend Harisharan, now *Block Development Officer*, wrote, Come, take a look, the State Government says "No story," but here's Surajpratap's report, come to follow it up.

He came for this purpose, and sensed already in Madhopura that a good deal of hostility was afoot against journalists not only in Pirtha Block but in the entire district.

The SDO [Sub-Divisional Officer] said, "Why are you going to Pirtha? There's nothing there. There's nothing more to be seen in the tribal areas. You'll make a noise in the newspaper if you say anything, and more journalists will come. There will be a furor."

— It doesn't matter to you folks after all.

— You don't understand. Nothing matters to anyone these days. Nothing happens to anyone. Look, look at this.

The survey map of Pirtha *Block* is like some extinct animal of Gondwanaland. The beast has fallen on its face. The new era in the history of the world began when, at the end of the Mesozoic era, India broke off from the main mass of Gondwanaland. It is as if some prehistoric creature had fallen on its face then. Such are the survey lines of Pirtha *Block*.

— Come and see. What, looks like an animal, no?

— Yes. But these creatures are extinct.

— Who knows?

The youthful SDO pulls the hair on his head.

— Our honor was destroyed by the Bhopal gas incident.

— How?

— There was talk about Bhopal. And in the middle of the gas affair in Bhopal, the state government did not permit a Health Center in Pirtha, and they were bringing the enteric patients from the tribal areas into town. The SDPO [Sub-Divisional Police Officer] fired in the dark, three people died. The enteric fever started from the polluted water supply. We sent water, it's coming, it's coming; the water *tank* didn't get there. Both the *truck* and the *tank* had disappeared. I myself had posted guards at the polluted wells. The tribals then beat up the guard, drank the water, and then: Epidemic.

— What did you do?

— Sent police to stop the violence.

— And the police?

— Hey journalist! Pirtha is not agricultural land, and there is no struggle here. So what do the police do in such a tribal area?

— Where did the enteric fever come from?

The SDO laughs with a vicious joy.

— When it rains, the water flows down the hillside. How do I know if something poisonous came with the water?

— It does rain then?

— From time to time. Otherwise how are they alive?

— Doesn't the state government give any aid?

— What aid? What resource? Look at this map. Near the foot of the animal there is a church but no *missionaries*. We are forty kilometers to the south of this church. And a *canal* would have gone from the animal's tail to its head by the Madhopura Irrigation Scheme. The scheme is in the register. That *canal* would have joined the Pirtha River as well. And look here.

— I'm looking.

— The tribals are in the animal's jaws. Near the throat water gushes down into Pirtha at great speed in the rainy season. If there were small dams three miles down the river, and then another mile down, the tribal area of Pirtha would be green.

— This didn't happen?

— No. Eleven years ago there was great pomp and circumstance on Independence Day. We sent food. There was a camp, the minister came, there was an inauguration ceremony, and many reporters came.

— I didn't come.

— It began where it ended.

— It didn't go any further?

— No no, it would have advanced if it had begun. Three SDOs have tried in turn, but these files get lost halfway between Madhopura and Bhopal. They always get lost. If the files get lost . . .

— It isn't yet done?

— No. It'll never be done. Now we hear, There's lots of water in Pirtha.

— Who says?

The SDO is probably getting transferred.

— Imagine someone going to see Pirtha in Shaon or Bhadro —the fourth or fifth months—at the height of the rainy season, and then such a view he would have. No way to guess there's a water problem . . . Journalist! Why come in the rainy season to inspect a drought area? You can spend a few hours most agreeably there if you take a picnic basket. Not everybody understands the seasonal nature of the stream. The Government brought a team of experts. They came in the rainy season. So OK, they said there's lot of water in Pirtha. Nothing can be done.

— But you people have been building roads and bungalows with tribal welfare money for some years now.

— How many copies do you print?

— Fifty-sixty-seventy thousand. A hundred thousand on Dewali Festival day. There's no fixed number.

— Then don't ask anymore. What will you write? How many will read? How much pressure on my state government? Have some tea.

— I don't want any more tea.

— Journalists and writers and poets drink a lot of tea, a lot of liquor, get very drunk.

— So everyone the same? All SDOs are not the same. All journalists are not the same. You and Surajpratap are not the same after all.

— How can that be?

Puran turns his head away. The office garden of the ruler of the subdivision was blazing with bougainvillea. This is also the soil for bougainvillea. Rough and dry. There is so much bougainvillea in India that one could have given it a proper Indian name. A big monkey sat on a laburnum with his tail hanging down.

Looking at this Puran says, "Has Surajpratap written of an unearthly terror?"

— Will Harisharanji send a jeep from the Block Office?

— What did Surajpratap write?

— Nothing but a story.

— That was nothing but a story?

— How do I explain? Starvation for years. Fewer children are being born to them, and the Administration still doesn't attach any importance to Pirtha. They have taken it for granted for some time that the government has given them up. Now how will they explain to themselves the reason for this misfortune? Whatever the case, they need an explanation if only for their peace of mind. So they are spreading stories.

— So tell me a story.

— You've come to Madhya Bharat [lit. Middle India], why don't you see Gwalior, Indore, Jabbalpur, Dhara-Mandu, Bhopal? Do you know that there's still a festival at Shivapuri, a statue-festival? The descendants of the servants of the old kings serve and worship the kings' statues. "The Middle Ages in Middle India" will be a fine piece. Go to Bastar, see the tribals.

— Come on, tell me what's up. You too have believed that some terrifying event has taken place.

— Look at this painting.

— A cave-painting?

— A boy painted this on the stone wall of his room. The picture was taken by Surajpratap, but no, this photo is not for a newspaper, *not for publicity*.

— He did not print a photo.

— No, we took away the negative. He cannot print this, he doesn't have a copy.

What is it? Bird? Webbed wings like a bat and a body like a giant iguana. And four legs? A toothless gaping horrible mouth.

— But this is . . .

— Don't say it. I won't hear it.

— How did he paint this?

— I don't know. The boy's shut up.

— Where? Where is the picture he painted?

— In Pirtha.

Now the SDO begins to speak in bursts. As if a badly wounded person is making a last-ditch effort to make a deposition to hospital or police, to the killers or to friends.

Like that man from Chitowra. Where Puran had been present. The Pasi harijans claimed a long-disputed piece of land, and no way would the Brahmarshi Sena [a fundamentalist Hindu gangster group mobilized by the landowners] militia let them have it. Of course the land is now with the Pasis, this very minute, but the ownership can change hands again. In Puran's state of Bihar, land changes caste often. Puran and a group of reporters went to the hospital. The man spoke in bursts, In front was Ramnagina, and Lakhan, and Nathniram and many people . . . five guns . . . Ramnagina opened fire . . . I was running to call the police . . . to call the police . . . The reporters would cluster there because it was only a Block Health Center—nothing bigger—and things were easier because Aditya Naolaksha of an all-India newspaper was there.

The SDO is talking like that man. He is moving his hands, trying to explain, as if there's a tremendous communication gap between him and Puran, a tremendous (mental and linguistic) suspension of contact. Are the two placed on two islands and is one not understanding the most urgent message of the other, speaking with vivid gestures on the seashore? This asymptote is a contemporary contagion. A man in Mahandi had split open the head of a guy who had poisoned his water buffalo and had received a life sentence. How valuable is a buffalo that you are going to jail for twenty years? Asked this, the man, collar-bone shaking and foaming at the mouth, had made an effort to explain to Puran what a buffalo meant in the life of a villager. A water-buffalo is a priceless good to a well-to-do farmer.

Puran had not grasped the desperation behind his urgent and troubled message. Although he did turn the man's words into a most compassionate small news item, "For the Sake of a Buffalo."

The SDO continues to report.

— It was the waxing fortnight of the moon. It was a moonlit night. I don't know, the moon might have been full. The Sarpanch, head of a group of five villages, had come up to Madhopura. With him were a few people from Pirtha. Shankar was there as well. You will find Shankar. He is the only literate man in the village. It is he who comes to town from time to time at Census time. Your friend sometimes employs him to get people for road construction work. Harisharanji is most dear to them!

Sufficient contempt is not demonstrated when the two words "most dear" are pronounced.

— Then did they see the creature?

— No.

The SDO's tone shifts. It reproaches the light frivolity of Puran's voice.

— Some of them were returning. There was a lot of drumming in the village. They beat drums with five sticks if they want to spread special news. The sound was like that. Then something had happened, they said, and started walking faster. The night was full of moonlight. You can count the leaves on the trees there on moonlit nights. They were walking along the sand and rocks where the Pirtha is a bit wider. At that time they saw a monstrous shadow fly by. Not too big, not too small, a bird.

— They said "bird"?

— That's what they said the first day. They'll think bird if they see something fly. What else can they think?

— Some sort of large bat?

— There's no such thing there. It was gliding rather than flying. It would flow like a wave, go down a bit swinging, rising a bit again. They raised their faces, saw it, and were afraid. Very afraid … the shadow moved with them.

— For how long?

— I don't know. Why don't you ask the owner of your news-paper to buy them all HMT watches? With illuminated dials. And train them. So that they can check the time whenever they see something strange.

— Forgive me.

— It's not a question of asking for or receiving forgiveness. This is beyond reckoning . . . The shadow moved on and vanished into the hillside. When they reached the village they saw that all the people of Pirtha were outdoors. And the headman was beating the drum. When they arrived the headman said, "An evil shadow has moved across us, some danger is ahead."

— This is the unearthly terror? This is an embodied creature, that can spread its wings and fly.

— Go to Pirtha. Explain this to them. I cannot make you understand. You are not understanding how it is in Pirtha. It isn't called a famine area. Pirtha is a place of perennial starvation. They have no resource, and they will never. A few thousand peo-ple have now accepted despair. They don't know how to ask, don't ask, but they take if given. How will I make you understand that it is not possible for those tribals to think reasonably, to offer explanations? You will understand them with your urban mental-ity? You will fathom the Indian Ocean with a foot-ruler?

— But you are a sympathetic officer.

— Please do not write this. A transfer as soon as the word "sympathetic" appears. And that word is false.

The SDO smiles weakly, becomes absent-minded, or drowns in the depths of his own mind.

— I'd have done something if I had been compassionate. You don't have to be "compassionate." I want to get a well dug, there are obstacles. I want to extend the road . . . the contractors and politicians are much more powerful than I . . . but I will cer-tainly establish a primary health center. And four wells in the area, and where the Pirtha comes down from the hills, a dam . . . don't write all this. In fact it will be useful if you write that the officer is inefficient and ruthless. If a question is raised in the State Legislative Assembly, if there is a warning—"Why aren't you getting the work done"—then perhaps . . . But the shadow was seen in Pirtha for quite a few days.

— You can't be serious?

— The more it was seen, the more the terror spread . . . Such a variety of stories! But I took away the roll of film when I saw Surajpratap's photos.

— You could have allowed them to be printed.

— No ... impossible. Then you have to accept what the creature is. How is that possible?

— Have you been there even once?

— I went a few times. No, no shadows are seen anymore. And it is not necessary either. The shadow has left a firm imprint on their minds. It's done its work and gone.

— What did you hear?

— Go hear for yourself. Why should you accept what I heard? Let me tell you what I saw.

— What did you see?

— I traveled around and saw everything: jungle, hill, cave. I got nothing, I saw the picture painted by the boy.

— Is it still there?

— It's there. Now that picture can't be erased. Engraved in stone. It's being worshipped. No, your jeep is not coming today, you'll have to stay overnight after all. Is the bungalow free ... I don't know what Department's.

— No hotels?

— You won't be comfortable in those kinds of hotels. If you don't mind, stay with me in my bungalow. Our truck will go to the *Block* tomorrow, go with them.

— I don't have any problems with that.

— I know. Journalists can do everything.

— Why did Harisharan behave this way? He knew I was coming.

— Perhaps he's on tour ... Your friend? He looks younger than you.

— Classmate. He was a good student. His father was transferred from Patna to Jabbalpur, he worked with the railways, they moved. We've kept in touch because he'd come to Patna occasionally. I never thought he'd enter the Madhya Pradesh State *Civil Service*.

— Why? What did you expect?

— He used to say he'd go into college teaching.

— I had thought to be a *geologist*. My brother wanted to be a doctor, now he sells "Have-A-Drink" soft drinks. Come ... the news of the terror in Pirtha had spread so far that even in Madhopura worship services are going on to get rid of bad luck. The *Block* is Pirtha, but its office is in Rajaura. There too people are seeing many things! Making offerings at temples.

Madhopura had only recently been established as a district.

The district town is not so big either. New roads. New houses.

— A small town ... there's a temple ... this is a new hospital ... that's the *District Magistrate's* house ... here is my house. You'll have to suffer a bit. My wife has gone to Delhi ... I myself didn't have the courage. The first child, just a little before birth, the fault of the doctors here ... this time I sent her to her father's house ... her father's a doctor ... I'd wanted her to go that time as well, she said, No way. A new hospital, there are doctors, every other convenience ... I shouldn't have listened. The daughter ... would have lived if they'd done a *caesarean* ... one does make mistakes.

Everywhere signs of the absence of the mistress of the house. A house itself tells you if there is a woman in it.

— Sleep in this room. There's an attached bathroom. Go to Pirtha, see the cave if you can. Some paintings have been discovered on the cave walls.

— Painted by cave people?

The SDO sighs.

— There's the problem. I believe one of them paints. I didn't see these pictures five years ago. I hadn't gone looking for pictures then anyway. And pictures of drunkenness, of communal dancing with drums, painted by cave people ... that's awful hard, Puranji. Can one measure the distance from the sun by releasing a kite? Even the birds don't know it.

— How much can birds know?

— See *The Birds*. Look at the group suicide of birds in Jatinga in the state of Assam. How can we tell what birds know or don't know? We have no communication with birds. We cannot know everything of nature's ways.

There are many books in the SDO's room. Mostly geology. Some novels in English and Hindi. Some Verrier Elwin. But the largest number is on chess, a man of many interests.

— Do you play chess?

— No.

— Here I don't get anyone.

After their bath they sit down to eat. They have to open stainless steel containers to get their food.

— They leave the food prepared. Have some pickles. Lie down after you finish. The *truck* will not come before dawn.

— *Passenger truck?*

— No.

The SDO gives a half-smile.

— Harisharanji's *truck*. He has let me know that they need food, milk powder, a doctor, medicine, matches, some clothes. I am sending rice, popcorn, dry molasses, a little milk powder and the doctors gave some sample medicine after a lot of begging. Harisharanji knows that they will spread the large sized birth control posters on the floor, and they will mend the holes in the walls with *koonch* sap.

— Aren't you going?

— There's no famine there after all. But I'll go at some point. I'll say over the mike how to celebrate the fortieth anniversary of Independence. Brothers and sisters! Independence Day is a sacred day. Fighting against the British ... everyone raise the flag at home, have fun, celebrate, light lamps in every room, and certainly go to the meeting in Rajaura. Mye-lay [MLA—Member of the Legislative Assembly], BDO, the Area Police and the heads of the rural administrative units will speak. They will also bring groups of Adivasi [aboriginal or tribal] dancers and singers.

That too?

— It's a district, even a *Block*, with an Adivasi majority, how can there not be Adivasi dancing and singing?

— Who will dance?

— The government can do anything if it wants to. Well!

They get up. Then they wash their hands and fall into bed. Now Puran will fall asleep.

In his sleep the men and women of the cave paintings dance. In his sleep a shadow flies floating. No, this incident is not of the type where I come, I see, I take some notes for writing a report, I record some voices on tape. How about staying on a bit? I must write to Saraswati if I can. Thirty-two is not old. Yet in his dream the men and women of the cave paintings keep dancing and Puran asks Saraswati, Will you dance?

It's at this point that someone shoves him awake.

— Get up, get up, the *truck's* here.

— Eh! I am late.

— Breakfast's ready.

He packs at speed. He has been packing and carrying his bag on his shoulder for so long, that the moves have become mechanical. A sarong, a towel, jeans and kurta top (this is becoming national dress, in the jeans and kurta "there is no sexual discrimination"), "Monkey" brand toothpowder (he can't bear a toothbrush), soap, shaving gear, comb, camera, a small tape recorder, a notebook, three ballpoints. The bag is sturdy. He'd had it made to order in Patna.

Tea, slices of bread, honey, bananas.

— Eat up. Tour ahead.

— Didn't you photograph the cave paintings?

— Yes. You will too.

— A picture of that creature?

— No. That I won't believe. I have to live with today's reality. So good-bye. Let me know your experience on your way back. I will read the Tale of Pirtha.

— I will certainly report back.

— Good day.

Puran climbs up on the truck. A thin wiry-looking man says to the driver, "Don't stop the truck."

The robust driver talks non-stop to the villages, trees, and human beings flying by at speed, "What's the use giving rice to the tribals? When have they eaten rice? Such good quality molasses, popcorn! The government lives for the Adivasis."

The thin man is silent.

— Be it jobs, or other kinds of aid, everywhere it's tribals and untouchables!

Puran says, "They need nothing?"

— No one can fulfill their needs, sir. They sell everything they get, they have standing clients in Rajaura you know. They won't live in government housing, so why should the government build for them?

Puran takes out a book from his bag, then puts it back. He has done his homework after all. Now he is looking at the villages on both sides.

The economy of Madhya Pradesh is mainly agricultural. Almost eighty percent of the population live in villages. Of course these are not villages like Pirtha *Block*. By 1981 figures there are eleven million, nine hundred and eighty-seven thousand and thirty-one scheduled tribals in Madhya Pradesh. 22.97 percent of the entire population. There are forty-six different tribes, and their sub-groups are one hundred and forty-seven in number.

Total area is four hundred and forty-three thousand four hundred and forty-six square kilometers. Of this 43.5 percent is arable.

Who has engraved the cave drawings? Are these pictures of contemporary human beings? They are without negotiable commercial value for TV if they are not prehistoric. Fourteen point four percent of the land in Madhya Pradesh receives irrigation. Who controls the fertile black soil for producing cotton in the Malwa area? So-called main crops are jawar, wheat, and rice. Who eats this? So-called "lesser food grains" such as kodo, kutki, and soma are also grown. This state's agri-products for trade are oilseed, cotton and sugar-cane. The other day a Bhil tribal and the six members of his family killed themselves for reasons of poverty, although, in the unwritten Adivasi lexicon, suicide is a dreadful sin. Central India will soon make news in soybean cultivation. Is it the soybean revolution after the green revolution? Who will consume this soybean powder, nutri-nuggets, oil, the whole seed?

The soil of Madhya Pradesh is rich in iron, manganese, coal, limestone, and tin ore. Large scale, medium range, tertiary range, and small industries are developing fast. Agri-business is also developing apace, every day. Why did the boy draw that picture? What novel about the ancient settlements of Vidisha and Ujjaini —like *The Bride of Vidisha*—whose novel did he read the other day? In Abujhmar there is a huge depression in the rock like a well, or like a monster's bowl. The sunlight never reaches its belly fully. The Adivasis live in the land of that primordial dusk. In some remote day they were invaded and they crawled into the earth's womb for safety, never to emerge. They raise and sell goats.

You have to descend along the rock to reach there. Their eyes have grown accustomed to the near-darkness. They come up along the rock with their goats, graze them, and then go down along the rock again. Are they Baiga tribals? Their link with the world above is to go to market, to sell goats and the strong-smelling yogurt and clarified butter made of goat's milk, to buy food grain, oil, salt, clothing. Whenever they come up they see the broad arrogant roads. These roads have been built with the money sanctioned for tribal welfare so that the owners of bonded labor, the moneylender, the touts and pimps, the abductors, and the bestial alcoholic young men lusting after tribal women can enter directly into the tribal habitations.

The person who gave Puran this account had finally come to Bihar after he and his group had made a film about the Bhopal poison gas disaster, opened a health center for the afflicted, and demonstrated against the oppressive tactics of the state government of Madhya Pradesh.

The Bihar state government was not particularly pleased

about the documentary on the blinding of prisoners in Bhagalpur
Jail either.

He had said, "When the Adivasis walk along that road to market, they walk on the graves of their education system, their irrigation system, their supply of drinking water, their health centers."

Except they don't know this.

What is theirs by right? The constitutional rights of 7.76 percent of the population of India, of fifty-nine million, six hundred
and twenty-eight thousand, six hundred and thirty-eight persons.
They have not yet been informed of this. Although Delhi and the
states print many different topics on millions of tons of paper.
Radio doesn't inform them, television doesn't inform them,
newsprint doesn't inform them, the aspiring MLAs and MPs do
not inform them, the rural administrative units or their heads do
not inform them, the state governments don't inform them, the
tribal welfare ministries do not inform them.

What an immense deal of labor and money is spent to keep
up this directive of non-information. How many subtle heads
work hard. How many political knots are tied.

What was theirs by right. The Adivasis will enter the twenty-
first century, ignorant of this in their shadowy habitation.

Puran has heard that once Jawaharlal Nehru, and once Indira
Gandhi, had tried to descend into those depths of Abujhmar, but
had given up.

No one else had even tried.

The way to reach them is so inaccessible.

They come to Rajaura.

A very small place. The *Block* Development *Office.* Police station, *school,* health center (closed).

There are almost no brick buildings besides the bank and the
post office. There is a market and shops, and a sawmill. Two
video halls, and a signboard declaring this is an "Animal Clinic,"
but behind it a roofless room, whose doors and windows have
either disappeared, or were never there.

The living quarters are attached to the *Block Office.*
Harisharan comes out and says with great glee, "*You bastard.*
Wait, let me check the goods. I am fighting with the uncrowned
king of Rajaura since yesterday."

— Why?

— He buys all the coarse kodo and kutki grain, so-called
"lesser" food grain, all the cooking koonch oil cheap and sells it to

them at a profit. Now he says, Give me the rice, I'll give popcorn in exchange, and take some money as well, you understand?

— Are you sure he won't get you in trouble?

— Of course he will.

Harisharan laughs uproariously.

— He transports labor everywhere from this district. A big labor contractor. Do you realize how powerful he is?

— He won't have you cut down by his thugs?

— No, he won't go that far. And now there's terror even here. There is a strong rumor that the curse is coming in this direction from Pirtha. A lot of religious activity everywhere.

— What do the people of Pirtha say?

— They themselves will tell you. There are folk from Pirtha here. Shankar! Come this way.

A dark, slender, young man of middle height. Dry reddish curly hair, heavily hooded eyes, a short dhoti around his middle.

— This is my friend, the journalist.

Shankar looks at him steadily.

— He will go to Pirtha, perhaps stay a couple of days.

— Now!

— Yes.

At this Shankar clasps his hands together and starts muttering, and Puran suddenly understands that his eyes are the mirror of his soul. He doesn't want Puran to go there. Shankar's lips move for a while, then become still.

A black string around his neck, and a little copper medal hanging from it.

Harisharan says, "It's all right Shankar. He's my man."

— Why will he go?

— As I said, my man.

Shankar is quiet and slowly gets in the truck. He sits on the sacks, and lights up a *bidi* in a vague distracted way.

Harisharan says, "Will you sit inside? Or shall we go?"

— I haven't yet met your wife.

— Do you think the lady lives here? She is herself an MPCS [Madhya Pradesh Civil Service]. She works in Indore. The two girls go to school there. We sometimes get together here or in Indore, or perhaps in Jabbalpur. Mother lives there.

— Isn't it inconvenient for you?

Harisharan says, "Oh no, she knew no housework at all. I taught her. And she's educated. She has a job, how can I say 'no'?

And you know what, she's very ambitious. Give the girls education, not dowries. Retire in Jabbalpur, run a school there. I have
no ambitions. Don't worry, stay here a couple of days after your
return. Will you stay in Pirtha, or come back?"

— I'll stay a few days.

— Good. I'm giving you a parcel. Might be of use later.

— What, books?

— See when you get there. Wait, you'll need a lantern,
kerosene, a mosquito-net ...

— Mosquitoes there?

— No, snakes.

— But they live there.

— They live there because there's no other way they can live.
You're not in that class.

— Did Surajpratap take all this?

— No. He is a different sort of fellow.

— Where is he?

— He alone knows. He lost his job after he wrote the Pirtha
report. The MLA's wife's brother's paper after all! And ... he had
something like a breakdown after he got back from Pirtha. As
soon as he was released from hospital he vanished.

— Where did he go?

— If I know him he'll be here again. Suraj comes around
every few years.

— He had great promise.

— Had, has. But he hasn't learnt what's needed, to move
with the stream. If you don't keep at it ... Use the *system* to
unmask it. He starts from the premise that, since the Independence is fake, everything in post-Independence Indian democracy
is fake—now such a line of thought is undoubtedly to be
respected, but it makes it difficult for him to last anywhere.

— Yes ... He doesn't fall in with the pattern of deals.

— In terms of Pirtha he wants to return to the history of the
human race in the India of some five to seven thousand years
ago. My need is to make a big noise in whatever way and put
Pirtha on the map of Madhya Pradesh and therefore of India. I
don't want heaven. Only what can be done within the administrative framework, what we otherwise can't do, either for want of
sympathy, or under pressure of politics and administration. I need
help to get that much done. Who will explain that to him? Rather
does he explain the root cause to me. Change the whole system.

— A rare type.

— Yes. But it's not right to deny reality . . . I think he'll turn up again.

— What does he eat? Where does he live?

— There's the problem. His wife . . . Sheila is working away at a center in Maharashtra to bring the consciousness that "leprosy is a social disease." A brave woman. An obstinate hardworking woman. Suraj can go there too, often does.

— I didn't even know he was married.

— Come on! He has a grown son, fifteen years old. Suraj and Sheila met in the Dalit ["downtrodden": radical name for the Untouchables] movement. They were married right away. Suraj is from the Dalit community; at one point, he caused a great stir with his book *You Are Untouchable, Not I.*

— But that book . . .

— Written by Shyam Dusad, his real name.

— From Bihar?

— At some point, he doesn't talk about everything.

— He wrote nothing else?

— No. Surajpratap never repeats anything. Sheila is a wonderful person, I've seen her twice. Bringing up their son, working herself, and waiting for Suraj. What's up with you? Still doubts, still no courage? When will Indian women change? Is Saraswati still waiting for a good-for-nothing like you?

— I'll come to a decision this time. Whether it's doubt or cowardice, I don't know myself.

— It's not good not to know so much, Puran. Life is short and it's not right to see the end of the century knowing nothing. How long do people live? At most a hundred years, or a bit more. Look at Rajaura Hill. That itself . . .

— Harisharan?

Puran manages a smile and says, "Don't tell me the age of a stone, my friend. I am not yet ready to look at the dawn of creation."

— Yes . . . true . . .

Now he talks in a different tone: "Shankar is a good fellow. They needed an explanation on the subject of that creature or shadow. They will not get food, water, roads. There will be no hunting. Singing and dancing will become extinct. At the same time they will not be allowed to explain the incredible shadow. This is intolerable."

— What are they saying?

— They will tell you themselves.

Pirtha approaches. The truck climbs. This is a pass in the hills. Once upon a time the enemy couldn't advance if the pass was blocked.

— This is full of hills.

— We'll climb, we'll go down, the truck will stop, we will stop, we'll climb down. We'll unload. From the Sarpanch's village goods will travel to Pirtha and Dholki by oxcart. Now the Khajra thorn bushes begin. Listen, you are completely free. Only request, don't go crazy to "print at all cost" like Suraj. If you suddenly saw a temple of pure gold somewhere, or a speaking tree, would you print that news and put modern man, the media, and foreigners on the trail?

— First off I won't see such a thing. Secondly, I won't tell if I do.

— That's what we want. We are entering on the tail of the animal traced by the survey map of Pirtha. Ahead is Gabahi, the Sarpanch's village.

The *truck* stops.

Some sort of instrument of the drum family is heard in the distance—dub-dub-dub-dub-dub.

Harisharan says, The drumming goes on, will go on.

— *Emergency* drum?

— Yes. This is an emergency.

II

The characteristics of the Indian *Austric* are medium height, black (sometimes very black) skin, longish heads, slightly flat noses, but otherwise sharp features. Perhaps the skin color and the flat nose are a result of intermingling with older *Negroid* peoples. Were the *Austrics* of a yet earlier time sharp-nosed and light-skinned? The *Austric* aborigines spread all over India, and went East to Burma, Malaysia and the islands of southeast Asia (were they then going farther and farther east in search of the sun?), kept moving, moving, moving on, establishing settlements. The *Gazetteer of India* says, *"The Austrics form the bedrock of the people."* To strike a stretched-skin instrument five times means to inform of an emergency. The news is coming and spreading. The Sarpanch shakes and shakes his head. "What to say, revered

Sir?" If a terrible, inevitable something repeatedly casts a shadow
... in the Mushal chapter of the *Mahabharata* the great constella-
tion of Time himself shadowed the earth again and again...
Krishna was dark, so was Rama. If you are very dark then you are
black, if slightly dark, dusky. The *Austrics* laid the foundations of
Indian civilization. They cultivated rice, raised vegetables, and
made sugar from sugar-cane. One of the branches of their language is Mon-Khmer, and is alive in Khasi and Nicobari tribal
tongues. Again the Munda branch has many divisions, and into
these language groups fall sixteen aboriginal tribes. These
Nagesia tribals are also among them. When did they cultivate
rice, grow vegetables, make sugar from sugar-cane? Why are the
descendants of the *"bedrock of the people,"* whose forebears laid
the foundations of the civilization of India, why are they sounding
their signal in such desperation? Puran has seen in his own state
of Bihar, in Palamu district, that the Parhaiyas were designated as
a "criminal tribe" by the British. And they are all bond slaves. The
Nagesias live on hillsides, some collective memory haunts them,
they'll see the enemy approach, and fly. But now all around are
modern India and medieval Palamu, the enemy doesn't come
with war drums, they have nowhere to run.

There are some caste-Hindus in Gabahi. Bhan Singh Shah
the Sarpanch [head of the village council or Panchayat] has a tur-
ban on his head and a singlet on his back. He introduced himself
as the descendant of the Gond king Shankar Singh Shah, whom
the British had blown from the mouth of a cannon at the time of
the Mutiny. If Puran doesn't believe this he can visit his home
and see the well printed family tree. It is a great injustice that the
government of independent India has not given him any recognition as the descendant of a tribal hero of the first Battle of Indian
Independence.

— This injustice is because I am a tribal.

Harisharan and Puran look at each other.

Relatively speaking, the Sarpanch is well off. In his fortlike
house with high earth walls you can see a separate enclosure for
water-buffalo, a granary for corn. Cots in the courtyard. One of his
sons is a messenger in the Electricity Office and another has
passed an exam to become a clerk in the Post and Telegraph
Department.

Harisharan said, "I read the proofs when you had your family
tree printed."

— Sure. But his name is in history books. This is what Bhalerao from Gwalior told me.

Puran cleared his throat.

— This is very true. I will discuss it with you later. We'll have a long talk.

— Will you stay in Gabahi?

— In Pirtha.

The Sarpanch looks at Shankar. Shankar keeps his head turned away. An inscrutable, passionless black face against the backdrop of the sky. That face will never give a reply. He's listening with care, in deep, deep thought.

— Dhomra-drum.

Five times ... five times ...

— That's how tribals ... we ... spread the news.

Although the Sarpanch changed class long ago (when the tribal gets a little education, gains a little safety and moves from his class, does he go up or down? Does the lower middle class or the middle class accept him as a member? If even one percent of the tribals gets a house, a motorcycle, a job, some land, do they enter the well-to-do middle class or the rural kulak class? No, the main point is that he is not of the destitute tribal community, and not of the class which is his in the adjacent community. Is that why he has to empathize with his poor tribal community in troubled times? Why did the Sarpanch first say "tribals" and then "we"? A many-leveled problem. It is improper to pass quick judgment from a safe distance.)

— Don't come to a slambang decision, Puran, you know what I mean.

— Mr. Sarpanch! What message are they sending?

The eyes of the Sarpanch are now vague and distant.

— Well, you have come with the BDO and you will stay here.

The Sarpanch licks his dry lips. Then he straightens his slightly bent body (Puran learned later that before his fortunes changed he used to gather the fruit of the Ritha tree in the extinct forest and a falling tree branch had hurt his spine; at the time peacocks danced on the banks of the Pirtha ditch) and spoke as if in deposition, in a still small voice.

— Now in the whole area we are unclean, in mourning for the dead.

— Why in mourning for the dead?

— What is it that we have seen? Tell us, Mr. BDO! You are an educated man, you are the first government officer ever to come to a tribal area. We had thought that the independent government of India was a fairy tale for our lot. We have seen you, now tell us, what have we seen?

— I don't know.

— You accept that we have seen?

— Yes, everyone can't be mistaken. But what it is, what kind of bird, that I don't know.

— Have you ever seen the picture drawn by Shankar's nephew Bikhia?

— You won't know what he saw.

— You say, our visitor wants to know.

— How shall I explain?

Harisharan says softly, "Mr. Sarpanch! My friend has been to many tribal areas. He is from Bihar. There are many tribals like you there as well, Baiga, Bithath, Gond, Khariya, Khond, Kol, Munda, Nagesia, Oraon, Asur—they are there too."

— How can that be?

— There are, there are.

— We are there as well?

— You are, you are.

— He has seen?

— He has seen them and lived there.

— Is he a moneylender?

— No, a journalist. He comes running when he hears of bad times for the tribals, he writes in the papers.

— Then why has he come now?

— Shouldn't he write about the famine?

— What famine? You tell them, the SDO tells them, and you are the government, still the government doesn't listen. This happens every year, no one knows, no one takes notice. The government doesn't even know that there are human beings in Pirtha.

Harisharan makes his voice even more respectful.

— I know. That is why I keep on trying, so that everyone knows about Pirtha, it comes up in the State Assembly, and the state helps you in some way.

Puran says softly, "So much money is earmarked for tribals, don't you get any aid?"

— How shall I explain to you?

At this point Shankar turns around, clenches his fists, and says in piercing anguish, "We are late by many many moons. Now no one can show us any help."

Moons? Many moons? When the sun is merciless in the sky?

When the swordlike heavy leaves of the Khajra trees are still, and when one leaf on the bare pipal tree shakes out of control? How late are Harisharan and Puran?

Shankar goes on talking with his eyes closed. Alas! He speaks Hindi; Puran and Harisharan also speak Hindi, but how can one touch the other? Shankar says his say in Hindi, but the experience is a million moons old, when they did not speak Hindi. Puran thinks he doesn't know what language Shankar's people spoke, what they speak. There are no words in their language to explain the daily experience of the tribal in today's India. Pashupati Jonko, of the Ho tribe of Singhbhum, a native Ho-speaker, had said with humble amazement at the time of translating Birsa Munda's life into the Ho language, There are no words for "exploitation" or "deprivation" in the Ho language. There was an explosion in Puran's head that day.

That was during the Sagwana (teak) movement: "Away with teak, save the Sal." Forest Singhbhum was washed over with turbulence. There was firing at Gua. The Ho language has no synonym for "exploitation.". There were many bullet charges after that. The Sal is sajom in the languages of Ho, Mundari, Saontali, but in the site of the unfinished Sagwana struggle the word "exploitation" cannot be explained. Then in Ilyagarh, in the resistance against the damming of the Kharkai, the fearless Kol tribal Gangaram Kalundia died. In Gua, Bidar Nag is ruthlessly beaten to death, and Pashupati Jonko says, Brother! The word "exploitation" is not in the Ho language. Puran thinks, Do the tribals, whose life is nothing but exploitation, nothing but deprivation, have a synonym for "exploitation" in any of their languages? But the theorist Kamal, who sticks to the tribal area, even he can't jump over the glass wall of book-learnt theory in his head and says, when he descends to the plains from time to time, "My friend! There is class difference among them and, although small, a class is growing up among them that is exploiting and deceiving their own kind." Saraswati got very angry.

— Oh yes, in our society one person can swindle others and make millions in black money, keep it abroad, that you can accept. And we have taken away everything that is their own, we are imposing our rotten value-system upon them, and then if one of them makes a bit of money, or becomes like us, we abuse them from a safe distance. We say, Look, look! How that man's nature has changed, he is no longer a tribal.

The whole thing is very complicated. To say something too quickly is wrong. What is Shankar Nagesia saying? A warning bell goes off in Puran's mind. He must understand Shankar's words, otherwise no justice can be done to himself or Saraswati in the Saraswati affair. Saraswati had amazed him that day. Shankar speaks.

As if he is singing a saga. They have captured their history by observing the rules of birth-marriage-death-social justice. There is no alphabet, they have caught the past in their songs.

— Once there was forest, hill, river, and us. We had villages, homes, land, ourselves. In our fields we grew rice, kodo, kutki, soma, we lived. Then there was game to hunt. It rained, peacocks danced, we lived. People grew, the community grew, some of us moved to a distance. We asked the earth's permission, we are setting down stakes to build a roof, settling land to grow crops. The Chief of our society told us where we should settle land fit for living. There we built homes, made villages, settled land each for himself. We worshipped the tree that was the spirit of our village. Then we lived, only us.

Shankar ran in a circle and pointed in all directions.

— We buried our dead. We lowered the body at the cross-roads. We scattered the seed of the kodo and rice. Then at the time of burial we gave oil, cloth, rice, fruit. We laid the body down with the ancestors. After the funeral we laid a rock on the grave. There are many, many burial grounds like this. The souls of the ancestors were at peace. Blessed us. We lived. And now?

— Ah misfortune! As ants come before a flood, as white ants fly in teeming swarms before the rains, so did our news reach strangers. Did we make a mistake in our worshipping? Did someone tear a leaf from a tree before it was consecrated, before the new fruit, new leaf, new flower came in the springtime, in the month of Phalgun? Did one of us kill a pregnant doe in the hunt? Did someone insult the elders? The community's rule is to protect orphans, was that rule broken somewhere? I don't know where we became guilty.

— Why did the foreigners come? We were kings. Became subjects. Were subjects, became slaves. Owed nothing, they made us debtors. Alas, they enslaved and bound us. They named us, as bond slaves, Haroahi, Mahidar, they named us Hali, named us Kamiya, in many tongues. Our land vanished like dust before a storm, our fields, our homes, all disappeared. The ones who came were not human beings. Oh, we climb hills and build homes, the road comes chasing us. The forest disappears, they make the four corners unclean. Oh, we had our ancestors' graves! They were ground underfoot to build roads, houses, schools, hospitals. We wanted none of this, and anyway they didn't do it for us.

— Alas! In pain we are stone, mute. We failed to give peace to the ancestors. We are coming to an end, rubbed off the soil. And so the unquiet soul casts its shadow and hovers. We didn't know how it would look. This is surely the ancestors' spirit! This is surely the curse of the ravaged land, village, field, home, forest! Now no one can save us. Now we are all unclean, in mourning. Oh Sir! BDO Sir!

— Here, I am here.

— I can't see you. But I say to you in great humility, you can't do anything for us. We became unclean as soon as you entered our lives. No more roads, no more relief—what will you give to a people in exchange for the vanished land, home, field, burial-ground?

Shankar comes up close and says, "Can you move far away? Very far? Very, very far?"

Shankar sways, he faints.

Some carry him under a tree.

— What happened?

— He fainted?

— Now what?

— They will splash water on his face, and he will come out of it.

Harisharan says, "Let's sit down."

They sit on a string cot. Harisharan says, "I have heard these words three times from three people. In three places, Pirtha, Gabahi, Dholki. I heard the same thing from the three. Some mysterious thing is taking place. Each time the man talks and talks, as if in a trance. When he talks, no one touches him, no one speaks. Then the speaker faints."

— What will you do now?

— Listen, *man*, I can't turn the clock back by five hundred years. Even if some magician can restore them to that archaic freedom, they will again lose it in the hands of newcomers. For they know or knew communism, harmony, co-existence. Is it possible to fight aggression, plunder, exploitation, using of the tribals—with their uncontaminated value-system? This is reality, this is history.

— But if they don't accept relief?

— And you too have to understand that a civil servant from today's Madhya Pradesh Civil Service cannot give back to an ancient nation the flowing Pirtha, the spreading forest, fields of grain where the only invaders are deer, peacock, and other birds, festival dances not watched and photographed by trippers, burial-grounds where others' shovels and spades won't strike. They want recognition of their violated ethno-national identity, their stolen dignity, freedom from slavery to the names Haroahi-Mahidar-Hali-Kamiya—my power is limited, dear friend. I can fight mightily with various government departments and bring them a little rice, medicine, powdered milk. And why do I run once to you, and again to Suraj? So that people know that the name "Pirtha" exists, so that the Pirtha canal is dug, if it doesn't happen while this SDO lasts . . .

In a quite different voice Harisharan says, "Sarpanch! I'd like a drink of water."

The water comes with corn-and-molasses sweets. They drink the water and return the sweets.

— Sarpanch, strike camp fast.

— Let's go to Pirtha.

Now the scene changes. Shankar sits up, dusts himself off, drinks water. The Sarpanch starts to abuse a dozen men who have turned up from nowhere.

— The BDO hasn't come here to sit and wait. This is public work, a government undertaking. Where are the others, what about carts? The name of Gabahi village will be mud. You after all are getting enough to eat, you're not in famine!

Some more people arrive. Men pull forward water-buffalo carts. Buffaloes might die pulling weight uphill. Shankar says, "Shall I go first?"

— No, come with us.

Now the trucks are unloaded and the carts loaded double quick. Some stuff is stacked in the Sarpanch's house. There are tribals in Gabahi as well. They are not coming forward now.

— Why?

— You'll understand when you get to Pirtha.

— Will the Sarpanch distribute the relief material in Gabahi?

— "Yes, he will. Now everyone is on good behavior because of the terror. If only the Sarpanch had reported earlier"—the health worker said, "We too received news that people were dying constantly, in ones and twos, in Pirtha. I came up. The state government will not declare famine even if people die. It seems that one can only declare famine if a certain percentage dies. How many people live here, that millions can die? They are deprivation's prey. Go take a look at the ones on the plains—happily farming."

— What's the reason for the famine this time?

— Man-made. It's always that way here. There's no water that they'd farm kodo-kutki crops. A bit of rain in the middle of the drought was disastrous.

— Rainfall was disastrous?

— I wasn't here. I'd gone to Indore. Suddenly word came down: "This week is Farm Aid week." Characters came down from the *Block* Office and saw there was no agriculture at all, and they sprayed insecticide all over the dusty fields. Think of it. You can see the fields are burnt out . . .

— Why did they do it?

— To teach me a lesson. After all, fertilizers and insecticides come to my *Block* Office as well. The people with land get it. Elsewhere the *Block* Office gives to the tribals only in name, they don't deliver the goods, offer a nominal sum of money and say we bought it.

— Yeah, the *banks* cheat them on the loans, and they are beaten into the ground with the so-called "pesticide-fertilizer *mini-kits*" as well.

— Here the quota for the tribals was just being sold to traders. I caught the graft, *suspended* the guys. In return they shafted me.

— What happened exactly?

— One day it rained.

Harisharan knits his brows and looks up in search of clouds. No clouds. The water-carrying sky-ranging clouds had left for Malava, Ujjaini, Vidarbha, as the bard sang.

— But rain is needed.

— The rain fell on the fields and fallow lands on the hillside and the poisonous water flowed into the wells they had dug. I had myself placed cement rings around them. Just a bit of water in two unpaved wells. They always ration their drinking water.

— Ration their drinking water?

— Always. They get enough drinking water during the rains, but at the time when both nature and the administrative authorities turn against them, the need for survival forces them to make those arrangements. What else can they do?

— So they died of drinking that water?

— They died of drinking that very water. The fleshy tuber of the Khajra is their chief hope. The roots sucked up that water. They died eating the fleshy tuber of the Khajra. And then each month a few kept dying. But even if they die, you don't know it until the patient gets to the health center. Only Bhalpura has a health center between Rajaura and Pirtha. There's a lovely temple. Like Khajuraho, smaller.

— How far?

— How do you find this climb?

The hillside is getting gradually steeper.

— It's a hard way.

— Four kilometers like this, then five more. Still Shankar sent word, health workers came. Adults were taken to hospital in rough palanquins, children in double baskets slung on shoulder poles. But doctors there will not say the cause of death is starvation or lack of food.

— How do you know this?

— The health worker told me. I came and spoke very harshly to the Sarpanch. He said, "In or out of hospital they are dying, so I didn't send news."

— He did nothing?

— Sent offerings to the gods.

— What kind of person is that?

— What does he know? How much does he know? Even doctors can't come to grips with all the diseases here. The tribal understands somewhat, they have their own healers as well. There are non-tribal rural doctors too. But cases of enteric infection, cancer, coronaries, thrombosis, are either not understood by the doctors at the health center or they can't do anything about them. We have not brought scientific health care to the tribals. If something happens beyond the limits of their knowledge they think of mysterious reasons, divine rage, the witch's glance, and so on.

— You came then?

— I came. At that point the truck had come twice. They'd taken five girls, young women, and children on the truck. They bought them for a few sacks of the grain of the kodo.

— What did you do when you came?

— I had drinking water brought from Gabahi. I had already brought some parched grains of the kodo. I sealed off those two wells. I fight with tooth and claw to bring some relief every time.

The Minister of State has warned the MLA, Relief is always famine relief. You are forcing the government to say "famine." This cannot be.

Famine! In some district there is tremendous and extreme lack of food, a thing like water is terribly scarce, the price of food increasing because of lack, widespread hunger, starvation.

But in the perspective of the tribal areas of India you have to say, O dictionaries, throttle your chatter, O liars! How can I accept your word, listen to your utterance?

For there was no food scarcity in Madhopura district. In the big shops of the grain dealers in Madhopura township, there are as many flies as there are cooked sweets. A young bride was feeding cooked sweets to a bull sitting in the courtyard of a Shiva temple and all the milk that was being poured on the Shiva phallus was collecting in a stinking pool of sour milk, and the devotees were taking that milk and drinking.

Obviously there's no extreme food scarcity in the district. There is no drought. In the houses of the Magistrate and the SDO water is pumped up and up in pipes and is sprinkled, how strong the grass how green the trees. And there are many irrigated green fields of grain. On the way to Bhalpura, the fields on both sides were green, arrogant with grain.

The price of food has not gone up because of scarcity. Now the big landowners have to raise the price of tractor cultivation, shallow tubewells, artificial fertilizer on each bale of parched grain. The green revolution means revolutionary prices as well.

There is no widespread hunger and starvation in Madhopura. Agricultural land is in the hands of the upper castes. Hilly Madhopura is tribal, the people with arable land are not hungry, not desperate with starvation. All the trouble is around agriculture. If a tribal owns land in the plain he often cannot set foot there. "Non-tribals are not permitted to buy tribal land. If such sale has taken place in the last twelve years (in West Bengal, after the Land Reforms Act Amendment, in the last thirty years), even in apparently legal ways through deeds of sale or gift, land bought by non-tribals can be claimed back by tribals upon presentation of proper proof. In such cases, the Courts will help the tribal to reclaim his land. If such cases go to court the *officers* and *special officers* of the Scheduled Caste and Scheduled Tribe Welfare Divisions are particularly charged to look out for the tribal interest. In this category, they are empowered with the authority of *special officers* in the Land Revenue Department."

But *legal-aid cells* are a hoax. And today there is no cell for tribal land anywhere in India, from West to East, from North to South. The non-tribal buys land in a fake tribal name, by force of political clout. The owner of the land gets no money, it's an inside arrangement. The *officers* of the Land Revenue Department are transferred if they are honest and when they see the political party is all-powerful, and the administration emasculated, they say "yes" to everything. Some take cuts, not everyone does. On this labeled sea-girt peninsula, the non-Aryans, the Titans, the demons, the monkeys (how many names for him from the Vedas through the epics, to the later Hindu scriptures) have forever seen land tax being paid in his name, seen influential thugs taking irrigation, fertilizer, and seeds by claiming "tribal land," and yet he had no right to that crop. To protest is to die. He can be a day-laborer on that land if he pleads with the thugs. Now these thugs don't have to tote guns on horseback. A thug who can sit in the village and keep the poor terrorized through political influence, a thug who can play catch with the heads of political opponents, does not need to ride a horse or tote a gun. He shits in the field like everyone, he oils his body when he washes, and looks at the photo of some holy man in the evening to see if some holy ash will fall from it.

In India, famine is being bought and sold by "to whom it may concern." Man-made famine is always kept going in Kalahandi or Madhopura or any intractable hill or forest area.

All the problem is in the tilling field, in taking bank loans to become self-reliant. Borrowing and lending is complicated, very complicated, it makes men violent. Otherwise why would a harijan-outcaste in Bilaspur district take a killer crowd and pull out the eyes of two harijan-outcastes who had been unable to repay their debts?

This is the way, everywhere, everywhere. Why is this bloody slaughterhouse, this stage of the executioners' fete, this valley of death—Puran's birthplace?

The aboveground bit of the Khajra tree is short, its tuber root is supposedly three feet long. The leaves are deep green, edged with spines. Are these the mythic sword-leaf plants lining the road to hell? Now the Khajra is growing more densely.

Harisharan says, "For the poor, it's the Kalpataru, the fabled tree of gifts. Split the leaf to weave mats and cut the tuber, leave the very end. Another plant will come up. And if you don't pick it, the bottom of the tuber will spread, many plants will come up."

— Can the leaf-fiber be used for rope making?

— No, the leaf-fiber is not of that type.

— They're growing it in Palamu.

— For rope?

— Yes.

— That's *aloe*, my friend. That fiber gives rope as strong as manila. They eat the root in Kerala. This family is a bit different. Rope indeed! I still cherish the hope of making a women's cooperative for weaving these mats, the women to be the owners. Rope-making! Look at our state of affairs. The government is bent on banishing poverty. *Man,* how can I show you all the new projects? The tribal doesn't get help to stay alive and the government will not help us to implement all the great schemes and all the hundreds of thousands of rupees supposedly there to keep them alive.

— Not easy.

— The money will even go back ... it's like that in Madhopura. Madhya Pradesh was Madhya Bharat—Central India—in the Raj, a land of small and big feudal princes. Even now women sometimes make arrangements to burn themselves on their husband's pyres to be sati. But Khajra plants.

— That's not it. In India, in the matter of forests ...

Surajpratap, yes Surajpratap had written. In India, there were various kinds of forests in the past. There were traditional uses of trees and forest products. In any other country they would have extended the forest and put trees to new uses for human beings. In our country natural forests were destroyed. People dependent on the forest were not taught any new uses. A lot of shellac was produced in Palamu from the flamboyant; the flamboyant is a village god there—the flamboyant has been cleaned out. And this production of aloe on barren soil is a kind of game. *Man,* the sacks are made of polythene, not jute. Rope made of synthetic fiber is much stronger than rope made of the fiber of the aloe.

The way doesn't end. Shankar sits with a stony face. Harisharan says, In 1983–84 there was a green revolution in the State of Madhya Pradesh as well.

Why does the *computer* in the brain store so much information, why does it turn the head into a bomb? The first green revolution in India was confined to Haryana, Punjab and Western Uttar Pradesh. The second green revolution takes place in West Bengal, Bihar, Orissa, Madhya Pradesh, and Uttar Pradesh as well. Why then do the plowing fields of Bihar burn repeatedly in protest, journalists run to Kalahandi, Bhil families kill themselves in Madhya Pradesh, and contractors incessantly take bonded labor from these states? Why are the starving tribals, the starving poor of these states, the special constituency of the *Migrant Labor Act,* why are they constantly becoming slave laborers non-stop? Why are there slave-labor cases from Haryana and Faridabad pending in *Supreme Court?*

"The Indian agricultural sector has made remarkable progress. Through scientific methods of cultivation India has not only been able to solve the problems of flood and drought. She is sending food to the Asian and African countries less fortunate than India."

In 1985–86 India has raised between 146 and 148.5 million tons of food grains and 32.6 million tons of oilseed and 175 million tons of sugar-cane; 8.5 million bales of cotton and 11.4 million of jute; and India exports 25 percent of the spices on the international market.

Why is this not reflected from Himachal Pradesh to Tamil Nadu, Maharashtra, Rajasthan to Eastern India?

Millions of tons of food grains, green revolutions in Central India, in Orissa, Bihar, West Bengal. Why this poverty then, and why do hundreds of thousands of people leave home mesmerized by labor contractors?

— Now you are in the jaws and teeth of the beast in the map, Puran. Take off your shoes.

Yes, they have entered. In front and on the sides a few huts disappearing into the hillside.

— What are these chalk marks on the hut walls?

— People have died there.

— What is that crowd in front?

— You'll see. Don't talk now.

Some people are sitting in a circle at a distance from a hut. The hut is on high ground. An emaciated boy sits on the stoop of the hut. His hair is tawny, eyes very bright. This hut, like all the huts, has foundations and parts of the walls of stone. The rest is mud. The roof is some sort of rush thatch.

The picture is engraved on the hut's base. The being whose

wings are webbed like a bat's, body like a gigantic iguana, four clawed feet, no teeth in the yawning terrible mouth.

Around the boy's neck is a plaited string necklace.

— Bikhia. He is the artist.

— He has engraved it!

— Bikhia first outlined it with chalk, that was photographed. Then he engraved it.

— He himself?

— They all can. You'll get engraved pictures like that in every hut.

— What do they draw?

— Trees, flowers, monkeys, elephants, birds.

— Bikhia is mute after setting down the unquiet soul of the ancestors. He can speak. He won't. Shankar, bring the ingredients for the ritual.

Harisharan arranges an egg, some flowers and leaves, in a clay bowl some rice, vermilion, and oil. Then he puts his palms together and says, "Now worship. We will make our offerings, ask for your ancestors' blessings, and then start work."

Many pairs of mute, dim eyes. As if they're looking from far away.

— Give us your permission.

Again the dhomra starts playing softly. It is as if there is a chorus of sound because many dhomras are playing together. The priest comes up. He sacrifices the eggs with his bony meager hand, offers the rice. All the men seem to be in mourning. The infants rest their faces like ticks on the chests of the skeleton mothers.

The Sarpanch sighs, wipes sweat, looks at Harisharan. Harisharan says, "Where are you striking camp?"

Shankar says, "Raise it here. We can give from here. No one will sleep in that room."

— Where does Bikhia sleep?

— On the stoop.

— Where will my friend stay?

— Behind this room. Dahi is dead, his son too. His wife has gone to Dholki.

The priest closes the service and says, "No one can do us any good now. Still since this government sir has come, we cannot turn him back. Tell us officer, what we must do?"

— See what I do. If you can help us, some of you.

Puran watches and watches. Stoves are put together with

rocks. Pots and ladles have been brought. Milk powder is mixed thinly with hot water. Shankar brings containers from every hut.

— Take the milk to the mothers for their children. Let the mothers take and drink, and then give again, give to the kids.

The Sarpanch helps. Today's relief is powdered parched maize and dried molasses powder.

— They'll give rice tomorrow. If it's given today they'll eat it raw.

— Sir! This is today and tomorrow. Then?

— Get it going at least. Day after tomorrow Kausalji, from Mahavir People's Welfare, will give rice, kodo, maize. But they will run the kitchen and give cooked food. Let's see if their lot sends a doctor. Your job is to have wells dug. Get wells dug, Sarpanch, with or without cement rings.

Puran and Harisharan now give out parched grain powder, dried molasses powder. The Sarpanch's men bring water in jars, slung on shoulders. Shankar explains to the people, "Thin it with water, otherwise you won't be able to keep it down. No, it's all right, we have made the sacrifice."

It was Shankar who said a lot then.

Harisharan says, "Shankar travels all the time, earlier he had referred to their ancient history, and having seen it fresh he was speaking from the forecourt of the present. This body lives here naturally, and the mind is free to travel. Normally he is one of my mainstays. It is by his hand that I have given the tribals seven rupees as daily wages for digging wells, paving well-rings, cutting steps on the rock face for climbing down to the source of the Pirtha ditch. They used to get two rupees. He kept all the accounts."

— What is to be done?

— Shankar, we have to take some people to the hospital. I can take them in the *truck.*

— No use, they'll die on the way.

— Says who?

— The shadow has been around the whole way.

— Shankar! Live. If you live, the unquiet soul will be at peace.

— You don't understand. The government doesn't want that we live. That's why they don't give us any help. The forefathers have been insulted, we could not protect their dignity. Now our life and death are not in our hands. And, don't you see how few people have come from the area?

— Perhaps they haven't enough strength in their bodies.

— The ones who are strong enough haven't come either.

Harisharan says to himself, "I cannot accept that an entire area will die of a death-wish. The Mahavir People's Welfare will come once, and then? God, in the warehouses of the *Food Corporation* in Madhopura, rice and wheat are rotting away. What on earth should I do?"

— Your tribal MLA?

Harisharan's mouth speaks as his hands work.

— The tribal MLA, MP, Minister never open their mouths. Their own kind mentally push them away as soon as they are elected. After all, they are elected through the support of some party or other! This party stuff also brings a distance into their minds, for the rank and file of the party as well. Then in the Assembly, in Parliament, in the Ministry, they feel tremendously isolated among the mainstream people. Why speak of MLAs, MPs, Ministers! Even a Sarpanch or a Panchayat. If you raise the standard of your unit they call you selfish. *Very funny.* In West Bengal we heard of a tribal Panchayat representative or MLA who gave money to his party but did not get any work done in his area.

— This is true all over. And in some places where the MLA is just like the *mainstream*, he is as much a bastard as we are.

— Look at the neighboring Sarpanch of Bhalpura. The Sarpanch there works hard, and also steals. This tribal unit has more money, more *schemes*, but he is afraid to ask.

— Do these people love him?

— Yes ... at least they could trust ... now that his sons have been educated and got jobs, a certain distance has been created. But since in spite of famine he can't do anything, quite incapable, this might have created solidarity, it's hard to say. All our contacts with them are through Shankar. It is normally difficult to get Shankar to talk, and now ...

Bikhia has not come forward and taken something to eat. He is looking at Puran with the same inscrutable eyes.

— Half of them have TB ... hey!

An old woman was looking at them from time to time, and drinking from her bowl. Suddenly the bowl drops from her fingers and she slips, slips down.

Puran puts his arms around her. A strange mixed smell attacks him: of dying of starvation bit by bit, of an unwashed body, of a rotting mouth. Puran lifts her up carefully and lays her down under a tree.

— I'll take a look. I'm a healer as well.

Sarpanch checks the old woman's pulse, turns up her eyes. Then he drips water down her throat from the end of his dhoti-cloth and gives Puran information. Dahi's mother-in-law.

— Come from Dholki?

— No sir, she lives here. If a little *relief gets* here, everyone will slowly come here. The shadow has gone around over Pirtha again and again, hasn't it? Hey, oldie!

The old woman opens her eyes.

Sarpanch says in a gentle voice, "Drink, I'll feed you."

The old woman keeps feeding in little bits from the mixture of powdered-parched grain and molasses, first from the dhoti end and then from the bowl.

Harisharan says, sighing, "From tomorrow we have to cook them rice gruel, rice over-boiled in salty water. No lentils, their bellies won't stand it."

— Send health workers.

— Yes, at least mentioning enteric ... but if the government behaves this way ... if I go to Madhopura tomorrow ... let the *Magistrate* come, let the SDO come ... let the Chief Medical Officer come ... if no one comes, let them give us something from the Food Corporation of India warehouse ...

Puran says softly, "You go to Madhopura."

— And here?

— I'll put my hands to it, it'll get done.

— Oh. Rain ... if it rains now?

— Another rain?

— We want rain. Then the Khajra plants will live. The wells will fill Pirtha tank to the brim ...

The *truck* beeps.

— The *truck* belongs to Mahesh *Road Transport,* the SDO got it. How can one get work done ... with the help of merchants and traders ... now the last resort, Mahavir People's Welfare ...

— You say they'll come.

— What can I say? A so-called social welfare organization. A massive affair. They get plenty of money from the state, from the center [federal government]. Kausalji's party is the Congress, the Welfare people are Bharatiya Janata Party ... don't ask me what it means ... he keeps all the parties in his pocket. Only if they help a bit ... they bring all this money by claiming to help these people after all. It's not that they don't do anything at all, but here ... they told me, you're a good man, you're asking, we'll go. But the government doesn't agree that this is a famine, they might take it amiss.

— What did you say?

— I said, the government now acknowledges the role of voluntary organizations in the eradication of poverty. Do some work, I'll help you from the Block Office, and ... I told them as lies ... *but why not*? If the government does nothing in the ITDP [Indian Tribal Development Project] area, I said, I'll ask you from the *Block Office* to set up schemes.

— And what can they achieve?

— Well, they can't do big items like Rural Labor Employment Generating Projects (RLEGP) or National Rural Employment Projects (*NREP*) but there are countless schemes, and endless funds ... some things can surely get done.

— There is a blueprint for this.

— How?

— If their registered organization starts a scheme with "We'll get this done here," it'll be good publicity.

— They must know this, otherwise why did they say "Yes"? I'm not telling them, Let me activate the Sarpanch and see if their huts through RLEGP ... affairs of the government! Someone sold the idea of solar ovens, and the MLA says, Why not some solar ovens in my area. And even biogas we can do. I had to say that the problem in my Block was what to cook, not what kind of oven to cook in. There is no cattle that there'll be bio from dung. And Sir MLA! You can get biogas from human stool as well. In your constituency people eat little, they starve, the quantity of stool they produce is minute. You can't make biogas from it. This is my opinion, of course you can do what you like.

— What did he say?

— Nothing. As if he understood! If his brother had been the MLA I could have explained. He's very sharp. Not this one.

Sarpanch brings a large portable paraffin lantern.

— Shankar! Let me show Puranji the room. Come Puran! Now the work will go on.

Past this hut there is another room on the hillside. It's not small, and its thatch is relatively fresh. Harisharan says, "Dahi and his son belong to the first batch of the people who died of the

water. Like I said ... they did some work ... got some wages ...
they moved the thatch ... see how they build! See the rocks?"

— It is of course they who cut through the rock?

— Yes ... behind that narrow tunnel-like passageway is
probably the shrine room to the gods of the household. Never go
in there.

— No.

— Will this room do?

— Perfectly.

When the eye gets used to the dark one sees there's nothing
in the room. Just the room.

— They've broken the oven as well. The door ... the rush-
framed cover, they've uncoupled as well.

— Why?

— No one will live here anymore. If anyone from Dahi's family ever comes, they'll put up new door covers, a new roof. This is
where they put the water-jar, the stone is dented here.

— They don't make windows?

— There they are, the small holes in the wall.

— An excellent room.

— The door is not toward the village on the west side, where
there's nothing but the steep hillside. Do you understand why?

— Why?

— Some people invaded the Nagesias in some distant day
and they still build huts facing due hillside.

— The same in Palamu.

In the houses of the Nagesias of Palamu Puran had seen no
date-leaf mats, not even grass mats, even in that notorious
Palamu winter. What to do, my lord? The bosses dragged everything away. Even building their houses like hawks, out of sight of
intruding enemies, the Palamu Nagesias have still not been able
to avoid becoming bond-slaves, or kamiya, seokia, haroaha,
charoaha, they have not been able to escape, anywhere.

They have nowhere to escape, not even in Palamu.

Young Gidhari Nagesia, with nothing but a loincloth on him,
had said he would buy a *petrol lighter* some day, matches cost too
much. Not for smoking, to light the oven and warm his limbs in
winter.

— See for yourself Puran, go from hut to hut. As you climb
higher, if one hut faces east, the other will face west.

Puran says softly, "So that the enemy can or could be spotted from every direction. They played the dhomra, in Bihar they played the nagara. This word they carry in their blood. So they still build in this way."

— You know this?

Puran smiles.

— No one told me. This room is telling me, or I am grasping this as I've entered this room ... this is sensed in the blood, it flows in the blood from generation to generation.

— Puran! don't romanticize it.

Sensed in the blood! Why do migratory birds fly in winter to the same distant place, from the same place, over thousands of years?

— When were they invaded?

— I don't know. These tribals can be found in the Palamu district of Bihar, although their name is not to be found in the tribal register of Bihar. Madhya Pradesh, Maharashtra, West Bengal ...

A small group, why did they scatter in this way? They lived in one place, built another village when their numbers increased, it is natural that they should live together, close together. They scattered, they went so far they were attacked.

— Now a different invasion! Invasion from all quarters, east-west-north-south.

— Yes, so Shankar said.

— You will need a water jar.

— I've got a water bottle.

— A filled-up lantern ... mosquito-net ... but what will you sleep on? Something from the Sarpanch's house ...

— I'll ask.

— You'll stay ... how many days?

Shankar comes and stands in the doorway.

— What do you say?

— What shall I say?

— The picture that he's drawn ...

— Yes, that picture.

Harisharan looks at him.

Shankar says, "Three people should go to hospital ... but they don't want to."

— The shadow was seen in Bhalpura as well.

Shankar is silent.

— Why don't they come?

— What is the use, sir?

Harisharan breaks down with the day's fatigue, labor, worry. He shouts his plea.

— Shankar! I didn't cut down the forest, take your land, keep you in bonded labor ... I'm only charged with your Block Improvement ... I can't do anything at all, let me do what little I can, let me take them.

Shankar looks in melancholy amazement.

Then he says, "Take them, sir. They will live in the hospital, then come home and die. You healed Dahi with the needle last year ... this time ... "

Harisharan rubs his face.

— Now as much as I can do ... Yes Shankar, from the Sarpanch's house a rope mat, a pillow ...

— A rush mat will do. I don't use a pillow.

Shankar says in a lifeless voice, "A rope mat, a mattress, sheets, pillow, nothing?"

— Just a rush mat, so I can tuck in the mosquito net.

— That journalist sir also ... you live like them when you stay in a tribal hut ... why? Then why a mosquito net, there are no mosquitoes.

— I'm afraid of snakes.

— Where are the snakes, sir? The snakes don't come, where did they go?

Shankar asks himself.

Puran realizes that he is not succeeding in earning Shankar's trust. He silently takes out his *tape recorder* and his *camera* and gives them to Shankar.

— Why are you giving these to me?

— Keep them in the Sarpanch's room.

Curtains come down over Shankar's eyes.

— I won't take pictures. I'll *tape* nothing.

Harisharan says, *"You fool!"*

— No, Harisharan.

Shankar returns the things to Puran.

— You keep your things ... that journalist also took pictures ...

Harisharan says in a dry voice, "We did not let it be publicized. If he had, there would have been a mad rush of people to Pirtha."

Shankar says, "Come, sir. Let me walk with you. Then I'll bring him a rush mat, water."

— Where shall I wash myself?

— It's getting dark ... why not come to the Sarpanch's place? You'll eat there too.

— I'll have a wash-up.

— You'll eat there too. Sir! You people understand nothing. Will our hunger lessen if you don't eat?

Harisharan says, "Come come, the Sarpanch can tell you what this place was like forty years ago."

He says in English in a low voice, "If someone dies at night you'll have to leave tomorrow, people are dying regularly. But from now on, whatever happens, if there is any *tragedy*, they will take your coming ... "

— They won't beat me up?

— No, never. You are their guest, an imposed guest, but still a guest.

They keep on walking. The skeleton men-women-boys-girls have now lain down in a circle, keeping the picture at a distance, and the petrol lamp is burning.

The Sarpanch says, "I'll have the pot scoured tomorrow. I've unloaded all the stuff. Come, sir, you too are tired."

— And you're not?

— I'm the Sarpanch ... this is my job ... how can I be tired? I can get something done because this *Block Officer* is here, otherwise ...

Harisharan says, "You can't go on saying that, Sarpanch. Now I want a full list of the poor and tribal homeless in your area."

— Yes sir.

— Can't you go to the *Block Office*? Can't you raise a noise? How many times have I said that I can't work if you don't go forward. When I go to Madhopura, for the last three years I hear you keep talking, but does the Sarpanch let you know anything? How many times will you slap my face?

— Don't say that, sir.

— Show work, show work, you're not worthy of being a Sarpanch of an ITDP area.

— It'll be done this time.

— After everyone dies?

Sarpanch says, "There are rocks in the way, watch your step."

Harisharan says, "Puran! If we could once make the administration sweat, *man!* Your report appears, the way I could draw you in with Suraj's report, perhaps with your report some big paper in Delhi ... All due to Sarpanch ... Other panchayats come to me all the time but to this man I have to come myself, he doesn't come."

— I'd have gone this time.

—You were keeping the gods pleased. So, keep 'em pleased. But show some effort as well.

— Master, I am also the village doctor.

— The problem is great, Sarpanch. It won't be cured by you and me, although we must try.

— Don't worry so much, Harisharan.

— Sir, you too haven't dined.

— That's fine.

Shankar says, "Shall I come with you?"

— No. Who'll take care of all this then?

Shankar says, "Clouds come and go. They come and go. Even the clouds know we've sinned."

Then he says in a spiritless voice, "We are unclean because we are in mourning. Even so the journalist sir came to visit us."

He says to himself, "How stop it? We have never been able to do it. Everyone comes to see us, to see us, and we get dirty. Our women ... "

Harisharan said, "And a few were sold, shouldn't you have let me know?"

— That's the Sarpanch's job.

— But you come to my office.

— This is not the first time that people have been sold out of Pirtha. As long as we are here, buyers will come.

— Puran, how do I put Pirtha on the *map*?

— Tomorrow, tomorrow. Go home, clean yourself, rest, eat something.

Harisharan, hairy and large, now looks like a lost and bewildered bear.

— Puran. I have fought for this situation in Pirtha, but the picture drawn by Bikhia?

— Get in the *truck*. You are taking patients.

— Pirtha will eat me up.

Harisharan leaves.

Shankar looks, shakes his head.

Sarpanch says, "Well well Shankar, will you have a bite?"

— No Sarpanchji. How will this sir go?

— I will send Ganesh with him.

— OK, sir journalist! Don't walk out after dark. You'll lose your bearing even if you have *batteries* [flashlight]. Rocks every-where! You won't understand which rock is good, which bad. You might fall.

The Sarpanch says, "Yes, yes, in the old days the rocks moved about on the Pirtha Hill. Everything was alive. And the Lord Sun told them, you are alive, but I'm now sending humans to the world. They will make settlements. You will give them shel-ter. Now stay still. How will the river come down if you're not still? How can grass and Khajra grow in your cracks, and the for-est grow on your slopes, at your feet?"

— Who told you this?

— Grandfather, great-grandfather, then great-great-grandfa-ther. Is it written in books, sir? The book-writers don't want to know anything from us, and what they write . . .

Shankar says, "I'm off sir, Sarpanchji."

Shankar leaves.

"That sir," the Sarpanch says, "also feeds Shankar . . . a lot and stands over him." He says, "If your health goes too, who will come to let people know about Pirtha? Come, wash up, let me serve you food, you'll have to rough it."

— No Sarpanchji.

— You can't get anything here.

— I don't want anything.

There was a drought on, a drought. Tell me if there was a drought in 1980 and 1981, up to 1982, how could the green revo-lution come in 1983–1984? Who reaped those harvests? Puran wraps a local-weave gamchha-towel around his waist and bathes by the well. No, one can't come to Pirtha and return posthaste to look for good food in some government bungalow, it's immoral.

The wife or daughter-in-law sets down a flat wood seat with little legs and brings a laden plate.

Flat bread, rice, lentil, pickle, pappadum, yogurt.

Something pushes up in Puran's chest. There are posters all around saying "only one child, no more," and showing a happy couple. This poster has failed in a country where a child is born every second and a half.

— Sarpanchji, I can't eat so much.

Puran hadn't known that a laden plate could give such a shock.

— Ask for another plate.

The woman brings another plate.

— It's hard to eat just vegetables, nothing but greens!

— No, I don't feel good.

— If you take a little powdered-chickpea drink at noon . . . I ate a ball of dried maize and molasses . . . you didn't eat anything, your belly is full of bile. Eat whatever you like.

A little rice, a little yogurt, a bit of molasses.

— That's all? Nothing more?

— No, I can't.

— Eat with us tomorrow then.

— No, I won't come for food. Have some maize-powder, salt, molasses, and rice brought for me. And a cooking pot.

— You cook yourself?

— Yes, I'm used to it.

— Does Sir have a family?

— Mother, my mother, and my son.

— And the housewife?

— Dead.

— You didn't marry again. And your son . . . ?

— He has his grandmother. And he's a big boy.

Puran tries to smile, "As in the poster, I have only one son."

— Yes . . . they cover cracks if you put them up on the wall, they stop the cold if you spread them on the floor, I distribute them a lot. But no more than one child! Here you are unjust. If you people have even four children, they get enough to eat, they get learning. Does that happen with the poor? The more children the better.

— But you won't be able to feed them.

The Sarpanch smiles at Puran's ignorance.

— He manages his kodo-grain himself. One goes to fetch wood, one pastures the goats of the village neighbors or of distant householders, one minds the younger kids, and even cooks. The parents can go to Bhalpura to look for work. One brings water, one goes to market to sell firewood. And all of them weave Khajra-leaf mats, to sell at the market.

Irrefutable argument.

— You can't do that family planning in a poor area. A poor household needs many children.

And they have no childhood, they remain illiterate. A child is born every second and a half in India. Where the parents have a halt after one or two children, there the children have childhoods *of food* and toys. Then from the *nursery* on as much ‎ation as possible. Population is increasing and will ‎ne poorer social strata. India will only take their head ‎1. And will not give them anything, education, a chance to live, some way of becoming fully human. On that stratum sexual intercourse with women is the only male pleasure, the way to be free of the pain of an accumulated sense of uselessness and failure, and as long as the parents are far below the poverty line, even if there are schools in every village, every year children will become child labor, ways of raising income. In Palamu Puran has seen children of eight and ten working in the landlord's fields with their parents.

Puran gets up.

— O Ganesh!

— Sir!

— Give the sir a mattress, sheets, a rope mat . . .

— Give me just a grass mat.

— Take a bundle of posters, you can spread them. There seems to be a touch of condescension in the Sarpanch's eyes. Puran realizes that he might be acting foolishly. He had always thought he was altogether self-reliant since he set out with nothing but a sarong and toothbrush in his shoulder bag.

Now he sees that's not enough. He feels inadequate. It's true that he can't reach Shankar's people by eating little or sleeping on grass mats. There is a great gulf fixed between Puran's kind and Shankar's kind. But he does want to get close.

Saraswati says, "Some day you'll see that what you know is not enough. Then perhaps your pride will fall, and you'll act natural."

— Am I full of pride?

— Isn't there a pride of "no pride"? It's there one way in you, one way in me, how can we avoid the touch of our times?

Now Puran realizes that he's never been in such a situation before. Where the ancestral soul casts a roving shadow, Bikhia draws, the settlement remains unclean and in mourning, and Shankar says, from a millennial other space, "We were!" Upon the backdrop of this experience there is the man-made famine. The same person, at the same time, banishes poverty in Constitution and Proclamation, creates poverty, protests in art-films.

They serve the upper echelons of society in glossy magazines, a lot of muddle like this.

What is Puran to do?

This burden is heavier on the return trip. The Sarpanch loads him up with maize-powder, molasses and salt, some rice. Ganesh takes a cooking pot. The Sarpanch says, "Don't pay me now."

— My paper has given me money.

— You can settle tomorrow.

On the way back the road from Gabahi to Pirtha is much longer.

It takes time to get there.

Pirtha is deadened. Bikhia is sleeping in front of the engraving.

He enters, lights the lantern, and lets Ganesh go. Puran was overwhelmed with sleep that night as soon as he had unrolled the mat, hung out the mosquito net and, lying down, had tucked it in.

The rains came riding on cold winds that night.

And, when the rain symphony was at its peak, then into Puran's room came the soul of the ancestor of Shankar's people, half claw scratching, half floating.

It had crossed the *passageway* and entered the dead Dahi's house shrine, the inner shrine to the god of the house. Down the narrow passage with its wings furled, rubbing its claws on the floor. Did it make any noise then?

This Puran cannot say.

Puran turns to stone, he freezes.

It rains and rains and rains.

Did the sound of breathing come from the shrine? Should he turn on his flashlight? No, that can't be. Puran slowly mobilizes his numb still body. He gets up.

He leaves his bed and stands on the floor. Then he slowly walks toward the *passage*. There is another room at the end of the *passage*. Part of the thatch of the room's roof has blown away. The room is not very large. Lightning flashes in the rain. The eye gets accustomed to it. Filling the floor a dark form sits.

From the other side of millions of years the soul of the ancestors of Shankar's people looks at Puran, and the glance is so prehistoric that Puran's brain cells, spreading a hundred antennae, understand nothing of that glance. If tonight he'd seen a stone flying with its wings spread, would he have been able to speak to it?

The creature is breathing, its body is trembling. Puran backs off with measured steps.

He comes outside. The rain wets him. Puran raises his face to the sky and opens his mouth. He has never drunk the rain. Now water streams from his eyes, Puran sits down on stone. He leans his head on the wall.

No, nothing must be said. It wants refuge with Puran. Puran cannot betray this, for any reason at all. But what capacity does Puran have to protect the supplicant?

Why should Shankar's ancestors give Puran strength? From antiquity to today, the long marches of the Aryan and the non-Aryan, of the living and the dead are on parallel ways.

Puran has never been particularly curious about his (not personally his) ancestors; and Saraswati's comment that day (one of her friend's sisters having been burnt to death by her husband over a dowry problem), to the effect that look! Ramchandra is the ideal of caste-Hindu men in Bihar. What did he not do? Political treachery, murdering the powerful by trickery, subjugating the powerless for political profit, burning his wife, deserting her when she is pregnant, killing the Shudra sage Shambuk—I don't think the high-caste men of Bihar will ever be able to shake off Rama's influence.

This comment has thrown Puran into greater doubt. No, he doesn't want to know about ancestors.

Who will give him strength now? Puran sees that the sky is clearing and perhaps dawn is breaking.

Was he in that state that's called a trance in English? But now there's very little time. Some arrangement has to be made, but what exactly? If a naked beggar is asked to hide the koh-i-noor, where does he conceal the jewel?

Not the koh-i-noor, but a much more valuable, rarer, earth-shaking piece of news.

Newspapers and scientists from the world over are pouring into Pirtha, extinguishing the tribals altogether. Why Madhopura, Pirtha is on the map of the world. Internationally known foundations determine the "why and how." If the world finally comes to the decision that "only tribal areas inhabited by starving, living human elements can discover the impossible, that these areas can help us determine the earth's real age and prove that, in some parts of India, a piece of the original earth still remains undiscovered"?

Bikhia on international television?

Puran shakes his head. Goes behind the room. Keeps looking, keeps circling.

Someone holds his hand.

Bikhia.

A most imperial laughter in Bikhia's eyes. His lips don't move, don't speak.

Puran tears off a bunch of long grass and spreads his arms to show this much is needed. He knows Bikhia can hear him. He has only stopped speaking after he drew the picture.

— Grass needed, a lot.

Bikhia remains standing.

— And, water in a container like this!

Bikhia lets go of his hand and grabs his feet, puts his head on Puran's feet.

Puran pulls him up.

— Did you go to the room?

Bikhia inclines his head.

Surprising Puran he puts his hand on his own lips and on Puran's.

— Let no one know! No one will know.

Bikhia brought in bundles of grass. Before heaping grass at the mouth of the shrine-room Puran had seen flowers, rice, grains of kodo.

Had seen a bowl of water. An earthen bowl. Bikhia had gone forward with his eyes closed, with the bowl of water, which he had set down and retreated.

Their ancestor was looking at them with half-open ancient eyes and then Puran sees that his body was quivering non-stop. No, not too large. And what is it in his faded eyes, a question? Longing? What can it be?

Bikhia takes the load of grass into the next room, sets it down in a corner. There is a peculiar urgency now in his arms and legs.

Then he puts his palms together, lowers his head, and takes one turn. He expresses respect by lying prone. Looks up, the roof has blown away in the storm, there is a gap up there.

He covers the opening to the *passageway* with grass. Did he have all this dried grass stacked up in his room? That clay bowl, is it a household object, belonging to a home that its people have left, holding death's hand?

Puran keeps looking at him. At least he's not alone now, Bikhia shares the intolerable burden of his explosive discovery. Puran would have gone mad if he had had to carry this experience in his brain cells.

Bikhia has received his ancestral soul. That is why his face is now so full of a quiet wisdom.

What has Puran received?

Bikhia holds Puran's hand with utmost care. Puran weeps silently.

Bikhia keeps pulling him outside and points ahead.

Water is running down a crack in the rock.

Is Bikhia asking him to listen to the music of the waters?

Bikhia looks at him in deep expectancy but Puran understands nothing.

Puran understood later, a bit later, when Shankar came to take him down below.

— Where?

Shankar didn't answer. He went near Pirtha ditch and said, "You have brought this rain, the people of Pirtha are now in your debt."

The water is echoing and bounding into the source-pool, flowing away. Puran watches and says softly, "Cooperate with the Block Officer, Shankar. He is a very good man."

— I don't know if the curse will break.

— Perhaps it will.

Shankar sighs and says, "The gods gave water at a time when we don't have the strength to go down to the fields. There's water in the wells and the Khajra plants will live."

They were watching the water. The stream of the Pirtha comes out of the cave, down the stones. There are many caves on Pirtha Hill, small and large.

Caves, cave paintings, Bikhia's picture.

Puran now realizes that the rainfall on the night of his arrival might give rise to another legend.

He shakes his head repeatedly. He says to Shankar, "I have a heavy head, I got wet for a whim."

Shankar sighs.

— Come to Gabahi, take some tea.

Puran does not say no.

III

Harisharan says, "*Man*, they keep on waiting for a *miracle*. The modern age has given them nothing, if a *miracle* can bring some good luck into this intolerable existence! A small *miracle*, something big! The ancestors' shadow had brought a kind of news to them, as a result of which whole villages were awash with *death-wish.* Malnutrition and starvation have a permanent settlement here, but in these three years I've never seen this type of despair, this type of exhausted despair. Night before last I couldn't sleep, couldn't eat, what a night of bad dreams!"

— Yes, you were very worried.

— *Tension* for me ... it was my father's *high* blood *pressure* ... My wife has brought me Benjamin's *Everybody's Nature Cure.* She writes all the time, Are you keeping to the *blood pressure* routine? And I write a million lies.

— What does *Nature Cure* say?

It is crucial for Puran now to find out what Nature says, what news she gives. He is caressing the leaves of the Khajra, the grass, the stones. From that dark rainy night on, he has been desperate to know if communication can be established, if the ancient mysteries of Nature can be known in any way. But it's breaking your head against an invisible glass wall.

Only when Bikhia comes at night ...

— Come on, is it possible for me? I still write I am eating fruit, fasting from time to time, of course I really don't smoke or drink. I write that I am not eating spicy food, no sweets, almost no tea or coffee. But it's all lies, friend. Can one follow rules all the time?

— No, is it possible?

— Oh, I'm deeply in your debt. You don't know, but you've brought a small *miracle.* There it was, you came, and it started raining ... there was some rain yesterday ... there might be today ...

Puran says in deep sorrow, "How can I bring rain? Can anyone?"

— *Man!* People who have nothing need *miracles.* For now it's through you ... now a story will be put together from voice to voice, the story will become song ... and the song will enter the history that they hold in their oral tradition.

Puran smiles palely, Can that be?

Will they ever wait in silence on the hilltop for the second coming of Puran? Shankar says those are not stones, the men who went on the ancient wars (Shankar doesn't know what wars, with whom, when) against the enemies, did not all return. The mothers, wives, and sisters of those who did not return turned to stone looking for their way back. At that time the enemy couldn't come across the Bhalpura, and the Pirtha was a bigger river. Those ancestors of Shankar's people would go up near Bhalpura and fight, they didn't let the enemy enter tribal settlements. But now there's a bridge there, the map is changed. Their ancestors' soul has therefore wandered looking for familiar spots and been pained.

How naturally Shankar can say these things! If the town had moved as far as Pirtha, if tribals and non-tribals had lived together for two or three generations, then perhaps the memories of earlier times, the ancient glory-sagas, would have gradually become blurred in the mind.

That hasn't happened in Pirtha. These people are fully in exile. They have not received anything from modern India. This *metal road* has come to them to serve the interests of those very moneylenders from Bhalpura and Rajaura who will snatch their harvests to recover their loans, those patient customers who wait like vultures for the moment when starving parents will sell their children in the extremity of despair, and fall to feeding on carrion, the advance men of those labor contractors who will make the aboriginals their bond slaves with the seduction of "ten rupees a day and a full stomach."

Modern India only gives them posters for family planning. The birth of children increases rather than decreases as a result of starvation, until the bodies of the man and the woman go on strike permanently.

Only Shankar is literate in the surrounding villages. He too cultivates the stony ground, lives on the hillside, eats mainly the root of the Khajra. How can he abandon the past? They don't know if that past is legend or history, and no researcher comes to separate the two. And who is going to tell us what is legend and what history from the perspective of these totally rejected tribals? Where is the boundary between history and story? If we can get so much history out of the *Ramayana* and the *Mahabharata*, what is the problem with Shankar's nostalgia?

How thoroughly rejected and forgotten these people are! They haven't seen a moving picture, they don't wear trousers, they don't drink tea, but only wait for a large or small *miracle*. When Puran leaves, will they be waiting in the merciless heat for the man who brought rain? And, if Puran doesn't come, will they say in self-consolation that he has gone somewhere else with his rain, where the drought is maybe just as bad? Is Puran so fortunate that they will mingle him in their history, saying, "Once upon a time he came with rain clouds at a sad burnt-out time when we were in mourning?"

— What are you thinking, Puran?

— No ... so many things ... did your Kausalji respond? Now he alone is our hope.

— Yes, today there will be a health camp in Gabahi. They are beautifully organized. Kausalji has been abroad many times. Don't you see how big the crowd is?

— But Harisharan! This is not the solution for Pirtha. For them to receive long-lasting help ...

— My friend! Things will happen as long as this SDO is there. He too will come today. Well, what did the Sarpanch say? I hear you're not eating at his place?

— No ... living in Pirtha ... going to his house to eat ... that's not possible.

— What do you eat?

— I have bought rice, salt, powdered dry corn, and molasses from him. I am cooking myself.

— Well ...

— Come, let's get to work.

— Taking *notes?*

— Yes, in longhand. I am realizing how barbaric it is to photograph skeletal men and women.

— Please avoid that realization. Make an uproar about Pirtha. Otherwise for me to do anything will be very ...

— I'll do everything, my friend. Don't you worry. After the massacre at Arwal, the Civil Liberties organizations are conducting investigations, many *reporters* from Delhi and from the big Calcutta newspapers. I will inform the Patna *press.* Also Delhi. Journalists are writing about Kalahandi in Orissa, why not about Pirtha? They will go to Bhopal and ask questions about Bhopal as well.

— Bhopal! There's the Union Carbide disaster, yet there's also Bharat-Bhavan, a huge cultural center, and the minister builds a palace. The state government couldn't be mobilized around such an immense poison-gas disaster, can it be moved about Pirtha?

— Let's see. Only one request ...

— What?

— Don't let them see Bikhia's drawing. Don't let them hear all that stuff about the ancestors' soul. Let them be concerned only about this permanent famine. Otherwise their enthusiasm will veer the other way. Bikhia will become the center of their discussion, surely you don't want that?

— No. I don't want that.

— These conditions are enough. This they'll find hard to digest. There will be an atomic explosion of news.

— I know. How will the drawing be explained?

— Bikhia is a natural. He saw such a picture somewhere and copied it. We think the cave-paintings are also his.

— That is no explanation. Let's leave it there for now.

— We want a stable solution here. As a *Block Officer*, don't you have any projects?

— The problem is most complicated, Puran. Look at it this way! I can help them in agriculture. I mean, I have the capacity. I will say this in Shankar's presence today. You will get an answer. Come, let's stop talking, let's go. Let's see what they're up to.

Even the relief camp, this temporary relief camp has moved away from Pirtha. Gabahi is at least flat, and *trucks* can come there. All day yesterday, rice was cooked in Pirtha, powdered milk was mixed with hot water. The stone ovens are still filled with ash and burnt-wood. A skinny dog is hovering there.

— I don't see Bikhia.

— Must be around.

— I see marks of worship today as well.

Bikhia has engraved the picture on stone with some kind of small hammer and chisel, like the ones used to prepare the spice grinding stone, and the lines show how gentle the hammer strokes must have been there.

— First he drew with a piece of chalk?

— Yes, that's what Suraj photographed.

— But you confiscated his film . . .

— That he can't say. And this drawing is the only proof, if it's covered up . . . let's see.

— Where did he get hammer and chisel?

— Listen, friend, they engrave pictures in that way inside their homes. They know all that. They carved the surface of the stone steps they built quite in the same way, so that they don't slip and fall. This work they know.

— Astonishing. Can't we turn this into something productive with enough encouragement?

— So I'd thought. You can't feed the government this project. How many will work? Where is the market? Still I kept it in mind. Yes, we should think about it, that they know how to use the chisel this way, if some cottage industry can be made out of this

... I think, I think.

There are lots of acacia trees between Pirtha and Gabahi. Harisharan said, "My Social Forestry Project is with acacia trees. On both sides of the Pirtha. They are themselves planting, as they hadn't before. Now they understand about planting. They can get firewood from the acacia. Goats can eat the new leaves. Although you still won't see goat or chicken in any of the villages. And they eat the seeds of the long hanging pods that are the fruit of the acacia. The acacia is the mythic tree of wish-fulfill-ment. Here, and in the State of Rajasthan, the acacia is the wish-ing-tree."

The Sarpanch says in Gabahi, "Come, sir! You are now a god to us. You came, the rains came."

— If the rains hadn't come, I would have been a demon, no?

— Don't they look for a witch when there's a drought or deaths from enteric fever? This is why witches are killed.

— Your *homework* is incorrect. Witches are indeed killed for such reasons. But these days most cases are land-related. They kill for the sake of land, or for the reward.

— These people don't believe in witches?

— The belief exists, but if things are this bad year after year—they know now that their lives won't be helped if witches are killed. But don't forget the matter of the *miracle*. They have assumed that nothing is owed to them, not even rain.

— To be a *miracle man* is a grave responsibility, Harisharan. Today *magicman*, tomorrow fraud.

— Don't be difficult, Puran. Don't make me mad. Shankar! Hey Shankar!

Shankar does not come forward. He is leaning against the wall and watching. A little ahead you can see Kausalji's relief camp. The work is going forward with highly expert skill and speed. Now a thin gruel of rice, lentils, and vegetables is being distributed. The health camp is right beside it. Their doctors and health workers are examining men and women.

Kausalji is a heavyset man in dhoti and top. He says, "Reporterji. Be sure to take photos!"

— Sure.

— We are taking pictures too. Write that we have come to Pirtha before this as well and they are in such poor shape because of the government's lack of concern. There are plenty of projects at the *Block Office*. You can remove their poverty like a shot.

Harisharan says, "You make the effort. The Government will listen to you more than to me."

— Yes, we need a *unit* here.

— There is a *Block Office,* there are projects. Shankar!

— Yes, sir.

— Come this way. Take notes, Puran. These people are saying that there are many projects in the *Block Office,* we are not showing you support. I have talked to you before, but these people haven't heard. The government assigns projects by rote. I wanted to give you cattle per family, did you accept?

— How, sir? What would we have fed the cattle?

— We did give goats.

Shankar looks upward. Says in a detached voice, "What a state Pirtha was in that year! Nothing but acacia leaves. The goat is a tribal, sir. It knows how to live on minimum food. But even that bit wasn't there. People came from Bhalpura. They gave us five or seven kilos of kodo grain. We gave up the goats. Was there anything for it to feed on?"

— We gave poultry as well.

— Sir, if people don't have anything to eat, tell me what they'll feed goats and poultry?

Harisharan speaks, "We gave no ducks. That would have been a dreadful mockery. Where is the water? Agricultural aid ... "

Shankar says, "If we had some land down below we could at least farm."

— Kausalji! The land these people owned disappeared long ago.

— Tribal land! Recover it for them.

— How? Did the land vanish yesterday? They farm on the slopes of this hillside, on barren land. Can one give agricultural aid to this soil? This is just for some kodo, some kutki ... and even then in trivial quantities.

— I will get the land back from the government, let them come down from the hills, they will farm there, plant trees there, there's plenty of water, I'll build a housing development for them.

— Oh, that land?

— Let's see. I'll teach the women to weave cloth on a cooperative basis and there will of course be schools.

— See what you can do!

Now Shankar says, "Where is this?

— To the west of Bhalpura.

— No hills.

Now Kausalji starts to speak fast and in English, "If they want to live on hills then we have to bring the roads up and give them land down below. Ask them to forget such unrealistic matters. Ask them to cooperate. Won't the condition of the tribals improve if they cooperate? Go and see in our Jijagar Ashram."

— There's a Shiva temple there, Puran, worth seeing.

— In our Jijagar Tribal Welfare Ashram two hundred tribal families ...

Puran says, "I've seen on TV."

— You can't do it, Harisharanji. You didn't even build them homes, yet RLEGP [Rural Landless Employment Guarantee Program] says, Give the homeless tribals homes. This is not right.

— The government money for building homes cannot be used for constructing stone dwellings on the hillside. I will get some more wells dug.

Kausalji says in English, "Go slow, friend, go slow. If you help that much they will get entrenched here. But the place has been *condemned*. If you can move them, and plant some more trees, this spot with the river, the hills, and the trees will make an excellent *picnic* area. In Madhopura my brother-in-law is the Managing Director of State *Tourism*, and as you know, in Bhopal my ... "

A rickety house is *condemned*. And the living areas of tribals. Unfit for the residence of the forest dwellers but fit for *picnics*. But Shankar was saying yesterday, "there used to be forest all around, now there is nothing. Still the graves of our forefathers are in Pirtha. We give to Pirtha's waters the bones of our dead at the end of the mourning time. Now we can't bury them anymore, we burn them. Then we put the ashes in a new bowl and bury them, put up a stone."

Will they put the past behind them, tear up their roots and leave this place to go to a housing development? Tribals in a tribal *colony*. In the India of the future, will they be preserved as endangered species or mingle in the *mainstream?* Or will the tribals change their character and become different? Even animals preserved behind wire netting are not safe. Somewhere the zookeepers themselves caught and ate the captive deer.

Harisharan tells Kausalji, "Yes, yes, of course. In fact he gives nodding assent to everything. Then he wipes the sweat from his face and tells Puran, Now you see what these people are doing. I will give you all their published *literature*, Kausalji. Let me walk with him a few steps."

— What, isn't he going to lunch with us?

— No. He's just moving around, looking, taking *notes*.

— That's what we want. We will take video pictures from tomorrow. We always keep video pictures.

— You think of everything!

— The SDO will be here, why don't you stay?

— I'll be back in a minute.

Harisharan goes forward and says, "God, what a man!"

— He'll build a housing development?

— Listen! The land is his. He'll form another organization. It will be registered and to it he will donate this land for the welfare of the tribals. Then he'll get money from somewhere. He gets all kinds of funds. Foreign money too. Tell me, what can I do? These volunteer organizations can get in, even get some work done, precisely because the government has failed in its work. All that will take a long time, and I don't think they'll leave.

— Yes, this for them is the place where they have been from the immemorial past.

— But how will they survive here if they don't leave! Well. Now I'll be grateful if they run the camp for ten days. It's wet now, I'll sow kodo seed, sir. And if I give *agro-training* to a few of them then they can raise crops that don't need irrigating, like peanuts. We'll see! I fight on many fronts. With Shankar's kind, with the government, with politicians, and Kausalji has a lot of influence upstairs!

Harisharan says good-bye.

— Shall I bring anything for you tomorrow?

— A bit of fish.

— Cooked?

— No, no. I can do everything.

— Fish!

— Don't if you can't.

— It's very hard, my friend! If I can't, I'll feed you fish on your way back. It's rained, maybe there will be small fish even in Pirtha spring. But whole settlements are dying, who'll fish?

— I'll eat fish on my return trip then.

— That's better.

Harisharan leaves. As a student he had hoped to be an agricultural economist, Puran used to think he'd become a professor. Life's wheel turns strangely. These days educated and affluent parents provide their children with education that will prepare them for a *career.*

Shankar's parents, Bikhia's parents, the parents of Dimag, dazed with the sale of his child (he'd wept aloud the first day, setting down the bowl of dried powdered corn and molasses, You did bring relief in the end, Master! I'd not have sold Magni if I'd known!) never did *career-planning, just* as they never did *family-planning.* They knew they would not have a *career* more brilliant than farming for kodo with their spades in stony ground, if possible pasturing goats.

Yesterday the Sarpanch arrived and distributed bundles of posters, "End separatism, keep communal harmony intact, and renounce the path of violence." Dimag's wife was saying, This paper is not good, too thin. She is now pregnant, and forever holds the hand of a three-year-old girl, as if someone will snatch the child away. She talks as well.

— O Shankar! When will we all die together?

— Shankar! Why did relief come this time?

— Shankar! Why did it rain?

They are not entitled to rain, they are not entitled to *relief,* the ancestors' soul has come and gone casting its shadow, therefore unremitting death was their only lot.

Puran gets down toward Pirtha spring. A lungi—an ankle-length cloth—around his waist, a gamchha—a scarf-sized local washcloth—around his shoulders, torso bare. Now he takes off his sandals and walks down the steps cut in the stone. You can make lamps, candleholders, small urns, vases, et cetera if it's that kind of stone. Of course, the supplier will come to buy wholesale only if thousands are made. And if on stone tiles they carved the fish, elephant, people, bow and arrow, bird that they have in their dwellings, the government art emporiums, rich export boutiques of tribal art will be interested. What will the people of Pirtha get? Each question reaches a great no-reply.

The spring water is quite cool and under his feet is stone. He doesn't get fish, but gathers some stone-caught moss in his gamchha. There is a tremendous problem facing him.

He finds Bikhia waiting when he gets back.

Puran gives him the moss.

Their ancestors' soul looks with half-closed eyes. Rice, kodo, some dead gnats. Small fish, some mud (so Bikhia caught fish) lie on the ground. Bikhia has refilled the water vessel.

Those eyes have a message for Puran.

Puran does not know those eyes' language.

Puran is a newcomer in the history of earth's evolution. The human being is only a few million years old.

This one came long before Puran.

Puran and Bikhia come out. The shrine room is full of an animal smell, a smell of flesh. This is an unknown carnal smell.

Now Bikhia looks at him. Then he suddenly stands up and spreads his arms as if in mime. The gestures are hand movements miming a floating flight round and round the room. He beats one hand on the wall as he turns and turns. Now that hand moves slightly. Bikhia sharpens his glance and still turns. Then squats with arms spread, drags himself on his hands toward the shrine room, and then is still.

— Yes Bikhia, all right. One wing is broken, so it dragged as it walked. Bring a bird if you can. If you can.

After Bikhia's departure Puran sighs and opens Harisharan's packet. And says in the direction of the shrine, Forgive me, forgive me.

IV

"Reptiles: in sea, in air.

"Pterodactyl—a flying reptile of the pterosauria class from the Mesozoic era, extinct species. Their limbs and organs were suitable for flying—their bones hollow and air-filled (when did marrow come to fill bones?)—the fourth digit of the front feet (they are quadruped) were unnaturally long holding up a flying membrane covering the entire body and thighs, Pterodactyls probably ate fish. Their earlier editions, e.g. the rhamphorynchus, still had the long tail of a reptile and innumerable teeth.

"[This creature has no teeth. It does not have a long tail, Puran is certain, for he has taken a good look in the half-light.] The pterodactylus of the earth's Jurassic age was as big as a sparrow, with a very small tail, and teeth in the front part of the mouth. [This one is larger in size.] The pteranodon from the Cretaceous age was much larger, with a 25-foot wingspread, and a huge crest [of skin?] in the back of the head and a long toothless beak.

"[Pterodactylus, pteranodon, pterodactyl!] Now most experts suspect that the pterodactyl could not fly by flapping their wings.

"Their sternum was not strong enough to support the large muscles needed for flight. Our knowledge of the physiology of modern animals suggests that, with such heavy bodies and wings, they glided like waves, going up and down, some such thing!

"...One group of these creatures, the pterosaurus, had bat-like leathery wings. [The pterodactyl, the pteranodon, and pterodactylus were all part of the pterosaurus group.] From reptiles they became winged reptiles, creatures of the sky. They probably hunted on the wing, feeding on shallow-water fish. They did not get wet themselves. It was not these but flying reptiles from other groups that evolved into birds. The first known bird is the archaeopteryx. This crow-sized bird was in existence about one hundred and forty-seven million years ago."

Puran closes the book. He gets moving. The moon was in the waning phase, the sky covered with light clouds. How liquid the dark, as if melting bit by bit. Now the sacred room is covered by a grass-frame door. Bikhia is now worshipping as well as eating the relief food sitting in the same place, his eye is dusky and calm after establishing the pact of secrecy with Puran—he concludes this pact with Puran while remaining mute, making Puran think, by habit we speak, needlessly, one can do with many fewer words—even after doing all this he gets the time to make up the door frame by shaving the thin branches of the acacia and binding it up with grass.

No, you are not as small as a sparrow, yet your wingspread is not twenty-five feet, something in between the two—I won't go near, I won't touch you, I will not take your picture with the flash bulb of my camera. I think you rested somewhere as you flew floating, Bikhia saw you then and, on the run, quickly managed to draw your picture with chalk.

Did your eyes give Bikhia a sharply urgent wordsoundless message? The reason why your form was *xeroxed* on his brain and he could come running and draw that picture with chalk? Did he think then that chalk rubs off too easily, and did he therefore pick up hammer and chisel? Why is Bikhia not speaking? Why is he remaining mute? Was some communication established between your prehistoric eyes and his eyes, so that he (illiterate, never having read a book, with no knowledge of the history of the evolution of the planet) grasps that to keep your affair secret is tremendously urgent. The world of today cannot be informed about you. "Today" does not know the "past," the "ancient." "Today," "the present times," "civilization," becomes most barbaric by the demands of getting ahead. Yet he doesn't know that "today" desecrates the ancient peoples' burial-grounds by building roads and bridges, cutting down forests. They won't let you go if they know of your existence, this is why he is protecting your visit like the sacred ashes of a funeral pyre or the bones of the dead. He has found some contact. He is a tribal, an aboriginal, you are much more ancient, more originary than his experience, both your existences are greatly endangered.

But oh the first and last living messenger from the prehistoric world! This too is the implacable and cruel truth that time will advance, that the wheels of time will destroy much as they advance. You cannot turn the eighteenth to the seventeenth, however hard you try. Only the creators of science fiction can do that. The boys and girls who are of the *"cute"* and *"oh baby"* and *"oh boy!"* brand and who are constant escapists in the mind get an unadulterated joy when they read those stories. But in India, or in the world, what is *"tidy," just* fine, smooth? Such things exist for the few. For the many, time means a struggle red in tooth and claw and the struggle does not mean the same thing all the time. Time, complex time, how can a *computer* possibly *process* this time and give birth to *a data-sheet?*

The roof of the shrine room has blown away. The sky of the waning moon is covered in fragile clouds, the clouds are ambulant, there is water somewhere after all, for in the moonglow there is a large luminous circle around the moon. How transparent the dark, how liquid, melting bit by bit. Everything can be seen in such darkness. No, I don't want even to touch you. You are moveless with your wings folded, I do not wish to touch you, you are outside my wisdom, reason, and feelings, who can place his hand on the axial moment of the end of the third phase of the Mesozoic and the beginnings of the Cenozoic geological ages? That is a story of seventy-five million years. The Mesozoic ended in a tremendous turbulence, with the inception of the ancestors of the human being, and the Cenozoic, which is still going on, got its start. That is when the continents drifted again and took their current shape. You were supposed to have become extinct then. Space separating, seasons and climate changing. Did your world have such dusks? What ocean, what weed, what fish did you see?

And were you extinct? Have you left the pages of some picture book, taken shape so that you can give some urgent news to today's humans, have you come here because Pirtha is also endangered, its existence under attack for other kinds of reasons?

No, I have not the right to touch you. Apparently one can still see prehistoric fish in the sea. But there was, there was a ptero-dactyl somewhere, the world didn't know, I am silent, I am defeated. I won't go near to see if there are feathers, if the toes and nails of the front feet are truly long.

Puran's eyes put a question.

— What will you eat?

What do its eyes want to tell Puran?

This body made of the grey dusk or this liquid darkness is quite still. Only an unfamiliar smell, sometimes sharp sometimes mild. When Puran or Bikhia stands, the smell becomes mild and faint. Is this the instinctive feeling for self-protection against unknown animals?

There is no communication between eyes.

Only a dusky waiting, without end.

What does it want to tell? We are extinct by the inevitable natural geological evolution. You too are endangered. You too will become extinct in nuclear explosions, or in war, or in the aggressive advance of the strong as it obliterates the weak, which finally turns you naked, barbaric, primitive, think if you are going forward or back. Forests are extinct, and animal life is obliterated outside of zoos and protected forest sanctuaries. What will you finally grow in the soil, having murdered nature in the application of man-imposed substitutes? "Deadly DDT greens, / charnel-house vegetables, / uprooted astonished onions, radioactive potatoes / explosive bean-pods, monstrous and misshapen / spastic gourds, eggplants with mobile tails / bloodthirsty octopus creepers, animal blood-filled / tomatoes?"

The collective being of the ancient nations is crushed. Like nature, like the sustaining earth, their sustaining ancient cultures received no honor, they remained unknown, they were only destroyed, they are being destroyed, is this what you are telling us?

The dusky lidless eyes remain unresponsive.

Have you come up from the past to warn us, are you telling us that this man-made poverty and famine is a crime, this widespread thirst is a crime, it is a crime to take away the forest and make the forest-dwelling peoples naked and endangered? Are you telling us that it is a crime to grasp in a stranglehold the voice of protest, and the arm of combat?

The eye says nothing.

How grey. What amazing eyes. It wants to say something, to give some news, Puran does not understand. *No point of communication.* Nothing can be said or written.

Is there a message in the smell of its body? Why do its eyes remain open? In the inner shrine room (the worshipped and the worshippers are gone) of the family god of a poor tribal (who is dead), you are sitting unmoving, oh ancient one, what do you want us to know?

The grey eye does not respond.

You have come to me for shelter, and I don't know how to save you, is that why I'll see your death? I don't know, if I knew I could have saved you, I don't know, if I knew I could have saved you, you would have left again on your flight, you would have searched out water, food, a resting place. I don't know, if I knew . . . In this shrine room of stone and earth in the last years of this century an urgent message like this arrived and the news could not be given because human beings do not know or understand its language.

The grey eye wants to tell Puran something.

Puran shakes and shakes his head.

The water-pot remains as it was. Bikhia's offerings—a heap of moss, a handful of fish, insects and flying insects, Khajra tubers, kodo seeds, and rice—remain on the floor.

Puran backs out, closes the grass door.

Carefully puts away the books lent by Harisharan. He knows more because he has read the information in the book, and the subject of the discussion is physically present in front of him. Yet he can know nothing from life.

How little he understood when he traveled in Ranchi district from one Munda village to another till he finally learned about them from S. C. Roy's book. Saraswati says, "Perhaps you have not been able to know me after so many years spent close together, because there is no book about me."—No I have not, Saraswati. Hominidi—hominidi—homo sapiens—mapiens—the human being, modern man is afraid to know life by entering life. It is much safer to know life by reading books, reading theory.

But if the pterodactyl flies and casts its shadow in Pirtha *Block* in the distressed days of famine, if the aboriginals of Pirtha think that their ancestors' soul has returned grieving because their ancestors' burial ground has been desecrated in their now extinct settlement, and if Bikhia, an illiterate tribal youth, draws the pterodactyl on the wall, and seeing it, photographing it, if there is an explosion in journalist Surajpratap's head, and if the SDO hides the photos by the following reasoning: "No, no indulgence for the fantastic. For if we acknowledge the pterodactyl, where will homo-sapiens-mapiens be? Their two worlds are different, after all"; and when Pirtha settlement is unclean in mourning, if journalist Puran enters the stage on Harisharan's SOS (expressed appeal, Put Pirtha on the national map, and unexpressed appeal: *what about the most mysterious mystery of the century?*") and if on a cloudy rainy night of the rainy season, through the doorless opening of Puran's room enters a pterodactyl, and goes to the godless shrine (how straight it went, was it living there before?) and seeing it there is an explosion in Puran's head (this fact must be kept secret, this discovery), and at the break of dawn comes Bikhia, from speechlessness moves to a lowered head, and before daybreak when Puran is quite adrift by the force of his amazing, inexplicable discovery, if then he finds out that those who considered him an outsider and an enemy yesterday are themselves today seeing him with different eyes, saying "He came and in his steps came rain, water for the thirst of the soil, of ourselves, of the rivers and the wells," then what is to be done by Puran, no book has been written about this.

If written by a third person Puran would have got a perspective on the whole thing.

There is no one to write.

And Puran has known in his blood-cells and his brain these three days that even after this deeply investigative analysis he knows nothing, has known nothing. Without taking his first lesson from humanity he has reached the final phase of the century. Yet he has seen human beings in the most excruciating distress, protesting oppression and debauchery and the blood-festival of the oppressor's protesting the protest, he has seen the battle between the government-enforced teak and the traditional Sal, the protest against industrialists by workers infected by poisonous asbestos down in asbestos mines, he has seen the self-congratulatory jubilation of the police after blinding prisoners.

How much he has seen like this, seen and written and come back to his safe room where Saraswati arranges and dusts his books and sits waiting for the day when Puran will say, "Come into my room and come into my life," but even that Puran has not said.

He has known nothing, for he has wanted to know nothing. And it is to such a half-man, a rootless weed, that the messenger from old earth comes to impart some intolerable warning message.

What will Puran do?

Today, at the crack of dawn, Bikhia comes with a jubilant face like an ancient hunter, with a freshly killed snake at the end of his stick. He looks at Puran and goes straight through pushing the grass barrier.

Puran waits standing.

Bikhia comes out after a long time. His mime is on stones of the hillside washed by the morning light, against the backdrop of the sky.

Now both his arms are wings, his body folds in two and crumples, he rolls his head, his two arms come down, immobile. He looks at Puran with questioning eyes.

Puran shakes his head.

— I don't know, Bikhia, what he'll eat, how live, what he wants.

Bikhia sighs and lowers his head, his body folds and crumples and trembles violently.

— Don't cry, Bikhia. Keep looking after him. And listen, I don't know where there are caves in these hills, you will lead me today. A most secret cave, where no one will ever go.

Puran strokes his body and head. Is anything communicated? Puran will have to leave Pirtha with so many things unknown.

He says in a deeply tender, soft voice, "Where is the time, Bikhia? We'll have to get a place nobody knows but you and I."

Bikhia gets up, leans his head in assent. Then he starts moving, as if he too is suddenly millions of years old. He can't carry on, he is weary, full of fatigue. So he drags his feet as he walks.

Puran goes into the room and lies down, closes his eyes.

Strange, they are no longer beating the drums.

What have they come to know, what news?

Puran writes the famine report in his mind.

In the morning Puran had seen a lot of acacia flowers, a lot of acacia leaves in front of the engraved stone, the stone almost invisible with flower and fruit. There was also a handful of rice, some earth in a clay pot, a torn piece of cloth and the place for the offerings marked off with a line. Bikhia stood leaning against the wall. Whoever came, touched the stone and put their hands to the forehead. Each left some acacia flowers, leaves, a handful of soil. The soul of the ancestors came driven by distress and now Bikhia must go in search of a cave, for the guest's hour of departure is approaching, he cannot stay anywhere here any more—everything has been invaded and devastated by the present—now he will return against the current of time. There will again be an impenetrable, profound and unrelieved darkness—and so Bikhia puts everything into the offering. Take leaves and flowers, there is no forest. Take rice, there is no beast or fowl for sacrifice, take a handful of soil, we hold no ground anymore. Take a bit of torn cloth, there is no coarse cloth loomed at home—I have marked off that little space, because around our existence an invisible line is coming ever closer, we are terrified, there is no escape.

There is no escape, we were torn apart so long ago, in fragments in atoms, we are scattered everywhere. Does Bikhia tell this in his offering?

Nothing can be known or grasped. Puran says softly, "Now we must go, I'll be back in a minute."

Bikhia looks with pained eyes. His eyes are quite impenetrable now. A precious, incredible mystery (for Bikhia the ancestral soul is a fact, the scientific definition of the pterodactyl is without value for him), that was only his at first, must now be taken in equal share with this outsider, this has hurt him. But this too is now an immutable directive from past generations, that on the last flight of the ancestors' soul the outsider is the last resort. So he can't ignore Puran's words.

Puran waits a minute. Soon the Pirtha chapter will in the strict sense be over for him. The rest of his life will have to be spent evaluated from the perspective of Pirtha. In fact Pirtha has kicked this much sense into him, that water, bread, rice, are actually extremely precious in India, more precious than the koh-i-noor, and no one has the right to waste them or destroy them at will. As precious is a roof overhead, a cloth on one's body, a-b-c-d, medicine in time of disease. One person eats well by keeping five hundred starving, one person graduates college while six hundred remain illiterate, and one person buys an apartment keeping how many hundred homeless, such complicated *ratios*. No *ratio* has ever been calculated from the position of people like Bikhia. The position from which *computer*, information ministry, and *media* see the situation depends on the will of the current social and state systems. And it is by the will of this system that the educated person is unwilling to think. This system considers original thought an "exterminable threat." This system forcibly occupies the thinking cells of the brain and makes a body brush his teeth with Forhan's toothpaste. Sometimes makes him or her say that India is proudly on the way to becoming the biggest power in the Third World. Again sometimes it makes one crazy with the idea that the first duty is to change the name of the state. The system wants, and people "dance like wooden dolls." But the first obligation is to calculate the ratio from the position of people like Bikhia. Without that effort Independence has grown to be forty years old.

Bikhia, you don't want anyone to know of our dreadful discovery, for to you he is your ancestors' soul. The purity of the situation will be polluted if anyone knows.

Bikhia, I don't want anyone to know of our dreadful discovery, because if we let them know there will be an invasion of the *media* of the inquisitive world. You will be shown on television, and the soul's warning message, the terrifying news of the tribal being of Pirtha, will all lose their perspective, by many analyses the rodent and the rhododendron will be proven the same. And who can tell, all the countries of the world will conduct investigations out of Pirtha everywhere, into the last forest, the last cave, to see where the prehistoric time and creature are still hidden. That invasion will be inevitable.

You are endangered, and so am I. Like that song,

Alas! Alas! Dust storm has come
Alas! Alas! The land is going
Alas! Alas! Our country is going
Alas! Alas! Land-country-people is going to dust, to dust!
Alas! Alas! How shall we catch dust-motes from the air and make a plowing-field?
To build the lost land?
We are distressed in that way.

But finally Puran says nothing. They are bilingual and speak Hindi.

Puran too speaks Hindi.

But Puran's Hindi and theirs come from two different worlds. Not just here, but from district to district of Bihar Puran has had the same experience. After the shooting at Gua a political leader gave a spirited speech in fiery language.

Having heard it all Roto Sumrai said, "Explain what he said, in Hindi."

A class-divided society goes on parallel lines. There is no meeting-point. Language too is class-divided. Whether exploiter, or a fake party man with an "I am for the poor" type slogan, or yet a true lover of the poor or a believer in the change needed in this rotten social system yet "no party man," their Hindi-Bengali-Gujarati and other languages move on parallel lines with their tongues. The problem is so big and permanent that the peasant Ramabatar from Nalanda would say, "Such is the situation. What to do, Maharaj?" Ramabatar called everyone "Maharaj [O King!]" including his goat.

Puran sighs.

— I'll be back, Bikhia.

V

Harisharan is most melancholy, and at the same time excited and reckless. The SDO remains as before, calm, harsh with repressed bitter mockery in the knowledge that all goodwill will finally be beaten. Puran realizes that an honest officer with a conscience has come to know that he will be defeated if he gives battle, but has decided to enter the battlefield within administrative confines. He is younger than Harisharan, yet he is old in wisdom. Harisharan is older, but he can still get reckless. As a student he had once said, "Let's do it on foot," and walked to Bodhgaya without climbing on a railway train. He is a bit older now, but he's still pig-headed.

— Pirtha is now a battle of honor.

— Hush, we don't want Kausalji's men to know anything.

— Kausalji has power, let him get work done if he can.

— ITDP [Indian Tribal Development Program] area. Government will say why should a non-government organization work when the government is there?

— But government is doing nothing.

— You and I are doing nothing.

— Will this state of affairs continue in Pirtha *Block,* in this Panch?

— Let him try, and let us try our best.

— How? There is no land, what land there is is full of stones. Who will give better than government quota land to a tribal? And where is land like that here?

— They will not go elsewhere.

— No.

— And they are all in debt at compound interest.

— Yes. The moneylenders are in Bhalpura, in Rajaura.

— Think about it calmly, please.

— About what?

— The current food problem.

— The magistrate will not say this is a *chronic famine area.* We must give battle on this issue.

— *Fight the famine on war footing?*

— Such is the case.

— *Fight the famine on war footing.*

The primary gross truth, nobody will allow you to say that an atom of the green revolutionary area of the State of Madhya Pradesh is in the "perpetual famine" zone of extreme backward tribals. War! War in sky-soil-water. Food will rot because of insufficient storage facilities at the Food Corporation, but it will still never reach, never does reach Pirtha, Kalahandi or Koraput. Food goes to Africa, to Sri Lanka, promises of building collective crop farms are given at SAARC conferences, let them be given, give everyone everything since you overproduce greatly in food crop production, but why not, at the same time, give to the district of Kalahandi and to the micro-region of Pirtha, why count the heads of the villages, of the forest-settlements of North Bengal for the census, to identify "Scheduled Tribe constituencies" and why not bring them within the panchayat system or the purview of the ITDP and when it comes to the responsibility for drinking water to roads for movement, education, health, employment, why wash your hands of them and say "They are under the Forest Department," when the Forest Department keeps them as slave labor, exploits them as "permanent casuals," gives them nothing, ever. By the same policy you keep the tribals of the North Bengal Dooars as outcastes, who are counted (the figure is needed to demarcate a constituency), and for them also you do not fulfill the minimum human claims from a to z, you say, "The tea-garden owners will look after them," and the garden-owner passes eighty-three paise per head for the garden's coolies in 1987, when "the century's sun is in the Western sky and its shadow is long,"—and the garden-owner can show this impudence because no government upsets the owners, let the owner of the tea-garden be a multi-millionaire, let the coolies be in the debit column; when the only tribal-directed tea garden cooperative is swallowed up by anonymous fake owners and the wily government takes the safe and profitable role of the spectator. When the names of the Nagesia tribals from Ranchi and Palamu are not included in the list of tribals census after census, and in the Assam Dooars and the plains, the Santal-Oraon-Mundas brought a hundred and fifty years ago are not listed as "tribals" but as "castes." (These facts would have remained unknown if Puran had not read books.)

This is reality, these are facts. Who will save them by fighting on a *war footing in* the case of the tribals dead, half-dead, dying bit by bit, of sheer starvation?

SDO says, "Do everything."

Raising his face to the sky he wipes his throat and says, "Give wells, trees, goats, hens, give a check dam at the mouth of the Pirtha, put them to *Block* work and give them *minimum wage*. Make an attempt. I have written, there are famine conditions in Pirtha, not drought. I don't know what will happen after that. But you'll have to keep at it."

Later Shankar told Puran, "The SDO sir, the *Block* sir, will all be transferred. If they do nothing, then they will stay put and if they dig one well they'll be transferred. Better not to do anything."

— Why, Shankar, why?

— They will not be able to change things for the better.

And these words later came true when the Irrigation Department, without actually opposing the building of a dam at Pirtha, simply said, "This is a department matter" and made the proposed double dam useless by tying a gordian knot around it with red tape.

First the SDO and then Harisharan were quickly transferred on the charge of "inventing famine where there is no famine."

All that happened later, much later.

Later even Kausalji gave up hope, because Shankar and his people did not get down into the distant plains, did not live in colonies, because "there were no hills there." All this distress is because of living in the hills, yet they did not leave the hills to descend, they did not abandon Pirtha, and when Harisharan gave Shankar a thorough scolding about "getting food, remaining alive, getting education," Shankar consoled him, saying, "Don't be so concerned, sir. We are dying, our numbers are decreasing. There are enough Khajra trees for so few, and it is you who have taught us to eat seeds of the acacia fruit, and look also! Not so many are being born, and even when they are born they are sold. Don't think so much for Pirtha, you are a good man. You feel pain. What can you do? There is no good soil in the plains below!"

Harisharan wept at this.

It was Harisharan who later wrote this to Puran from Indore. At least a year and nine months later.

Now Harisharan says, "Kausalji's master-plan is not going to take effect today."

— Do your own stuff without thinking of that. Oh hello Mr Journalist! You stay here. Pirtha needs rain. Of course the rains bring administrative problems as well. The people upstairs have only one verdict, "It's not famine, it's drought." Now that you've brought rain, the verdict might become "It has rained, so it's not even drought." See what a problem it is for us.

— I didn't bring rain.

— I hear that's what the tribals are saying.

— What else are they saying?

— I hear they're saying that the rainmaker must not leave.

— There would have been rain anyway.

Harisharan says, *"Man, let them have their miracle. They want a miracle, I have nothing in my bag. Only yesterday someone said in Rajaura, A sage is ready to do a fire service in Rajaura and is guaranteeing rain as a consequence but the Block government will have to pay expenses, ten kilos of clarified butter et cetera."*

The SDO says, "So bring him."

— Sir, I said that my friend brought rain without expense. So the holy man's tout said, "The real religious people are beaten because of these crooks. If someone brings rain without a religious service, no one will have a service performed."

SDO says, "What's up with Bikhia?"

Harisharan says, "He's kept his mouth shut, but I hear he's very friendly with Puran."

— Are you in mourning too, reporter?

— Mourning, why?

— Unshaven face, dried out hair, bare feet, and wearing a lungi-sarong are dangerous. If you leave after this it will be an act of treachery. Hang on here.

— I stay showing false passion, and then to leave because I

couldn't bear to eat Khajra tubers and live with the drought and distress would be even greater treachery.

— The reporter is smart, Harisharanji! He knows one mustn't raise hopes in the tribal's mind, for it is hard to keep a promise in the end.

— Not hard if you admit to it beforehand.

— How?

— I was young then. A friend of my father's, an *"uncle"* with an M.A. in Anthropology, got a job in Dandakaranya. Very honest, most hard-working, interested in education, and with experience in other tribal areas. But he had worked mostly in the Himalayas where people cover their body.

— Why is dress important?

— There is a reason, believe me. Then he went to Dandakaranya. He came from a conservative family, and was himself a devout and practicing brahman. Since he couldn't keep to every restriction when he was on tour, he would do penance when he returned home. Now he went to an area this time, you understand, where women did not cover their chests, only down from the waist. Since he read a lot, he had known that women of that particular tribal community dressed in that manner. But once he saw it himself, he could not take it. He left after three months, resigned his job. He wrote the Department, "They are simple and innocent. But I am greatly inconvenienced at the sight of their women. I realize that the 'nakedness' is a pure and innocent thing, but I also realize that I am myself not so civilized, simple, pure, or innocent that I will accept this 'nakedness' as my bread and butter. Otherwise why should my mind react this way?" What's the matter Kausalji?

— Come, they are going to take a video picture.

— No no, you are enough.

SDO says, "What is this?"

Suddenly there is a slight disturbance there. Dimag's wife is saying something, Shankar goes forward.

— Let's go and listen.

— Don't take a fillim sir.

— Look here, if we don't inform people about you, how will they know?

— Don't take, sir.

— How strange! Harisharanji! This way . . .

The SDO says, "Go. This is your affair."

Harisharan goes forward.

— What's up, Motia's Ma?

Dimag's wife flares up, "Why are you calling me Motia's Ma? Where is Motia? Take a fillim again, people will come again, they'll know famine is going on, again *tur-rucks* will come. They'll take all the children away."

Kausalji is angry, he's angry, and it is now evident that he can raise camp from here at any point in time. OK, let the government decide if there is a famine or not. He has come and is doing work to save the deprived. But famine or drought, or the matter of administrative failure or negligence and Kausalji's role and human suffering, all this should be captured in a documentary. Public opinion will be shaped, and relief help will come, in fact there are people and organizations in other countries of the world who think of the hungry humans of the Third World. A lot of pictures are taken to form international public opinion about Nicaragua. This is true that the tale of Pirtha does not come into the map of Kalahandi even, forget Nicaragua (a little regret resonates in Kausalji's voice, practiced in giving speeches at home and abroad), but this must be documented. And it is here that he wants to inform those who misunderstand his goodwill that, if his wishes come true, then he will take the distressed of Pirtha from stony hill to the green of the plains, there they will have rooms fit to live in, drinking and irrigation water, agricultural aid and land, his training for women, school for children and adults, health care, they'll live like humans. They need this video image as they need food for their aid. No child-buyer will see this, but only those who need to see it. Government people have become very selfish, and people in the West have become self-indulgent.

The SDO says softly, "Here is the power of money—rupee, West Germany's mark, kroner-dollar-franc-pound. What do you say, Harisharanji?"

Shankar looks at the Sarpanch. Will the Sarpanch say something? But the Sarpanch is confused and silent.

Shankar looks at Harisharan. Sir! Sarkar! It's you brought these people, now will you too remain at a safe distance? Or will you make me say that we are surrendering? His eyes say to Harisharan in experienced wisdom, I know, Sarkar. Everything finally becomes a deal, even giving food to the hungry. At this moment we're eating his food, in exchange he wants to capture us *in film*. His dictionary cannot include the self-respect of the hungry.

He raises his hand. Says dryly, "Motia's mother could not make you understand. We are now in mourning. Our ancestors' soul is displeased with us. Our faith is hurt if you take pictures of us in this state."

— It's not a question of faith.

— I know. Take pictures. Motia's mother! Don't obstruct anymore, there is nothing we can do. If the government looked after the tribals, then how today . . .

Now the pictures are taken. The women cover their faces with the torn ends of their cloth. The men turn their faces away. The scene of an old woman holding a skeleton baby in arms taking lentil-rice in her bowl, is captured very well and when the tape recorder is held close you can catch the rattle in the old woman's throat and her mumble as well as the child's chirping wail.

— The next show in Geneva.

Harisharan murmurs.

SDO shakes his head.

— Come back to the initial argument. The government has failed in eradicating poverty. It's giving a lot of money to voluntary organizations, and it's a fact that behind most active, successful organizations there is foreign money coexisting with domestic money. In fact, because this dirty wash would have been brought out again . . . reporter?

— I'll tell you later.

What's there to say about this. Foreign money infiltrating by way of voluntary organizations in the name of welfare, is that unknown to the central government or at the state level? They have to accept this, because in spite of their hundreds of thousands of projects and tens of millions of rupees and a few hundred thousand government employees and Panchayats nothing reaches the real recipient. This ocean of money that flows for the removal of poverty among the tribals and the other deprived groups does not show up in the tribal and non-tribal demograph of destitute India. So many job quotas are another hoax, for how many tribal PR officers, computer scientists, oceanographers, and particle physicists have been produced in forty years? Who gets the jobs of that type that are set aside for them? They go a few in a million into higher education, it's enough if there should be a handful of lawyers or doctors, or they go into the humanities stream, not science or business, and even that a few in a million. All the states and the Center are pushing away poverty, and yet poverty is and will be on the rise. They don't even get called according to the work that they can do. Teaching jobs in commerce, the sciences, geography, political science, and economics are reserved for tribals; and Bengali, English, History kept open for everyone, so everyone gets those jobs. "Because there are no qualified tribal applicants." When this is the entire *film serial*, then the voluntary organizations have to be acknowledged and if a *pathological* analysis of the sample is made foreign money comes out. Apart from the organizations nourished by foreign money there are too few voluntary organizations that can do anything for the poor. The Center and the state governments have accepted reality. Since these are the facts, the SDO's purism is unrealistic. All the power is in the hands of the government, and a huge amount of money spent is not reflected at all in the demograph of destitute India. The amount of milk reflects the cow's intake, a richer harvest reflects the fact that more advanced methods are being applied in agriculture, but the money that the Center gives the state and the state sends for the tribal *Block* in Pirtha, is not reflected at all in this area condemned to a life sentence of starvation. In the government documentaries, who acts the healthy, happy, smiling tribal peasant couple? Who says, We are building a happy family because we have only one child?

Puran says, "I'm off."

SDO asks, "Won't you write about Bikhia's picture?"

— No. That's their own affair.

— You're a journalist, weren't you intrigued?

— It's the soul of their ancestors, not mine.

— And this famine?

— Possibly the first culprit is the fundamental failure or heartlessness of the tribal welfare department from state to district to subdivision.

— That's all?

— They are themselves guilty as well. With all these arrangements for extinction they are not extinct, don't they have to pay for it? How much more relieved you'd have been if they weren't here.

Harisharan says, "Don't lose this bite in your report."

— It'll be there. On the survey map too Pirtha is between two jaws. How can there be no bite?

— You too are mad at Kausalji's film.

— Don't be daft. What right have I? It's he who's taking the film. So much relief, so much preparation, and no bite?

— *Man!* Don't you look at Shankar's eyes, all their eyes? They are again curling up inside. This is the real problem. We are living together, we talk, but they never trust us.

— This is a subject to be debated, discussed.

— They are angry.

— Harisharan! Don't be childish. We already have this situation, and then do you notice Kausalji's words? From the way he speaks, it's quite clear that he is blaming the failure of the government, explaining that his Kausal-method is much more effective, and that the tribals know nothing, everything about them is backward, most barbaric, and if they leave all this they can start new lives in his projected colony, this too he explains. Their starvation is real, the relief camp has held their inevitable death at bay for a bit, this too is real. But hence they must be grateful, they must enjoy things, by this you're expecting too much.

— You're back where you began, friend. But it's as if you have really understood them?

— I'm living in a dead woman's house, I too am in mourning.

SDO asks, "Are you eating all right?"

Harisharan says, "This is not Surajpratap, but the reverse *case*. Listen *man,* don't go crazy in a different way. Everyone will say, Pirtha is the place where reporters go mad."

Puran smiles a bit at the words of both and says, "I'll be on my way. I must make some *notes* to write my *report,* mustn't I?"

SDO says, "Write this too in your *notes,* that Kausalji wants to make a *picnic spot* out of the spring-fed pool and hillside of Pirtha."

Harisharan shakes his head repeatedly.

Puran says, "I also need to know your views on why no projects have been blueprinted or implemented in this ITDP area. The matter is most complex, I suppose?"

— Do come by. I'll tell you everything.

Puran looks around, and says, "In the Pirtha *package,* you get *a sample of tribal India.* Incredible."

Puran leaves.

SDO says, "Do you think he'll hang on?"

Harisharan says, "Oh no."

Now the Sarpanch comes forward. Excited.

— What's the matter?

— Sarkar, we must pitch camp in Derha, Sangatoli, Madhola, Pungarh as well. Please give the order. Won't there be encampments there? There's famine in those areas as well.

SDO says, "Sure thing. Definitely. From the *Block* Office. What's Madhola *Block* doing?"

— The BDO has not been there for three years, Sarkar-sir! And the Sarpanch is in hospital.

— Even so.

Harisharan says, "Why don't you go on tour with the SDO from the *South?* Take some material with you when you go. There too—"

— Yes, Kausalji's organization is there as well.

— It's admirable that his organization works in many places in the district.

The SDO sighs.

— Why shouldn't there be, sir? The entire state of Madhya Pradesh was under kings and nawabs of various degrees of power. His family owned land all over the district. Madhola was in his taluka-fief. Wherever he had talukas, he has . . .

— I don't know all this.

— Wherever there were kings and chiefs . . . Yes, Sarpanch, something will be done.

— My daughter lives in Madhola. My son-in-law has sent her back here. The Janayuba [People's Youth] Group boys are here. They say, We'll take kodo seeds and maize from those who have some, and will give it out to everyone.

— Where is their leader Madhu Singh?

— In Bhopal. There'll be trouble with all this, Sarkar-sir.

— No, what's the trouble? They don't plunder, they are non-violent, they do purification-penance, and they distribute *leaflets.*

Harisharan says, "No, let's come to a decision."

— Harisharanji! The more it's known the more problems we'll face. Think upon it. Do whatever you can within these conditions.

Kausalji says, "Wherever the suffering people are, there we are too. Try to understand that. Cooperate with us."

— Isn't your organization working there?

— Other work, but they'll do relief work as well. But that's not the solution of the problem. We need a permanent solution. Give me the chance, I'll show you work. My workers are different. They have not come for a job like the government employees. The government and the contractors are eating the money that is the tribals' right.

Kausalji looks at them as he says this. It's his brother's contracting firm that gets the government contracts in Madhopura.

His anger is due to the fact that Harisharan and the SDO kept him in check. But now everything will be passed. He holds much more power than they do.

— We'll bring clothes tomorrow.

After he leaves, Harisharan says, "We will start well digging, and some goats and hens . . . "

— Whatever you do, double quick.

— What do we tell Puran?

— Tell him the truth. Journalist people understand. They will want the truth.

— Puran too has changed so in these few days.

— It happens, suddenly this sort of thing happens. Bye.

He turns around as he goes and says, "I too must make *notes* to defend my end. It can't be that I came to know after a journalist from Bihar informed me."

— Yes sir. But Madhola—

— Yes. Let him go! They are not in mourning there.

The Sarpanch says in troubled surprise, "Why do you think so, Sarkar? Everybody near here, tribal areas, tribal settlements know about this and are in mourning."

— But they saw nothing.

— So what? How do I explain . . .

Shankar comes forward, "Stop explaining, Sarpanchji! Leave us now. Mahi and Diman and Lurhi are calling. You have not put their names on the list yet. Greetings, Sarkar!"

Shankar does not stop walking.

SDO looks at Harisharan.

— You have to take it all.

— Yes, sir.

Shankar stops in a bit. Steps down and off the track. Harisharan knows what there is. On the slope of the hillside, between and below two hills (the hills are low here, they can be called cliffs). Their land is on the gravelly flats. Divided by cactus fences. There's land here, land by the Pirtha ditch, land in little lots, perhaps no one has a full acre.

— What do you see, Shankar?

— Sarkar?

— What are you looking at?

Shankar says, "Land."

— Let's see what happens if it gets irrigation. It's never been irrigated after all. If there are field-wells in the land itself . . .

— "Yes, Sarkar."

Shankar shakes his head. Goes forward. You can see from his eyes that he has entered some cave again. The video filming has shaken him.

Harisharan moves toward the camp. He must be in constant attendance at this time. For Kausalji. Although his worry for Puran nags at him and he is pained that Shankar has again become the elusive quarry of fable for him. The *magistrate* often says, "Tribals are ungrateful and do not realize how much the government does for them."

Harisharan had brought for the Sarpanch today posters proclaiming that "Leprosy can be cured if caught in time. Go to the nearest Leprosy Hospital." The paper is good, the posters large-sized. The crowd has opined that it is a help that the government is giving such paper. Pasted on grass frames such paper will keep out the wind. The women say they can lay their babies down on it. You can sift the relief food grains on it. It is useful in many ways. Government proclamations serve the poor in this way alone.

Harisharan thinks, Who will do family-planning? These people are keeping the peace and quiet of the country unbroken in the process of becoming extinct, how much responsibility can a person who had nothing to eat today take to stop separatism and communalism all over India, and when Shankar and his other tribals had surrounded Rajaura Block office (by sheer luck not in his time!) chanting "Sarkar! Give us seeds, seeds, to eat," they had threatened law and order in the Block? And Leprosy Hospital! There are no hospitals near here. The Sarpanch or a village doctor or healer is the resort in sickness. They do know how to use these posters.

— O Sarpanchji! Give the reporter some posters.

Puran is lying on the ground on a mat, eating maize powder, unbelievable! He used to wash his gamchha, vest, and sarong with soap every day.

Puran and Bikhia went looking for a cave in the same distressed urgency. A flashlight in Puran's hand, a staff in Bikhia's.

The water of Pirtha pool was shadowed by its banks, by the acacia trees all around. The water was green in places, in places transparent with sun. Stones slipping with moss in the bottom, the water comes up to your waist. Crossing the pool, walking upstream along the ditch gives you the sense that Pirtha hill is not narrow and confined. It has spread its domain over a good area. The roots of the tall grass in the cracks of the stone are tough.

Puran has seen just such grass in the Western Ghats. Though after the rains there were sweet and bitter-sweet fruit trees on the slopes and peaks of the Western Ghats, food for the local poor, and there were countless waterfalls.

Here the hill looks primeval, the spread of the land is different, hard and harsh. There are no wild fruit trees, no trees of unscented white flowers as in the Western Ghats. After walking a bit Bikhia grasps at the hanging grass and enters a cave mouth and signals to Puran, Come up the same way.

Puran ties his gamchha around his waist and climbs up. Drums seem to beat in his chest, his heart lashes so in excitement.

He flashes his light, moves up watchfully with Bikhia and suddenly gets some sun as he enters a well-proportioned cave. The sun comes in at one side through the crevice above.

Puran shines his flashlight where Bikhia points. Drums beat from the smooth stone, one hears the clamor of the dance.

With great care and over time, who has engraved dancing men and women, drum, flute, the khoksar to keep the beat? Peacock, elephant, deer, bird, snake, naked child, tree, Khajra tree, bow and arrow, spear.

The human beings are larger than life, the animals and birds small, the trees large again. Who carved these pictures, filling the cave wall for how long?

Do these pictures date from the time when Bikhia's people were free, and the animal kingdom was their dominion, beasts of prey? When the forest was mother and nurse?

— You drew too?

Bikhia doesn't answer. The men wear earrings. The women are ornamented, apparently they used to wear ornaments of catachou wood at one time. To what period do these pictures belong?

Or is it that Bikhia and his people carve pictures to capture that past life?

No, Puran will take no photographs. He will not defile anything sacred, he feels no such urge.

Bikhia presses his hand, his eyes say, Let's go.

Now go down through a roofless tunnel, down, down, go down, turn, enter a dark cave again. The sound of water above them and its floor is slippery, walk carefully shining your flashlight. Bikhia strikes the floor with his staff as he walks. The Pirtha is flowing along the upper cave. The thundering sound of its fall up ahead fills the cave.

Then a narrow path. They are descending further. Then Bikhia stops him.

The sun falls through a crevice above. In front a cavern. The flashlight does not hit bottom, the lowered stick strikes no floor.

Bikhia and Puran wait. Yes, a dark cavern in front. Perhaps it goes down to the hill base. As if the dark waits with its skirts forever spread. Give me, give me what you must keep secret, I will guard it with care. Now I have no mysterious secret of my own. Whatever is mine has been invaded. Where will the wild animal run when it's surrounded by a net fence? The present, encroaching from all sides, will eat the past whole. Yet there may be a priceless truth worthy of being guarded in secret, that you cannot let anyone know, give it to me, I am that ageless, timeless darkness of time, when the earth was under water, there was no light anywhere, darkness was everywhere and the creator was in thought, how to create the earth and the living world. I am waiting since then, I keep everything in my lap, nothing is lost.

Bikhia drops down a little stone.

The sound of the fall reaches them in a few seconds. Bikhia, this is good. No one will know.

— No one will know.

Bikhia lowers his head.

— The picture you carved . . . plant Khajra trees all around it . . . surround it with stones . . . it will slowly be covered, yet it will remain. How many pictures have survived in this cave. No one has seen them, they have remained.

Now they turn back. This hill was perhaps a fortress for them once. There are other caves. Did they think of houses on the hill as safe in the face of some invasion? Did they already understand, seeing the worship rituals and rites of other nations infiltrated into their forest dwellings, that an invasion of their ethnic being, their ritual, their faith and folkways was being ushered in? Is that why they spoilt their rituals? Fled into the forest? Will Raghupati Raghava—King Rama of Gandhi's famous song— come again and again to determine their punishment? We never found out what the narrative tradition captured in their folk memory has to say. But from what an old Santal spoke of the ancestors a hundred and sixteen years ago (Roman script, Santali language), we know that the ancestors said that at the time of King Rama all the aboriginals went with him to Lanka and fought to defeat King Ravana.

Too little can be known, we have destroyed a continent that we kept unknown and undiscovered. The tribal wants human recognition, respect, because he or she is the child of an ancient civilization. In what a death farce we are enthralled as we turn them into beggars, who are nowhere implicated in Indian education, development, science, industry, agriculture, technology. They remain spectators. India marches toward the twenty-first century.

They go back the way they came. And as he drops down holding on to the tufts of grass Puran realizes what an impossible (for him) thing he has done. Now they walk along Pirtha's breast and bathe in the pool. Black clouds pass overhead and the water suddenly looks black. Perhaps it'll rain again. But even if it rains, Puran hasn't brought that water. And, he has in fact read somewhere that if the desert in Rajasthan is made green the rains will slowly decrease and Madhya Pradesh will suffer the consequences first.

They come up after their bathe. Puran says without looking at Bikhia, "Sleep during the day. Come in the night." Bikhia leaves without response.

Today Shankar comes to his room.

— What Sarkar, eating parched maize-powder?

— I am Sarkar too?

— No, just "Babu"—gentleman.

He is silent for a while and then says, You have traveled a lot. Is there no forest or hill that no one knows about?

— I haven't seen anywhere. And ... Shankar ... will your people live if they cling to their mountain?

— Where should we go to stay alive?

Puran shakes his head.

— Your Sarkars are saying ...

— Yes, they're saying ...

— If there's a solution to the water trouble ...

Shankar gives a little smile.

— Then all would have been well, Babu.

— Have you eaten anything?

— *Relief.* Take *relief,* let 'em make *fillims.* We are hungry, naked poor. That will be known on the *fillims.* But the *fillim* won't say who made us hungry, naked, and poor. We don't beg, don't want to beg, will people understand this from those pictures?

Everybody took pictures, what did you take?

— Of the camp's tents. Kausalji's. Tell me, you'd get water if you dug a well in the direction of the river, wouldn't you?

— If we dig wells . . .

— Won't your mourning end?

— Bikhia knows.

Shankar says in immaculate conviction, "Now Bikhia is above everyone. He will give everyone oil, then we'll oil our body and bathe. We will shave our heads and faces, cut our nails, and come out of mourning. It was he who saw . . . he knows what there is to know, and we know when we saw him."

— What'll happen to him now?

— He is bound now, Babu, he'll keep the stone unsullied, perform the ritual, he will not be free in this life. And that stone! How can there be a move away from Pirtha, tell me that?

They would on no account have left the shelter of Pirtha hill and river, now the stone tablet has become another reason for their not leaving. Perhaps Pirtha was their last shelter, or their domain, their past. And now it is precisely there that one finds the tablet. A myth to bind the past to the present. Perhaps this explanation is necessary for their nearly extinct sense of ethnic being. How can one rob a people of the supernatural, of myth, what is in their understanding an unwritten history, when the present time has given them nothing? No one holds that right.

— Babu!

— Yes, Shankar!

— Tell this to the *Block* Sarkar.

— You can say it too.

— No, Babu! He's a good man, he won't understand, he'll be hurt. I don't know if you will understand my words. He won't for sure.

— Who is in your family, Shankar?

— Me? Everyone. Wife and daughter and mother. One by one they became stones. We bury the ash and raise a stone. I've heard that we buried the bodies in the old days.

— And now?

— No Babu! There is always famine. My son is with my sister. In Bhalpura.

Shankar says in surprise, "How? I'm in debt for thirty rupees. He grazes the moneylender's cow, cleans the cowshed, makes cow dung cakes for fuel. It's been years, the moneylender does not keep accounts. If he did the Sarkar would get the boy out. Sarkar says that "Hali" bonded labor is illegal now. That if the boy comes away the boss can do nothing. That would be wrong of me, Babu. I had taken money after all. He returns home at evening."

— Does your brother-in-law work?

— Both of them ... whatever they can get.

— You?

— Whatever I can get. I'll get the boy out.

— Won't you send him to school?

Shankar says with profound affection, "I'll bring him home. Where will he read? And also, why should he read? I read up to Class Six, and the Tribal Officer and the Sarpanch had said I'd get a job. I'm off, Babu. You came and only suffered, come in the wintertime."

— There'll be no famine then?

— Then we get work on the boss's land. We bring paddy and marwa from the field that dropped out of the bales at the gathering of the harvest. Birds come to the Babla forest. For a month, month and a half. Otherwise the famine goes on. Good-bye Babu.

He says with a sigh, Will the Big Sarkar [the central government] listen if you write about famine? If you write everything?

— I will of course try.

— You too will leave.

— Yes, I must go.

— But the old folks used to say that the person who brings water shouldn't leave. Someone brought water then too. And he stayed on here. I've heard he died of old age.

Shankar gets up.

— As long as there's Kausalji. And then?

VI

Puran and Bikhia sat at the shrine-mouth. There are clouds today, clouds are piling up. Let it rain again, let the earth wells fill, as well as the Sarpanch's big brick and cement well. It is the Sarpanch who gives water in times of drought. In Gabahi the Panchayat's big well is right in front of his house. There was much talk at the time of the digging of the well, that he's taking advantage. But the well was dug because the water level was somewhat accessible precisely there. The Sarpanch gives water from that very well, although he also bathes his water buffaloes. Let that well fill also, Pirtha, Gabahi, Dholki, all the villages are thirsty. Moreover, the water of the wells for the tribals of Derha, Sangatoli, Madhola, and Pungarb is bitter, foul-tasting. That water has some taste in the rainy season. Let the rains fall.

Bikhia's eyes are unblinking in his face pinched with lack of food and with mourning. Puran no longer wants to know where Bikhia saw it to draw it. Pirtha has taught him that, even if you are a reporter, you must not ask all the questions all the time.

Bikhia is witnessing that their ancestors' soul embodied itself and flew in one day, and now it's leaving its form and returning. If it were truly that? Would it have told all the tribals of the burial-grounds in the extinct settlement, lying underneath the *bridges* and paths, the new settlements and fields of grain, that our descendants are disappearing? Their existence is freshly endangered. To survive they must mingle in the mainstream, where their social position will be on the ground floor and their sense of ethnic being will no longer be distinct. Yet there is no liberation for them if they hang on with their teeth to the hillside of Pirtha, their land and their soil have turned to dust and blown away in the wind. Who can catch dust-motes from the wind and compose village, forest, field? Bikhia's eyes are like the still flame of a lamp, he wants to see his fill of the noble death of this noble myth.

Puran is witnessing his own futility. Having seen history from beyond pre-history, continental drift, seasonal changes after much geological turbulence, the advent of the human race, primordial history, the history of the ancient lands, the Middle Ages, the present age, two World Wars, Hiroshima-Nagasaki, holding under its wing this entire history and the current planetary arms race and the terror of nuclear holocaust, it came to give some sharply urgent news. Puran, a modern man, could not read the message in its eyes. Nothing could be known, can be known. One has to leave finally without knowing many things one should definitely have known. Seeing that Puran had understood nothing its eyes were closed since yesterday. The body seemed slowly to sink down, a body crumbling on its four feet, the head on the floor, in front of their eyes the body suddenly begins to tremble steadily. It trembles and trembles, and suddenly the wings open, and they go back in repose, this pain is intolerable to the eye. Bikhia goes on saying something in a soundless mumble, moving his lips. He sways, he mumbles, sways forward and back.

About an hour later Puran says, "Gone."

Bikhia is still.

Bikhia is still, unmoving, immobile.

They sit, the two of them sit.

An eternity passes. Bikhia has possibly gone to his ancestors, then, taking an eternity he traverses five thousand years and gradually returns. As if he had gone to sea in a boat and has returned after crossing the ocean, he is on his way back, his body moves, he had left Puran waiting. Puran is merely a spectator, he watched the boat set afloat, he saw the return in the boat, a spectator watches from a distance after all, he doesn't have news of the water.

Then Bikhia lies prone to pay his respects. He gestures to Puran to leave.

Puran goes outside and sits down.

Bikhia had brought a lot of stuff today, already before evening. He comes and takes a big basket woven of grass.

Much later he comes out with the basket covered in acacia leaves and grass.

Now he keeps looking at the eastern sky. The sky slowly pales in the east.

Bikhia keeps walking. Puran walks with staff and flashlight. Now Pirtha pool after descending the hill. Then past the pool upstream along the riverbed, turning again, in a strange devotion Bikhia holds on to the tufts of grass with one hand, clinging to the stones, holding on to the basket. Puran says softly, "Let me climb and show the light."

Bikhia stopped once before the cave drawings. After that the way was more complicated. Some reptile moves away, some night bird calls outside.

Much later they reached the edge of that expectant darkness. Then the darkness opened its mouth.

They bathed at the crack of dawn.

Then Bikhia brought water and washed out the shrine room, and an effaced, impersonal, yawning nothingness came and filled the room. Then it starts raining. Bikhia raises his face to the sky and drinks. Counts on his fingers, looks at Puran.

Now his voice is as fresh and clean as the rain.

— Oil bath in five days.

— Bikhia!

Bikhia is like an ancient chief of the community, venerated by all.

— Then you leave.

— I could go today too.

Bikhia shakes his head.

— You will stay in that room for five days.

— You?

— Me too.

Now Bikhia's eyes explain that this strange situation had made them one but they were never really one. As if in a strange situation of war two people from separate worlds and lives, who do not understand one another's language, were obliged to cross some icy ravine, or to pass an unknown and violent desert, and then complete mutual help became necessary. A time of danger has brought them together. Although their hands were clasped at the end of the episode of danger they realized that they belong to two different worlds. This is not just two classes going back to their separate habitations. Two classes, and then a poor tribal and a non-tribal, their stream of life is different from the mainstream, like the Ganga and Pirtha ditch. Life has not been linked to life, now Bikhia's eyes are bound to be distant. After all is said and done it is true that this outsider had to be let into what was intimately their own, in fact their own dead ancestors' soul, but to survive it took shelter with that very outsider, and then can the entire experience not be summarized as follows? That you are now invaded even in the extinct burial-grounds of the vanished settlements, even in the after-world, the only resource is to take shelter in the mainstream and therefore it came to Puran, not to Bikhia. It was informing Puran of some even greater message, which Puran did not understand. Bikhia's eyes spoke it. Because you are involved in this incident, therefore you'll have to stay to the end. That does not mean that you will get from me the comradeship of the last few days. You remain you, and I remain me, and after this heavy phase is over each will return to the orbit of his life.

There is rain on Bikhia's body and on his matted tawny hair. He leans on his staff and looks at the sky again.

— I am not your enemy, Bikhia.

— I will tie the grass frame to the door.

— I have not broken your trust.

— Now you won't even be able to cook in that room.

— Aren't you understanding my words?

— What need, Babu?

Bikhia smiles, and moves off with his staff over his shoulder. No, there is no meeting-point with them. The ways are parallel

from the distant past. Puran knows everything, he came to I
having read many books and done a lot of *homework*. It wa
so much to know them (before coming) as for Harisharan's ......
Harisharan had written, *Man,* this much I pray you to do.

Here, Bikhia's engraved picture, the *"death-wish"* of the entire
area, then Pirtha's unbearable suffering, then the rains, then their
dead ancestors' soul enters his very room, in this connection
Bikhia came to him. From the next day the settlement accepted
Puran, he has brought rain, and his communication with Bikhia
was then at an unusual peak. Did he put head on Puran's feet, did
he bring offerings of insects and flies and grain and moss and
snake and leaves and appoint Puran the doorkeeper? Did he take
Puran to that astonishing cave where the hunt goes on on the
walls of stone, the drum plays, the dance takes place, and the forest bears witness? Take him to the edge of that cavern which is the
frontier of the earth, in whose belly primordial darkness lies in
wait? Then, even at daybreak today the two of them were together.

Now, as soon as Bikhia broke the fence of his self-imposed
silence, immediately Puran became superfluous. When he was
silent and mute, then his mime, his eyes, and his fingers said so
much. When he opened his mouth, it became evident, that even
that intimacy had been in fact a *myth.* What a pity, this *myth* is
and will be alive. He too will have to accept it and stay.

He strokes his own face. Oil bath in five days. Was it S. C.
Roy or someone else who wrote that that is the day for the end of
mourning and a small funeral service?

Puran keeps climbing down.

Today Bikhia is beating the drum without a break, endlessly.
Shankar looks at him.

What is in front of the stone tablet today?

Puran does not look that way.

Shankar says to him, "Come, have some tea at the Sarpanch's."

— Let it be.

— Why?

— Let me remain in my room and write.

— All right, I'll walk with you.

— Come.

No terrible secret news waits now in the shrine room. Now all
can come.

Shankar does not even look at the shrine room.

— The roof must be mended.

— Then?

Shankar says in deep compassion, "Whatever Bikhia says. If anyone from Dahi's family comes, we'll raise a roof."

— Then? What will you do?

— What we used to. We've got water, we'll work the field. One thing is true, we must plant the Khajra that keeps us alive. If Baola keeps us alive, we must plant Baola. Otherwise everything will be desert, and we will have to leave.

Harisharan comes to his room today as well.

— *Man!* I've *sanctioned* six wells. You don't get continuous rain here, so we'll have to dig in batches.

— Contractor?

— No, they'll dig themselves. Shankar will bring people, Sarpanch will give everyone ten rupees in cash and kodo maize. Shankar says they can do it themselves. And I know they can.

— Perhaps so. If starvation is your regular diet, you can get to work on a few days' food.

— Kausalji is leaving in a week.

— He'd said he'd stay longer?

— Doesn't look like it.

— Actually his *grand scheme* . . .

— Forget it. And by the way! I hear they're going out of mourning. Oil bath in five days, and Bikhia is even speaking again.

— I've heard.

— *Report,* or his words?

— Both.

— Bikhia now possesses secret powers. He knows when the mourning began, and when it will be over.

— At least it's been proven that we don't know this.

— Anyway, the wells are not *mythic.*

— What's on the other side of the river?

— *Forest* Department land.

— Plant more trees there. Taking up the entire land and if you keep up cultivation of something or the other all year round, *as long as the land is under cultivation,* the Forest Department will not be able to evict them.

— *Man,* I'll do everything. You just do . . .

— In five days.

— What's that! You too? This is a mistake, Puran. Even if you do the oil bath here you may be sure that they won't think of you as their own.

Puran's smile is tarnished with pain.

— I know it better than anyone else. Still, I came at mourning time, stayed with them these few days . . . Think of it as a whim.

— No proper food.

— Powdered gram seed, molasses, pickles, what else do I need?

— Shall I send *lunch?*

— Feed me in Rajaura.

— *Man!* Go back. Get married. Return to normal life.

— I'll do that.

Harisharan points his finger and says, "This not marrying, not keeping to any rules, you can defend yourself about this with a lot of theory in the English language, but it is actually fear, an escapist outlook. You need courage to accept the responsibilities of everyday life. I cannot believe that you are still grieving Archana's loss."

Harisharan moves off like a busy bear. He married for love and they are both very happy.

Puran returns to his room. *Notebook, ballpoint pen, writing pad.* Is the pen mightier than the sword? You had to "amplify this idea" in school. Let Puran believe that, even today, in the present social system, if the journalist's pen declares holy war then public opinion is formed and in some cases the government does some work. In Gua, by government report, eleven people had been killed, and by private report many more and after that even the unbending Singhbhum government, arrogant with caste and race pride, was obliged to move. Puran went to the impenetrable forest of Serengsighati, the memorable site of the old Kol revolt, where the Ho tribe stores paddy and spends the night, for fear of elephants, on wood platforms on top of high trees, and there, after bathing in the trickling stream that had once been red with the blood of the insurgents and putting a stone in his pocket (how grave and noble those hills, those immense trees, how talkative that stream), Puran saw a World Bank *Mark 2* tubewell on the hill, Laru Jonko (a militant young woman from the Ho tribe) told him that the government had put that in after Gua. No, let Puran be able to keep his faith in the pen. He is not a tribal. His naming ceremony is not called "napta," his marriage ceremony is not called "kirincho bouhu bapla," his surname is not "chonre," his clan-totem is not the lizard, at his cremation women will not play the main role, his ancestors' soul does not become unquiet, he is not the prey of man-made famines every year.

How can he have faith in their faith? Puran must keep unshaken his faith in paper, pen, and the printing machine. Puran has nothing else. If there is no pen there is no Puran. Puran is not the bond slave Crook Nagesia of Kalabhori village in Palamu, whom his owner forced to pull a cart full of paddy to save his expensive oxen from the June heat and whose shoulder blades broke under the yoke and who was thus newly named Crook Nagesia (Crook! There ain't no Nagesias in Bihar—the official decision, you don't exist), who had pointed at the vanishing forest and said, "The forest went, and we went too."

The forest is not Puran's nurse.

For him the pen.

For people like Crook nothing but ancient tales held in memory.

But the old stories are also getting lost, they are losing their way, like motes in the face of a dust storm, ancient tales, history, songs, sagas, folklore, folkways. How will fifty-nine million six hundred and twenty-eight thousand, six hundred and thirty-nine people capture and put together their history and their culture from the storm winds of areas ruled by twenty-five states and the central government? Will they too finally seek shelter from main-stream writers? If Nagesia has to learn from the writings of some anthropologist, he has to get that much education in order to read that material. If he wrote his own story!

Even educated tribals don't do that.

Puran picks up his pen.

VII

Dateline Pirtha.

I think the problems of Pirtha-Dholki-Gabahi-Derha-Sangatoli-Madhola-Pungarh and the other villages of the Block are the same. I have heard that the Sarpanch is not sufficiently active here. But the Sarpanch has said that he goes to the Block every year and informs them. After Harisharanji became *Prakhanda Ayukta* or *Block Development Officer* they first received an earth well in Pirtha and then two elsewhere, seed for sowing (which comes a lot after sowing time and which they eat. It comes to the *Block* by this rule), fertilizer, which the Bhalpura moneylenders take away for repayment of overdue debts, and pesticide. All this did not help much, for the problem lay deeper. The state govern-

ment has no doubt granted monies through the district adminis-
trations in the ITDP areas for the backward people among these
tribals, and that money is no doubt showing up when the bal-
ance sheets are audited. The state government is not prepared to
think any further. But the awful truth is that the government officers, contractors, and businessmen are eating that money. At
least ten motor-roads have been built with the tribal development
money in a few years, two *bridges*, and the low-priced food shops
are being controlled by the pet dealers of the Food Corporation.
The contractors (who carry political clout) control everything. I
traveled and observed for four days that most tribals are landless. The "Act Prohibiting the Transfer of Tribal Land" is a total
failure. For shrewd exploiters have either bought land in the
name of nonexistent tribals or forced the landowner to sell. Or
the landowner knew nothing at all. This is happening with the
cooperation of the Revenue Department and the courts of law.
This Act is a failure. In Madhola I saw that people were not even
going through the motions of buying. The land is in the name of
a tribal, the taxes are reckoned in his name, and the tribal has no
right to enter that land. This sample-survey asks: by the strength
of what support is the poor tribal to live in the water and fight the
crocodile? We can thus form an idea of the land owning situation
of the tribal in the entire country.

I have seen only two tribal villages in Rawagarhi, the *Block*
adjacent to Pirtha, the Sarpanch gave me a bicycle. The picture
is similar there. The central and state governments have kept at
least thirty-five projects and subprojects in the ITDP sector in
various names, and for each there is an enormous amount of
money. I have toured some tribal areas of Bihar, Orissa, and
West Bengal, mostly in Bihar. Such projects exist in this state as
well. There are projects, money is being spent, yet there is no
reflection in actual fact.

Let me speak of the Pirtha area.

Their land (even when given by the government) is stony and
infertile. Yet they are dependent upon that land. The land might
have grown kodo if there had been irrigation, but there isn't.
There isn't enough drinking water. If there had been a double dam
on the Pirtha River they might have been able to cultivate the
Forest Department land on the two shores, but it hasn't been
built. No school, no hospital, no good tracks. No self-supporting
small industry project. All the neighboring good land has been

distributed in the name of fake tribals. Madhoria, Singh, and
Deokia, three families from Bhalpura, Sougandha, and Rajaura,
are the actual owners of a few hundred acres here under false
names. It is they who take water, irrigation, fertilizer, and pesticide in the name of the tribals. They are also the tribals' creditors.
Most of the tribals from at least ten villages work in their fields in
season at wages of two to two-and-a-half rupees. They are also
rich contractors, working for the government, they are the moneylenders, and because of their understanding with the Forest
Department their unlicensed sawmills are growing every day.

This is the main reason of the persistent famine here.
Whatever comes in their name, the government can show that it
is spent in the tribal areas. And in fact others are plundering
everything. But impartial investigation followed by confiscation
and redistribution of land? That too is impossible. When in the
records the owner is a tribal? And undoubtedly many different
government departments on the district and state levels are
involved in this plunder and robbery in ITDP sectors, and I also
saw that as a result the budget in this sector is on the rise. These
bosses are buying buses and trucks.

The state government obviously does not want such news to
be published. Therefore there is so much objection to the word
"famine." This is just "drought."

Every year at this time, in villages like Pirtha, Madhola,
Derha, Dholki, people die of starvation, of eating rotten scav-
enged material, of dehydration. Touts gather, the tribals sell their
infants and girl children. Touts take them for coolie labor at this
time as well. Two Gond families from Dholki went to work in
Bombay and came back two years later as destitute skeletons.

The SDO and BDO at headquarters knew that, in this so-
called ITDP area, (a) some families are taking everything that's
coming for tribals by holding false tribal names and by means of
influence with government people and political clout. (b) This
graft is in enormous amounts. For example, in the NCDC
[National Cooperative Development Corporation—currently working with World Bank assistance] project from 80,000 to 100,000
rupees will be given for developing small businesses through
LAMPS [Large Multipurpose Cooperative Societies] according to
the cooperative method. To take over this project some living tribals must be shown. Since Block and Subdivision offices raised
objections to such a trumped up case, secret power battles are

still going on. (c) This must be exposed. (d) It is necessary to make it known that the true tribals in Pirtha are dying of man-made starvation and to explain why this will not be called "famine"; and (e) to bring relief quickly to Pirtha.

The little relief that has happened is thanks to a voluntary organization. The state government will not allow us to say "famine," because then it will be revealed that:

In the ITDP sector of Pirtha the fruits of what comes in ITDP and related channels are enjoyed by others, but in forged tribal names.

Many officers, politicians, and contractors are implicated in this.

This is why it is so hard to get food by government channels and help had to be accepted from a non-government organization. The ones who accepted this will suffer the double bind of severe administrative reprimands.

Money in this account increases annually. And the government of course has the rule that ministries such as Food-Education-Irrigation must spend one-fourth of the budget in tribal areas.

There is no reflection in the tribal areas of the money spent on these projects and balanced in the accounts of the ITDP sector.

There is, elsewhere.

There one can see everything that the government wants for the tribals: for example, advanced mechanized agriculture, income augmentation, general development, improvement in education.

I have already mentioned that the land bears gold.

Also mentioned transport, sawmills, lumber smuggling, et cetera.

Health—Bhalpura has a hospital, nursing-home, maternity home, you name it.

Education? In Bhalpura and Rajaura together there is a co-ed college, a commercial college, two higher secondary schools with boarding facilities and eight schools run by various organizations.

Who will change this completely? Why should the State Government bother to say that famine continues on a *mini-scale* in the ITDP sector of Madhopura district?

What will happen to the people of Pirtha?

Let us now see if there is any way of helping them.

They will not leave the hills. Whether they eat or starve, it is the symbol of their near-extinct ethnic being. Yet the productivity of that soil is extremely low. With irrigation, fertilizer, and timely seeds, the soil can produce at the most four months' food.

The first necessity is to free them from slavery and indebtedness by applying the law ruthlessly on the basis of the illegality of the handover of land and the cancellation of the Agricultural Loans Act.

At the same time we must give help for survival. Otherwise, like the bond slaves of Palamu whom I've seen myself, liberated bond laborers will become slaves again in order to survive, because of the administrative failure (or deliberate cruelty? This system wants the feudal landowner to keep land, to have bond-slaves slave for him) to implement the emancipation. Bond-slaves receive some food, some food grain, which is a huge help in their lives.

At the same time we must help their survival by creating forests, giving them poultry and goats and giving them work and food during the starvation months. Before planting the forests they can themselves say what plants they want, what will help them live. Goats are hardy, they will live on grass and weeds. I had heard of *"war footing."* We cannot save them if we do not continue to fight.

At this time it is also necessary to encourage them to build hassocks and baskets with that strong and supple grass, to weave mats with Khajra leaves, and to arrange to sell them.

Cementing the sides of the Pirtha pool, putting up at least two double dams on the Pirtha river, will help them cultivate the Forest Department land. Then it is necessary to build in Gabahi a school, a center for basket-weaving, handloom, and animal husbandry—in order to make the women self-supporting—a primary health care center, and a *modified ration shop.*

I have used the name "Pirtha." The need is in every village. (Harisharan, this extended *report* is for you. Give a *xerox copy* to the SDO. I am writing another *report* for the *Daylight.* I will try to interest other papers, I give you my word. —Puran.)

P.S. Let's keep the art of engraving for the *Daylight.* I will be able to give many *"human angle stories"* for the papers, following my *notes.*

Motia's mother sold her children before this.

Shankar's own son is a bond-slave in the family of Tehsildar Singh in Bhalpura.

In Madhola, Ragho and Dashi, and Madho (female) in Pungarh did not eat poisonous tubers to commit suicide. They ate the root because they could get no more Khajra. Listen, give great importance to the planting of Khajra. I ate it today, Shankar gave me some. It's edible.

The brother of the man who's been buying infants and girls from Pirtha and Dholki has a bicycle repair shop in Madhopura town. He too is implicated in this ring. The shop's returns cannot subsidize a house in Madhopura and the rental of a passenger truck. It's been bought by Dalpat Chhajan and the truck-owner lives in Bhilai.

A certain Doctor Rao in Bhalpura Hospital told the Sarpanch, The government has not built the hospital to treat famine-starved people of this kind. He always mistreats people.

Dahi died of starvation this year. Year before last Dahi's elder brother committed suicide of starvation with his wife and children.

Doga's mother in Pungarh said that the government gives us no help, only takes our *vote*. What do they do with our *vote*? And does the government live in Britain that they don't have news of Pungarh?

The clearest truth was told by the tribals of Rawagarhi. Their communal chief spat and sat silent. An elder said, "Go away. A reporter came two months ago as well. You'll take our pictures? You'll write about us? What's going to happen with that? Will the government give water, land, or food? Look at the girl."

A young woman sat looking at the sky. She would have grown comely in a month if she had enough to eat.

— She sold one of her twins, and the other died. Want to take her picture?

I took a picture of the fortress-like house of a boss of Rawagarhi and the pile of leaf-dishes used and thrown away, lying before it. They are having thanks-giving rites for ten days, the wife has given birth to a son.

In the name of these villages, millions of rupees have been spent in the last few years. I have taken pictures of the effects of the great tribal welfare project.

"Building Houses for the Tribals"—the picture of a few broken shacks with nothing more than wooden posts.

"Help with animal husbandry"—Sona Gond on her way to sell her last goat.

"Integrated Mother and Child Care Project"—three female skeletons sitting with four skeleton children with swollen bellies.

"Forest project for tribals"—a billboard saying "This Land

Belongs to the Forest Department" surrounded by unbroken fields enclosed in barbed wire.

"Drinking Water for the Tribal"—in the first picture an uprooted tubewell lies prone on the ground. Second picture, a Panchayat well, women standing at a distance with pitchers, and a certain non-tribal Gabbar Singh washing a fat water-buffalo. Third picture, women gleaning water from the sandy bed of the Pirtha.

"Revolution in the tribal mode of cultivation"—parched and barren earth on the hillside slope, a bemused infant stopped short, looking questioningly into the eye of the camera.

"Fair price food for the tribal"—an old woman holds up a Khajra tuber she has picked.

"No Famine Here"—skeletal men walking by the wayside, with mat-covered bundles on their head, holding the hands of women and children. Look at the arrow-sign on the *milestone*— Bhalpura ten kilometers.

Harisharan, these pictures will reveal some truths and some lies.

The truths and the lies are the same.

The truth, the tribal receiver gets nothing.

The lie, the government's proclamations are only on paper, they do nothing when it comes to the reality.

Look at the last picture.

Three houses framed one in the next. "Houses of the real beneficiaries of tribal development." I have mentioned his name earlier, but look again. Of course, I'll write, "It is alleged that the owners of such houses cultivate land *recorded* in the name of fake tribals in advanced and scientific ways."

Then you cope.

Again, Puran.

The "oil bath" takes place quietly.

Bikhia, the only discoverer of the embodied ancestral soul, gives everyone oil from a small bowl at the point of a twig in a ceremonial way.

Why does this boy observe the same rule in the matter of the form of the ancestral soul as is appropriate to the funeral rites of the formerly living? No one asks this question.

Did he see its death?

No questions asked.

Did he cremate or bury it?

No questions asked.

But the flow of excitement travels like a current of electricity.
Did the soul of the ancestors come in this way? Or didn't it?
Pirtha knows, it knows.

Did they fall into mourning at a dreadful news? Pirtha knows, it knows.

There are many rites after the oil bath, Pirtha will perform them as needed.

Puran realizes that the crisis of the menaced existence of the tribals, of the extinction of their ethnic being, pushed and pushed them toward the dark.

Looking at Bikhia's tawny matted hair, freshly shaven face, he understood that they were being defeated as they were searching in this world for a reason for the ruthless unconcern of government and administration. It was then that the shadow of that bird with its wings spread came back as at once *myth* and analysis.

This is a new *myth*. For the soul of those long dead will return hundreds of years later in the form of an unknown tired bird. Such a thing is probably not there even in their *oral tradition*.

But from now on they will wait in their suffering and in evil times for that shadow, otherwise this deception cannot be humanly explained.

Having drawn that stone tablet Bikhia is the guardian of the new *myth*. He will protect it.

And this mourning, this "oil bath" has given them an assurance. Now something has happened that is their very own, a thing beyond the reach of the understanding and grasp and invasion and plunder of the outsider.

Is this collective shaving and bath really purifying them? Everybody's face and eyes are very different, beyond Puran's reach, did Puran ever reach this?

Puran shaves and bathes and then descends with his bag on his shoulder. How self-absorbed, how calm, how distant Bikhia is now, Puran's breast trembles.

— Good-bye, Bikhia.
— Yes, Babu.

He doesn't say "come again," no one does. Shankar smiles wanly and says, "Come at the drought."

— If only I can catch the rain clouds!
Shankar says, "How will you go?"

— Let me walk down. I'll get a *truck*.
— Sarpanchji?

— You tell him.

— The *Block* Officer won't come today?

— No.

— And *relief will* stop too.

— I heard.

Shankar says softly, "I don't know what the *Block* Officer is thinking. But we will not leave Pirtha."

He looks around and says, "Why should we leave? Isn't this our place? Now no tribal will leave. The ancestors' soul let us know that all the places it visited are ours. Can anyone leave anymore, or will they leave?"

— Is that what it let you know? Who told you this?

— Bikhia.

Shankar says triumphantly.

Puran shakes and shakes his head. They will not leave, they will not go anywhere leaving those stones, hills, caves, and river. To the fertile fields, to the plains, where there is plenty of water, and many supports for survival.

— If they want to give us aid, let them give it to us here.

Spreading his arms, he says, "All this land was ours, the kings took it from us. They were supposed to return it to us, to whom did they give it back? No, we won't go anywhere. Let them give us our dues here."

— OK.

— If not let them forget, let them forget us. At most we'll die, nothing worse can happen.

Some rare deaths become *myths* and ascend from the dark caverns. But Puran does not say this.

— Good-bye, Shankar.

— Yes, Babu.

To reach from the back to the tail of the animal in the survey map, to get down in Gabahi, wiping his damp eyes, finally stopping on the road and looking out for a *truck*, how much time passes?

Seventy-five million years?

Five thousand years?

There is no need to look back at Pirtha hill. Puran is carrying Pirtha village in his heart.

Today he must leave Rajaura as well.

No need to go to Madhopura.

Pirtha is everything, all other places now seem trivial.

What will he tell Harisharan?

What will Harisharan tell him?

— Harisharan, do you know the final experience of the story of Pirtha?

— What? What? What?

— We have lost somewhere, to Bikhia's people, to Pirtha. By comparison with the ancient civilizations modern progress is much more barbaric at heart. We are defeated.

— And?

— Do you know the final word? There is no communication-point between us and the pterodactyl. We belong to two worlds and *there is no communication point*. There was a *message* in the pterodactyl, whether it was a fact or not, and we couldn't grasp it. We *missed* it. We suffered a great loss, yet we couldn't know it. The pterodactyl was *myth* and *message* from the start. We trembled with the terror of discovering a real pterodactyl.

— And Pirtha?

— We built no communication point to establish contact with the tribals. Leaving it undiscovered, we have slowly destroyed a continent in the name of civilization.

— There isn't anything at all?

— Nothing at all.

— Is it impossible to build it?

— To build it you must love beyond reason for a long time. For a few thousand years we haven't loved them, respected them. Where is the time now, at the last gasp of the century? Parallel ways, their world and our world are different, we have never had a real exchange with them, it could have enriched us.

— And ... the engraving of the pterodactyl?

— Bikhia knows.

Puran repeats the dialogue a number of times in his mind, speaking for both. Yes, this is indeed the truth.

We have lost.

Bikhia has probably understood what the pterodactyl, seeking shelter, had come to say.

Puran has not.

Harisharan, Harisharan! We have not understood, because we didn't want to and now it is evident that Bikhia's people are finally much more civilized, holder of the ancient civilization, and so finally they did not learn our barbarism, there is possibly no synonym for "exploitation" in their language. Our responsibility was to protect them. That's what their eyes spoke.

Only love, a tremendous, excruciating, explosive love can still dedicate us to this work when the century's sun is in the western sky, otherwise this aggressive civilization will have to pay a terrible price, look at history, the aggressive civilization has destroyed itself in the name of progress, each time.

Love, excruciating love, let that be the first step. Now Puran's amazed heart discovers what love for Pirtha there is in his heart, perhaps he cannot remain a distant spectator anywhere in life.

Pterodactyl's eyes.

Bikhia's eyes.

Oh ancient civilization, the foundation and ground of the civilization of India, oh first sustaining civilization, we are in truth defeated. A continent! We destroyed it undiscovered, as we are destroying the primordial forest, water, living beings, the human.

A *truck* comes by.

Puran raises his hand, steps up.

[In this piece no name—such as Madhya Pradesh or Nagesia— has been used literally. Madhya Pradesh is here India, Nagesia village the entire tribal society. I have deliberately conflated the ways, rules, and customs of different Austric tribes and groups, and the idea of the ancestral soul is also my own. I have merely tried to express my estimation, born of experience, of Indian tribal society, through the myth of the pterodactyl. —Mahasweta Devi.]

Afterword

"If read carefully," Mahasweta says in conversation, "'Pterodactyl' will communicate the agony of the tribals." And in December 1992, Gopiballabh Singh Deo lovingly complained, again in conversation, "Didi [Mahasweta] leaves too much unsaid. Not everyone can understand her point of view." Ranajit Guha has commented on the Sanskritized translation of "culture" innovated by Bankimchandra Chatterjee, the celebrated nineteenth-century Bengali nationalist writer and intellectual: *anushilan*.[1] Here as elsewhere, the colloquial language takes away the project of an intellectual. In colloquial Bengali today, *anushilan* is attention, concentration. What Mahasweta asks for is *anushilan*, on our part, of the First Nation, the *Adim Jalti*.

I am learning to write on Mahasweta as if an attentive reading of her texts permits us to imagine an impossible undivided world; without which no literature should be possible. This is a learning because such a permission can be earned only by way of attention to the specificity of these writings. Since the general tendency in reading and teaching so-called "Third World" literature is toward an uninstructed cultural relativism, I have always written companion essays with each of my translations, attempting to intervene and transform this tendency. I have, perhaps foolishly, attempted to open the structure of an impossible social justice glimpsed through remote and secret encounters with singular figures; to bear witness to the specificity of language, theme, and history as well as to supplement hegemonic notions of a hybrid global culture with this experience of an impossible global justice.[2]

I believe that the same habit of mind—a vision of impossible justice through attention to specificity—may draw a reader to Marx, to Mahasweta, and to Derrida, in different ways. My earlier companion essays perhaps showed this too enthusiastically. And the general uneasiness about (or unexamined celebration of) Derrida's critique of humanism compromised their reception. My own sense of their inadequacy is related to an insufficient preparation in the specific political situation of the Indian tribal. I have

197

tried to remedy this, indeed compensate for this, by letting Mahasweta's intimate and abyssal responsibility toward that originary history of India, that must haunt any present that India might want to shore up, speak itself at the head of this volume. Here I want to supplement her remarks by a few observations about a general (rather than nation-specific) political urgency to which these stories relate—a vision of inter-nationality that is not only impossible but necessary.

In the contemporary context, when the world is broadly divided simply into North and South, the World Bank has no barrier to its division of that world into a map that is as fantastic as it is real.[3] This constantly changing map draws economic rather than national boundaries, as fluid as the spectacular dynamics of international capital. One of the not inconsiderable elements in the drawing up of these maps is the appropriation of the Fourth World's ecology.[4] Here a kinship can be felt through the land grabbing and deforestation practiced against the First Nations of the Americas, the destruction of the reindeer forests of the Suomis of Scandinavia and Russia, and the tree felling and eucalyptus plantations on the land of the original nations, indeed of all the early civilizations that have been pushed back and away to make way for what we call the geographic lineaments of the map of the world today.

Upon the body of this North-South world, and to sustain the imaginary map making of the World Bank, yet another kind of unification is being practiced as the barriers between international capital and the fragile national economics of the South are being removed. The possibility of social redistribution in these states, uncertain at best, is disappearing even further.

In this context, it is important to notice that the stories in this volume are not only linked by the common thread of profound ecological loss, the loss of the forest as foundation of life, but also of the complicity, however apparently remote, of the power lines of local developers with the forces of global capital. This is no secret to the initiative for a global movement for non-Eurocentric ecological justice. But this is certainly a secret to the benevolent study of other cultures in the North. And here a strong connection, indeed a complicity, between the bourgeoisie of the Third World and migrants in the First cannot be ignored. We have to keep this particularly in mind because this is also the traffic line

in Cultural Studies. Mahasweta's texts are thus not only of sub-
stantial interest to us, but may also be a critique of our academic
practice. Is it more or less "Indian" to insist on this open secret?

What follows is not a romanticization of the tribal.[5] Indeed,
"Pterodactyl" is a critique of any such effort. The following para-
graphs outline a dream based on the conviction that large-scale
mind change is hardly ever possible on grounds of reason alone.
In order to mobilize for nonviolence, for example, one relies, however remotely, on building up a conviction of the "sacredness" of
human life. "Sacred" here need not have a religious sanction, but
simply a sanction that cannot be contained within the principle of
reason alone. Nature is no longer sacred in this sense for civilizations based on the control of Nature. The result is global devasta-
tion due to a failure of ecology. It is noticeable that the less
advantaged groups among the Indian tribals still retain this sense
as a matter of their cultural conformity, if only because they have
been excluded from the mainstream. It is also true that more self-
conscious First Nation groups such as the Canadian Native
American Movement use this possibility of cultural conformity
precisely to mobilize for ecological sanity as well as against historical injustice. What we are dreaming of here is not how to keep
the tribal in a state of excluded cultural conformity but how to
construct a sense of sacred Nature which can help mobilize a
general ecological mind-set beyond the reasonable and self-inter-
ested grounds of long-term global survival.

Indeed, if this seems an impractical dream, we should perhaps learn a lesson from the other side. In the World Bank's
Environmental Report for the fiscal year 1992, we read:

> The world's remaining indigenous peoples—estimated to
> number more than 250 million in seventy countries—pos-
> sess knowledge fundamental to the sustainable manage-
> ment of resources in these regions ... in cooperation with
> the Center for Indigenous Knowledge, the Environmental
> Department prepared a Bank discussion paper entitled
> *Using Indigenous Knowledge in Agricultural Development*
> (Warren 1991). Region-specific technical papers are being
> prepared to support the implementation of the directive.[6]

World Bank assistance comes at the request of governments.
These stories prepare us to take a critical stance toward such

"assistance." Within that framework, we should remind ourselves that the preparation of "technical papers" that will extract methods from so-called "indigenous knowledge" will not be accompanied by any change of mind-set in the researchers. By contrast, we draw out from literary and social texts some impossible yet necessary project of changing the minds that innocently support a vicious system. That is what "learning from below" means here. Mahasweta writes in "Pterodactyl" that the tribals remain largely spectators as India moves toward the twenty-first century. Assia Djebar has written that women remained largely spectators as Algeria moved toward Independence. "If only one could cathect [investir] that single spectator body that remains, encircle it more and more tightly in order to forget the defeat!" she writes.[7] This wish is another version of ethical singularity. It should not be conflated with romanticizing the tribal as figure for the Unconscious.

Having seen, then, the powerful yet risky role played by Christian liberation theology, some of us have dreamt of an animist liberation theology to girdle the perhaps impossible vision of an ecologically just world. Indeed the name "theology" is alien to this thinking. Nature "is" also super-nature in this way of thinking and knowing. (Please be sure that I am not positing some generalized "tribal mind.") Even "super" as in "super-natural" is out-of-the-way. For Nature, the sacred other of the human community, is, in this thinking, also bound by the structure of ethical responsibility of which I have spoken in connection with women's justice. The pterodactyl is not only the ungraspable other but also the ghost of the ancestors that haunts our present and our future. We must learn "love" (a simple name for ethical responsibility-in-singularity), as Puran does in "Pterodactyl," in view of the impossibility of communication.[8] No individual transcendence theology, being just in this world in view of the next—however the next is underplayed—can bring us to this.

Indeed, it is my conviction that the inter-nationality of ecological justice in that impossible undivided world cannot be reached by invoking any of the so-called "great" religions of the world, because the history of their "greatness" is too deeply imbricated in the narrative of the ebb-and-flow of power. In the case of Hindu India—a terrifying phrase—no amount of reinventing the nature poetry of the *Rg-Veda* will, in this view, suffice to undo that history.[9] I have no doubt that we must *learn* to learn from the original practical ecological philosophers of the world, through the slow, attentive, mind-changing (on both sides), ethical singularity that deserves the name of "love"—to supplement necessary collective efforts to change laws, modes of production, systems of education and health care. This for me is the lesson of Mahasweta, activist/journalist and writer. This relationship, a witnessing love and a supplementing collective struggle, is the relationship between her "literary" writing and her activism. Indeed, in the general global predicament today, such a supplementation must become the relationship between the silent gift of the subaltern and the thunderous imperative of the Enlightenment to "the public use of Reason," however hopeless that undertaking might seem.[10] One filling the other's gap.

Mary Oraon comes closest to a momentary performance of this supplementation, though there is no possibility of collectivity for her. And it is Douloti in whom the love of land, of Nature indistinguishable from parents and home, is seen at its strongest and most vulnerable. Yet, as I have argued above, the literary text cannot successfully represent a supplementation without standing in the way of such practical effort. That text (text-ile as the weave of work) is in the field of activism, e-laborated in labor.

Woman is in the interstices of "Pterodactyl." If the non-Eurocentric ecological movement offers us one vision of an undivided world, the women's movement against population control and reproductive engineering offers us another.[11] And here too Mahasweta shows us the complicity of the state. The bitter humor with which she treats the government's family planning posters shows us that the entire initiative is cruelly unmindful of the robbing of the women and men of Pirtha of the dignity of their reproductive responsibility. All collective struggles for the right to sexual preference and pleasure, the right to equitable work outside and in the home, the right to equality in education, must be supplemented by the memory that to be human is to be always and already inserted into a structure of responsibility. Capitalism, based on remote-control suffering, is obliged to reject the model of the acknowledgment of being inserted into responsibility as unprogressive, in order to be able to justify itself to passive capitalist members of society. Demanding rights or choosing responsibility is more useful for its purposes.

This position should be distinguished as strictly as possible from oppressive traditionalisms, the so-called communitarian or neo-familial or nativist positions within capitalist societies that would deflect the interests of the underclass, from above, by separating them from their rights. The imposition of personal family codes on colonized societies is one scandalous example from which women are still suffering all over the world. Yet the possibility of learning from below should not be forever foreclosed because of these forces of reaction.[12] And it is this learning that can only be earned by the slow effort at ethical responding—a two-way road—with the compromised other as teacher.

I have published longer essays on the first two stories translated here, which may deserve the critique of insufficient political specificity.[13] In all of them I have tried to address myself to the dominant readership and emphasized the elements that are different from the activist's account. The former ranged from groups of benevolent cultural relativist women, through migrant intellectuals who conflated Eurocentric migrancy with post-coloniality as such, to audiences where "nations" were not acknowledged as a palimpsest upon the ignored Fourth World.

In "The Hunt" I emphasized, among other things, the fact that, unlike the ethnographic account of tribal identity in rituals, Mahasweta shows an individual activating ritual into contemporary resistance. She chooses a character who is not a full member of tribal society, and shows her judging the mainstream exploiter before the act of rape can take place. In discussing the transformation of rapist/exploiter to ritual prey, I focused on Mahasweta's use of the words *janowar* (animal) and *bonno* (savage), and commented on Mary's negotiations with resources of the other side, a transvestism of spirit. In "Douloti" I emphasized gender division in resistance and gendering as the foundation of post-colonial exploitation. (This last is helpful also in discussing the role of international "homeworking," women's sweated labor at home.) In both I pointed out with the greatest possible urgency that a conflation of Eurocentric migrancy with post-coloniality lets drop the vicissitudes of decolonization and ignores the question: Who decolonizes?

A discussion of "Pterodactyl" comes at the end of an address on academic freedom presented at the University of Cape Town, from which I have already quoted. Since that has only been published as an occasional pamphlet, I here take the liberty of quoting a few more passages from it. I have included a brief consideration of Mary Shelley's *Frankenstein* in the hope that it might be pedagogically useful in distinguishing a piece of writing from the post-colonial world from colonial discourse studies:

In a piece published some years ago, I suggest that *Frankenstein* attempts to come to terms with the making of the colonial subject.[14] Sympathetic yet monstrous, clandestinely reared on sacred and profane histories of salvation and empire, shunned by the civilization which produces his subjectivity, the Monster's destructive rage propels him out of that novel into an indefinite future. When, however, it comes to the colonial subject's pre-history, Shelley's political imagination fails. Her emancipatory vision cannot extend beyond the speculary situation of the colonial enterprise, where the master alone has a history, master and subject locked up in the cracked mirror of the present, and the subject's future, although indefinite, is vectored specifically toward and away from the master. Within this restricted vision, Shelley gives to the Monster the right to refuse the withholding of the master's returned gaze—to refuse an apartheid of speculation, as it were: "'I will not be tempted to set myself in opposition to thee ... How can I move thee?' ... [He] placed his hated hands before my [Frankenstein's] eyes, which I flung from me with violence; 'thus I take from thee a sight which you abhor. Still thou canst listen to me ... '"[15] His request, not granted, is for a gendered future, for the colonial female subject. The task of the post-colonial cannot be restrained within the specular master-slave enclosure. I turn to Mahasweta Devi's "Pterodactyl, Puran Sahay, and Pirtha" to measure out some of the differences between the sympathetic and supportive colonial staging of the situation of the refusal of the withholding of specular exchange in favor of the monstrous colonial subject; and the post-colonial performance of the construction of the Constitutional subject of the new nation. Devi stages the workings of the post-colonial state with minute knowledge, anger, and loving despair. There are suppressed dissident radicals, there is the national government seeking electoral publicity, there are systemic bureaucrats beneath good and evil, subaltern state functionaries to whom the so-called Enlightenment principles of democracy are counter-intuitive. There is the worst product of post-coloniality, the Indian who uses the alibis of Development to exploit the tribals and destroy their life-system. Over against him is the handful of conscientious and understanding government workers who operate through a system of official sabotage and small compromises. The central figure is Puran Sahay, a journalist. (Devi herself, in addition to being an ecology-health-literacy activist and a fiction writer, is also an indefatigable interventionist journalist.) But all this is a frame narrative. Inside the frame is a story of funeral rites. A tribal boy has drawn the picture of a pterodactyl on the cave wall. Puran and a "good" government officer do not allow this to become public. Through his unintentionally successful "prediction" of rain, Puran becomes part of the tribe's ongoing historical record. He sees the pterodactyl. If the exchange between the nameless Monster (without history) and Victor Frankenstein is a finally futile refusal of withheld specularity, the situation of the gaze between pterodactyl (before history) and a "national" history that holds tribal and nontribal together, is somewhat different. There can be no speculation here, the tribal and the nontribal must pull together. We are both in the nation, conjuring against the State, "the aggressive advance of the strong as it obliterates the weak, ... think if you are going forward or back ... What will you finally grow in the soil, having murdered nature in the application of man-imposed substitutes? ... The dusky lidless eyes remain unresponsive." For the modern Indian the pterodactyl is an empirical impossibility. For the modern tribal Indian the pterodactyl is the soul of the ancestors.[16] The fiction does not judge between the registers of truth and exactitude, simply stages them in separate spaces. This is not science fiction. And the pterodactyl is not a symbol. The pterodactyl dies and Bikhia, the boy struck dumb—withdrawn from communication by becoming the pterodactyl's "guardian," its "priest"—buries him in the underground caverns of the stream, walls resplendent with "undiscovered" cave paintings. He allows Puran to accompany him. The burial itself is removed from current practice. Now, Shankar says, they burn bodies, like Hindus. "We bury the ash and receive a stone. I've heard that we buried the bodies in the old days." The desecration of the dead is a common theme in post-colonial writing. This burial, then, can be situated in a community of longing. The particularity in this case is that the scene is one of internal colonization in the name of decolonization. A caste-Hindu, remote outsider in a now Hindu-majority land, earns the right to assist at the laying to rest of a previous civilization, in a rhetorical space that is textually separate from a frame narrative that may as well be the central narrative, of the separate agendas of tribal and journalistic resistances to development, each aporetic to the other, the site of a dilemma. Like the Monster in *Frankenstein,* Puran too steps away from the narrative of this tale, but into action within the post-colonial new nation: "A truck comes by. Puran raises his hand, steps up."

Ignoring all warnings, Mahasweta Devi has pulled me from the web of her fiction into the weaving of her work. I present my services to her work—translation, preface, afterword—in the hope that you will judge the instructive strength of that embrace.

Columbia University   GAYATRI CHAKRAVORTY SPIVAK

Notes

Translator's Preface

1. "Sabar" is a somewhat Sanskritized spelling of this tribe's name (the Sanskrit word means hunter), accepted in West Bengal. I have changed the spelling in order to save it from understandable non-Indian mispronunciation. "Shaw-bore" would be the closest to the Bengali word. The tribal languages are not identical with the vernaculars of the Indian states. The languages of the tribes mentioned above, for example, are not identical with Bengali and Hindi, the main languages of West Bengal and Bihar, themselves containing many dialects, some of which, in Bihar, are now considered sufficiently elaborated to be deemed languages in their own right. Modern India has 25 states, nearly all of which have a tribal population.

2. For an analysis of the relationship between dam-building, Development, and the World Bank, see, for example, Vandana Shiva, *Ecology and the Politics of Survival: Conflict over Natural Resources in India* (London: Sage Press, 1991).

3. Shankar Prasad Guha Niyogi, a middle-class Bengali, went to work for the Bhilai Dam in Central India, became thoroughly identified with the movement for tribal liberation, founded and led the Chhattisgarh Mukti Morcha until he was assassinated in his sleep by an unidentified gunman in 1991.

4. A little less than a quarter in 1993. With the continuous devaluation being practiced by the IMF to "equalize" international capital in the New World Order, it is almost meaningless to give an equivalent.

5. The peasant-based Naxalite movement against the exploitation of peasants started in the village of Naxalbari in North Bengal in the late 1960s and soon spread to other states. It formed the basis of the Communist Party (Marxist-Leninist), and several parties of the extreme left.

6. Jacques Derrida, "Differance", in Alan Bass (tr.), *Margins of Philosophy* (Chicago: University of Chicago Press, 1982), p. 17; emphasis mine.

7. By "new immigrant" I mean the continuing influx of immigrants since, by "[t]he Immigration and Nationality Act of October 1, 1965," Lyndon Johnson "swept away both the national origins system and the Asia-Pacific Triangle"; precisely the groups escaping decolonization, one way or another. "That the Act would, for example, create a

207

massive brain drain from developing countries and increase Asian immigration 500 percent was entirely unexpected" (Maldwyn Allen Jones, *American Immigration* [Chicago: University of Chicago Press, 2nd ed., 1992], pp. 266, 267).

8. I have kept to the Indian custom of referring to thoroughly public figures by their first name as a sign of recognition of their stature.

9. I will use the word "subaltern" sparingly. Although I read it first in Gramsci, I encountered it in its current usage first in the work of the Subaltern Studies group. As a result of the publication of Ranajit Guha and Gayatri Chakravorty Spivak (eds.), *Selected Subaltern Studies* (New York: Oxford University Press, 1987) in the United States, the word has now lost some of its definitive power.

10. Indeed, Gramsci is useful here if read freely. Necessarily without a detailed awareness of the rich history of African-American struggle, he was somewhat off the mark when he presented the following "hypothesis" for "verification": "1. that American expansionism should use American negroes [sic] as its agents in the conquest of the African market and the extension of American civilization" (Antonio Gramsci, "The Intellectuals," in Quintin Hoare and Geoffrey Nowell-Smith (trs.), *Selections from the Prison Notebooks* [New York: International Publishers, 1971], p. 21). If, however, these words are applied to the new immigrant intellectuals and their countries of national origin, they seem particularly apposite today. The partners are, of course, "Cultural Studies," liberal multiculturalism, and post-fordist transnational capitalism, in a world that is already under way.

11. Sara Suleri, *The Rhetoric of English India* (Chicago: University of Chicago Press, 1992), pp. 11–12.

12. Sujit Mukherjee, "Mahasweta Devi's Writings—An Evaluation" [the title given by Mukherjee had been "Operation? Mahasweta Devi"], *Book Review*, xv.3 (May–June 1991), p. 31.

13. For a succinct account of the events surrounding Chuni Kotal's suicide, see Mahasweta Devi, "Story of Chuni Kotal," in *Economic and Political Weekly* (29 August 1992). Incidentally, derisive comments made by upper-middle-class Indian-Americans of the public version of Chuni's suicide put me in mind about the dismissal of Bhubaneswari Bhaduri's suicide by women of the next generation, anger against which produced my remark that the subaltern could not speak. In her book *Aranyer Adhikar* Mahasweta has celebrated the great Ulgulan or uprising of 1895–1900, led by Birsa Munda, the tribal leader. "Every trace of independent initiative on the part of subaltern groups should therefore be of incalculable value for the integral historian. Consequently, this kind of history can only be dealt with monographically, and each monograph requires an immense quantity of material which is often hard to collect" (Gramsci, "Notes on Italian History," *Prison Notebooks*, p. 55). In the matter of the "organic intellectual," however, we must commemorate Gramsci's uniqueness by

supplementing with our own different history. "Every social group, coming into existence on the original terrain of an essential function in the world of economic production," Gramsci writes, "creates together with itself, organically, one or more strata of intellectuals which give it homogeneity and an awareness of its own function not only in the economic but also in the social and political fields" ("The Intellectuals," p. 5). Writing in the context of Fascist Italy, where the power of the organized intellectual clerisy was more than millennial, Gramsci is not confident of the possibility of organic intellectuals being elaborated (worked through) among the "peasant masses" (ibid. p. 6). By contrast, the recently denotified Indian tribes had been millennially separated from the mainstream peasant underclass. This difference between the Italian and Indian cases allows the elaboration of a Jaladhar Sabar. Again, Gramsci sees a difficulty in the formation of the peasant organic intellectual because he (Gramsci is incapable of imagining a female type) must go through traditional education in order to enter intellectuality. Sabar's education, in the most robust sense, has been through association with Mahasweta Devi, herself a female organic intellectual of unusual ethical responsiveness, elaborated as a permanent persuader type by way of the resistant left bourgeoisie (to keep to these forbidding and formulaic descriptions): "The mode of being of the new intellectual can no longer consist in eloquence, ... but in active participation in practical life, as constructor, organizer, 'permanent persuader'" (ibid. p. 10). It can be said that people of Sabar's kind and Mahasweta's kind elaborate each other as organic intellectuals from different social groups. Chuni's suffering in this regard was first because she was a woman and secondly because she was trying to infiltrate institutions of traditional intellectuality. In conclusion to this long note, it must be said that the organic intellectual is not a concept of identity but rather of a focus on that part of the subject which focuses on the intellectual's function. Mahasweta Devi, Jaladhar Sabar, Gopiballabh Singh Deo (caste-Hindu head of the local landowning family, conscientized and politicized through left struggle, now thoroughly identified with the tribal movement and an indefatigable worker on their behalf), and Prasanta Rakshit (a young man of provincial petty-bourgeois origin who lives and works with the Kheria Sobors) form, therefore, a metonymic collectivity. Keeping in mind that the word "class" loses its lineaments here, we might remember the following remark: "the 'organic' intellectuals which every new class creates alongside itself and elaborates in the course of its development are for the most part 'specializations' of partial aspects of the primitive activity of the new social type which the new class has brought into prominence" (ibid. p. 6).

14. A recent piece in *Frontier* about the commodification of another organic intellectual, Rigoberta Menchu, is apposite here ("Recognizing A Maya Indian," *Frontier*, xv. 13, 7 November 1992, p. 2).

15. I use the word "dilemma" as a synonym for "aporia" to avoid the charge of obscurantism. An aporia is different from a dilemma in that

it is insoluble—each choice cancels the other—and yet it is solved by an unavoidable decision that can never be pure. Dilemma is a logical, aporia a practical item.

16. It is again a phenomenon of the unequal distribution of knowledge that this gifted novelist of the French language, who published the novel *Fantasia: An Algerian Cavalcade,* tr. Dorothy S. Blair (London: Quartet, 1985), in 1985, has not received sufficient attention in the North; to the extent that so politically aware a feminist as Sheila Rowbotham recently mentioned and discussed Pauline Rolland as a "find," without, of course, being aware of this claim of kinship.

17. In *Bonded Histories: Genealogies of Labor Servitude in Colonial India* (New York: Cambridge University Press, 1990), Gyan Prakash has studied this from a Foucauldian and ungendered perspective. He argues that the colonial/postcolonial capitalist exploitative social relations were imposed upon the historical construction of bonded labor within a precapitalist hierarchical socially functional structure. The dominant lord became the exploitative landlord without the *kamiya's* participation. There was therefore no attendant change in their mindset, their discursive formation. (Mahasweta's account of census and elections in "Douloti" can take this analysis on board, though Shankar in "Pterodactyl" escapes this line of reasoning.) Prakash therefore argues that the discourse of "freedom" is counter-intuitive to the *kamiya.* Such a conclusion is obliged to ignore the history and possibility of the emergence of the "organic intellectual." Mahasweta's work also reminds us that, when the dominant mode of the country is capitalist, the activist must see the residual mode as "internalized constraint expressed as choice" (Sheila Allen and Carol Wolkowiz, *Homeworking: Myths and Realities,* London: Macmillan, 1987, p. 73), and work for a freedom not necessarily defined by the official decolonizer. This reminder, and a consideration of gendering, would enhance Prakash's good concluding sentiment: "The continuity that the kamias have maintained in their refusal to participate in the official project, and in mounting struggles against domination experienced at the point of power's exercise, far from indicating passivity, ought to be seen as their recognition of power concealed by the juridical guise of rights. It represents their critique of the discourse of freedom, their pronouncement that there is 'bondage' in freedom" (p. 225). Here perhaps is Shankar, standing alone.

18. Although the methods recommended are largely usable in Western European society and the vocabulary of popularized psychoanalysis, this is the general insight of Frigga Haug, *Beyond Female Masochism: Memory-Work and Politics,* tr. Rodney Livingstone (London: Verso, 1992). Ethical transcoding of strategy is not impossible in our part of the world. Otherwise we remain caught in a collective disavowal that paradoxically strengthens the long-term possibility of the very thing we seek to avoid: the virulent misogyny of the right. This is the one absence marked well in Gita Sahgal's documentary on the *sati* of Rup Kanwar. None of the urban feminist radicals in that film was able to

acknowledge that, quite apart from the obvious male coercion, brutality, and exploitation, Rup might indeed have seen the *sati* as an ethical choice; just as her obviously loving mother comments that she believes Rup to have been happy in her choice. Without this acknowledgment and the responsible and caring process of the establishment of ethical singularity (which can only exist between equals) that is its practical consequence, no collective action on the basis of legal calculation, itself absolutely necessary, will last. In this connection, see Mahasweta's "Sati Moyna," *Pratikshan* (forthcoming in my translation).

19. Mukherjee, "Devi's Writings," p. 31. I gratefully accept his correction that "[t]*akma* (a medal-like object of brass or bronze worn by a servitor) cannot be taken to mean livery," and therefore "*takmadhari*" as "liveried" ("Draupadi," in Spivak, *In Other Worlds,* Routledge, 1987) is unacceptable. And I agree completely that Samik Banerjee's "kounter" is infinitely better than my "counter" ("Draupadi"). I should mention here that Mahasweta has read this translation carefully and I have, for the most part, accepted her suggestions. All mistakes are of course mine.

20. J. M. Coetzee, *Doubling the Point: Essays and Interviews* (Cambridge: Harvard University Press, 1992), p. 88. My translation of the last piece in this book bears little resemblance to the draft translation offered by the author—the only piece for which I had such a text—although I invariably consulted it when I was in doubt, especially about the accepted English names of the various institutions of the bewildering Indian bureaucracy. Italicized words are in English in the original.

Afterword

1. Ranajit Guha,*A Construction of Humanism in Colonial India* (Amsterdam: CASA: 1993).

2. A reader acquainted with Derrida will find in these thoughts echoes from Derrida's two essays, "The Force of Law: the 'Mystical Foundation of Authority'," *Cardozo Law Review* XI.5–6 (July-Aug. 1990), pp. 919–1045; and *Schibboleth: Pour Paul Celan* (Paris: Galilee, 1986); available in partial translations in Geoffrey Hartman and Sanford Budick (eds.), *Midrash and Literature,* (New Haven: Yale University Press, 1986), and Derek Attridge (ed.), *Acts of Literature* (New York: Routledge, 1992), pp. 373–413.

3. For a detailed discussion of the implications of World Bank cartography and the uses of the Geographic Information System, see Crystal Bartolovich, "Boundary Disputes: Textuality and the Flows of Transnational Capital," *Mediations* XVII.I (Dec. 1992), pp. 21–33.

4. By "Fourth World" is meant the world's aboriginal peoples who were literally pushed to margins for the contemporary history and geography of the world's civilizations to be established.

5. Kumkum Sangari is right to criticize such romanticization in "Figures for the 'Unconscious'," *Journal of Arts and Ideas*, XX–XXI (1991).

6. *The World Bank and the Environment* (Washington: the World Bank, 1992), pp. 106, 107.

7. Assia Djébar, "Forbidden Gaze, Severed Sound," in *Women of Algiers in Their Apartments*, tr. Marjolijn de Jager (Charlottesville: University of Virginia Press, 1992), p. 141.

8. We cannot even and after all be sure that the pterodactyl *has a* message for us. Yet we must think that it wants to speak. This is rather clear in the story. It is uncanny for me that Derrida's notion of the "trace"—our conviction, faced with a situation, that something wants to signal something else—must also run the risk that there might be no signal. Love is not do-gooding, ethics is not social work, although a bit of both is possible. I am more and more convinced of this as I hang out in the field of work more and more; and it brings me closer to Mahasweta and Derrida—one as seemingly devoted to goodness as the other to truth, yet both astringently describing their devotion as "obsession"; Mahasweta in the introductory conversation here, and Derrida in a similar interview in Attridge, *Acts of Literature*, p. 34—and a bit further away from academic historiography. "All in all I prefer that to the constitution of a consensual euphoria or, worse, a community of complacent deconstructionists, reassured and reconciled with the world in ethical certainty, good conscience, satisfaction of service rendered, and the consciousness of duty accomplished (or, more heroically still, yet to be accomplished)," (Derrida, "Passions," in David Wood (ed.), *Derrida: A Critical Reader*, [Cambridge: Blackwell, 1992], p. 15).

9. I am aware of the strategic importance of drawing upon principles of tolerance that are recuperable from religious traditions in order to combat fundamentalism. And there the narrative of Hinduism would have to serve in the Indian national case. But here I am speaking of a new inter-nationality to resist "development" without irreducible reference to a state power that may be irretrievably compromised in a financialized globe. Aijaz Ahmed has recently spoken of confronting the current Indian situation by understanding it as a displacement of Fascism versus Communism (rather than sectarianism versus secularism) and an anti-clericalism filled out by industrialization, following a Gramscian model. ("Gramsci and *Hindutva*" [abridged title], unpublished lecture, Calcutta, 28 Dec. 1992; chapter in a forthcoming book.) For the lack of fit between Italian anti-clericalism and Indian secularism, see "Translator's Preface," footnote 13. As for choosing the Fascism/Communism model for India, it seems important to remember that, in essays like "Notes on Italian History," Gramsci is careful to warn against drawing analogies even between the various European states. Gramsci perceived Italian Fascism as continuous with nineteenth-century liberalism precisely because of the presence of a millennial intellectual clerisy. Italy is almost the

only European state where the original position of the *Seculum* as contaminated—by procreation because of dynastic succession—and the *ecclesia* as de facto rational—because held together by discipline—persisted for a few centuries before the reversal into public (secular) and private (religious) led to the consolidation of liberalism into Fascism. As for *national* industrialization, no doubt a worthy goal in itself, here the Gramscian model must be re-constellated from its historical moment in the face of the collaboration between "sustainable development" and global financialization. Thus, even though the organic intellectual elaborated by the national electoral Left parties in the post-Soviet South can use a seamless and superficially plausible Gramscian analogy, our fear is that we will once again lose specificity in an attempt to fit ourselves into a European coat misappropriated, so that what is insistently represented as an instrument of freedom from above will become a strait-jacket that leaves no room for resistance.

10. Immanuel Kant, "What Is Enlightenment?" in *On History*, tr. Lewis White Beck (New York: Macmillan, 1963), p. 5. The historian may remind us that there were many Enlightenments, but this was the formula internalized by social engineers, imperialist and otherwise. Even the most unenlightened and minor entry into the mysteries of capital teaches this lesson as a rule of thumb.

11. For more extended discussions, see, for example, the documents of FINRRAGE, available from Pergamon Press, New York.

12. The last five sentences are a modified quotation from my *Thinking Academic Freedom in Gendered Postcoloniality* (Cape Town: University of Cape Town Press, 1992). I take the liberty of quoting from my own work because, overwhelmed by the honor of being asked to speak in post-apartheid South Africa, I discovered how much my reading of Mahasweta expanded to teach me about a general globality. I hope the reader will forgive a further quotation from this text in conclusion.

13. "The Hunt" is discussed in "An Interview with Gayatri Spivak", in *Woman and Performance* 9, vol. 5, no. 1 (1990), and in "Who Claims Alterity?" in Barbara Kruger and Phil Mariani (eds.), *Remaking History* (New York: Dia Foundation, 1990); "Douloti" is discussed in "Woman in Difference: Mahasweta Devi's 'Douloti the Bountiful'," in Spivak, *Outside in the Teaching Machine* (New York: Routledge, 1993).

14. Spivak, "Three Women's Texts and a Critique of Imperialism," in Henry Louis Gates, Jr. (ed.), *"Race", Writing and Difference* (Chicago: University of Chicago Press, 1986).

15. Mary Wollstonecraft Shelley, *Frankenstein: or the Modern Prometheus* (Chicago: University of Chicago Press, 1974), pp. 95, 96.

16. This is counter-factual. "The idea of the ancestral soul is . . . my own," Mahasweta writes in an authorial note included with the story. She does not provide material for an anthropologistic romanticization.